English Moral Interludes

Edited with an introduction by Glynne Wickham
Emeritus Professor of Drama, University of Bristol

Dent: London and Melbourne
EVERYMAN'S LIBRARY

Made in Great Britain by
Guernsey Press Co. Ltd, Guernsey, C.I. for
J. M. Dent & Sons Ltd
Aldine House, 33 Welbeck Street, London W1M 8LX

First published in 1976
Reprinted 1985

This book is set in 9 pt Plantin

No. 1303   Paperback ISBN 0 460 11303 8

To

C. I. H. W.

CONTENTS

ACKNOWLEDGMENTS

My thanks are due to Dr Basil Cottle, Senior Lecturer in English, University of Bristol, for his help in the preparation of the Middle English texts included in the Appendix to this volume and in the correction of all the proofs; also to Miss Brenda Jackson, academic secretary in the Department of Drama, for her help in preparing the texts of the six Interludes.

My thanks are also due to Weidenfeld and Nicolson and St. Martin's Press, New York, for permission to reproduce two passages from *The Medieval Theatre* (1974) in the General Introduction.

Photographs and programmes of recent revivals of *Fulgens and Lucres*, *Nice Wanton* and *The Marriage Between Wit and Wisdom* can be consulted in the Theatre Collection of the University of Bristol, and copies can be obtained on application to the Keeper.

1975   G. W.

GENERAL INTRODUCTION

Few types of English drama have suffered more unwarranted neglect than Tudor Interludes. This can largely be explained in terms of an already overcrowded curriculum in English studies both in schools and universities where such plays get pushed aside to make room for the writings of more illustrious or more modern authors. Some portion of the blame, however, must attach to a failure innate in the plays themselves—the relative poverty of their language considered as poetry when compared to the best of earlier Middle English or to later Elizabethan drama. It is only the more unfortunate, therefore, that so many scholars and teachers should have failed to recognize the dramatic and theatrical virtues of these plays when considered as vehicles for actors, and should have come in consequence to dismiss them as unworthy of study as drama as well as literature: for to dismiss Interludes in this abrupt manner, whatever the reason, is to invite students to consider Shakespeare's plays and those of his contemporaries in a context hopelessly divorced from the moral, social, political and aesthetic values of the theatre which they inherited from their immediate predecessors. Shakespeare was already fifteen when *The Marriage Between Wit and Wisdom*, the last of the Interludes included in this book, appeared in print (see p. 163 below).

A growing understanding in recent decades, however, of the conventions that informed the construction of these plays, of the impact of the Reformation on all plays of the period (plays of religious polemic in particular), and of the vested interests of the nascent companies of professional actors in the fifteenth and sixteenth centuries has gone some way to change these attitudes, as has the successful revival of several Interludes.[1] These performances have revealed how lively they still are, how suitable as texts for practical class-work in small study groups, and how relevant their conventions are to any genuine understanding of both late Elizabethan drama and theatre and modern street and arena theatre.

[1] In the past twenty years *Mankind* has been presented in Toronto, *Magnificence* in Oxford, *Liberality and Prodigality* and *Wit and Wisdom* in the George Inn, Southwark, and *Wit and Science*, *Respublica*, *Nice Wanton* and several of John Bale's plays in Bristol, to name only a few.

When preparing the first edition in 1976, my principal objective was to assemble a collection of representative types of Interlude in a modern edition in order to stimulate further experimental productions. For this second edition the List of Further Reading has been revised to incorporate editions of texts and commentaries printed since then: otherwise both texts and introductions are largely unchanged.

The nine texts printed in this volume span the whole range of plays that share the generic title of Interlude and span, collectively, a period of some three centuries from the reign of Henry III to the opening of the first Blackfriars Playhouse by Richard Farrant and the building of The Theater by James Burbage in 1576. All of them have proved capable of revival with success before modern audiences and reveal as many affinities with the traditions of the medieval religious stage as they do with the critical theories of renaissance humanists. They are thus something more than bridges from one era to another, and possess a vitality which reposes in the notion that dramatic art is an infinitely flexible and enjoyable game that is played for the pleasure and profit of actors and audience alike.

What then was 'an Interlude'? This is a question that is impossible to answer with either certainty or precision; but the key to any attempt to define it lies in an understanding of the Latin word *ludus*. This was a generic word used by the Romans to describe any form of recreational activity, athletic or mimetic. In the Middle Ages the word came back into use to describe any sport or game that possessed an entertainment value of its own whether instructive in intention or not. Much the same happened to the Latin word *jocus*; originally 'a word game', it came to rival *ludus* in embracing other sorts of game, more especially in French, Italian and Spanish as may be seen in the modern *jeu, gioco* and *juego*.

The Church gave a lead to this approach to drama during the twelfth century by applying to dramatic re-enactments of biblical narrative St Augustine's concept of the world as a theatre in which mortal men act out their brief lives with God, His angels, and the Saints and Martyrs as the audience. The Latin words *lusores* and *joculatores*, derived respectively from *ludus* and *jocus*, were revitalized simultaneously to describe actors. In the Anglo-Saxon vernacular the equivalent words were *plég* and *gomen*, 'play' and 'game', and *plégman* and *gomensteora*, 'player' and 'gamester'. The players were thus regarded as the activators of the game, the actors. These concepts survived the Reformation with the words 'play' and 'game', 'player' and 'gamester' being used virtually as synonyms until the end of the sixteenth century.

The rules of this game were simple and easy to grasp. They were applied with equal vigour to the lengthy Miracle Cycles, to Morality and Saint Plays and even to quasi-dramatic entertainments like Tournaments, Mummings and Civic Pageants. They also informed the Interlude.

The first of these rules was that since the stage action was itself a game, it was not 'in earnest': in other words it was a fiction, a convenient pretence through which the author, or 'maker' as he was known, was enabled to comment on human existence, explain man's motives for his actions, and discuss the consequences. The second of these rules was that this commentary should be conducted within the orthodox beliefs of Roman Catholicism. The third was that the scenic, costume and acting conventions of the stage must allow the playmaker complete freedom of movement in time and space, uninhibited by considerations of verisimilitude. Thus the make-believe aspect of any form of drama was openly admitted and fully exploited. The advantage gained was that actors could cross seas and continents, travel to heaven or to hell, grow from childhood to old age, and perform several different characters by recourse to simple changes of costume and make-up within the confines of a single play—even within as short a play as an Interlude.

Brevity was one of the distinguishing marks of an Interlude and perhaps the most important of them in leading us towards both a definition and derivation of the word itself. The latter half of it clearly comes from *ludus*. *Inter*, in Latin, means 'between'. Hitherto two explanations have been advanced for the coupling of these two words in the context of dramatic art: one assumes dialogue between players, the other assumes play-acting between courses at a banquet. Both are credible. The difficulty with the former is that any dramatic text of the period by that definition, including the longest Cycles, Moralities and Saint Plays, is embraced by it: the difficulty with the latter is that some plays specifically entitled Interludes in the sixteenth century were patently not written for performance between the courses of a banquet. Without wishing to discredit either of these explanations, I believe myself that there is a third, not postulated before, that lies behind them both. It seems likely to me that the word came into the language in the wake of the antiquarian revival of interest in Roman antiquity that was a characteristic of the twelfth-century renaissance: in that context we could regard self-conscious imitation of Roman practice in the imperial era in punctuating lengthy feasts with entertainments of a diversionary nature as providing the origin of the word 'interludium' in medieval Europe, a word later to be translated into the new vernacular languages as *intermezzo* in Italian, *entremet* in French and 'enterlude' in English. With the passing of time, a word that had at first only been applied to a type of entertainment reserved for the privileged and literate few in the great halls of palaces and the larger monasteries came, by extension, to be applied by the performers themselves to entertainments supplied by them

to other audiences at other times and in other places. It is notice-
able that use of the word 'tournament' developed along similar
lines during the same period, the particular connotation attaching
to it in the twelfth century being overtaken by the generic connotation by the fifteenth.

Whether or not this was the case, this speculation at least explains
why the word should have been applied to a play devoted to a
secular subject like *The Interlude of the Student and the Girl* as
early as A.D. 1300; why Wyclif in his *Tretise on Miriclis*, c. 1385,
should have thought it inappropriate for a priest to 'pleyn in
entirlodies'; why the Mayor and Aldermen of London should
have issued an Edict in 1418 forbidding mumming in the Christmas
season and extended the wording of it to cover 'playes, enterludes,
or any other disgisynges . . .' and why Robert Mannyng of Brunne
in *Handlyng Synne* of almost the same date should have coupled
the word 'entyrludes' with singing, wrestling and summer games.
Against this background it is less surprising to find Agnes Ford of
New Romney in Kent being paid 6s 8d *pro ludo interludii Passionis
Domini* in 1463 and 'pleyers of enterludes' belonging to Dukes,
Earls and Bishops from 1450 onwards travelling widely and being
rewarded by their hosts in cash for the entertainment provided,
than would otherwise be the case. By then it is clear also that
distinctions between religious and secular subject matter had little
or no bearing on whether or not the word 'Interlude' was used to
describe it. Just as clearly, the choice of a word other than Mumming or Disguising suggests that it was desired to distinguish a
dramatic entertainment scripted in dialogue throughout from an
explanatory ballad or prologue the subject matter of which was
then represented in silent mime and dance (see Appendix, pp. 196–7
below).

Another factor of consequence is that while Calendar Festivals
provide the occasions for many entertainments, Interludes do not
appear to have been tied, like liturgical music-drama, Corpus
Christi Cycles or Saint Plays, to particular Feast Days. In this
respect then the Interlude of the fourteenth and fifteenth centuries
shared the freedom that distinguishes Morality Plays from other
drama of the period, being as suitable for performance on one day
as another and at any time indoors or out. If, in addition, as the
payments to players of Interludes indicate, the plays were short
and the number of parts small, it is obvious that a repertoire of
such plays would be of more use to a company that was forced to
travel to earn its keep than any other. This argument does not
preclude the writing and performance of Interludes by amateurs,
but it does suggest that without a stock of Interludes the idea of
deriving a regular income from acting as a profession could not
have developed very far. If this reasoning is accepted, then I think
we are entitled, by the last decade of the fifteenth century, to

regard play texts such as the anonymous *Everyman*, or Henry Medwall's *Nature* and *Fulgens and Lucres* as Moral Interludes. By that time we know something of the way of life of at least one company that performed such plays.

The *lusores regis, alias, in lingua Anglicana, les playars of the Kyngs enterluds* maintained by Henry VII were four in number and led by John English. From their master they received a basic retaining fee of five marks each, together with their liveries. In addition they received a gratuity in reward for every performance given at Court. When not required there they travelled, receiving similar gratuities for performances before the nobility in their halls and from mayors in their guild halls and city merchants in their livery halls. In summer they could add to their earnings by performing their plays to public audiences in town halls, on fair grounds and in other places of public resort in the open air, either charging admission at the door (where one existed) or circulating a collection-box when it did not. The hall was thus the natural home of the professional player. In that environment he was already supplied *in advance* with a sense of occasion, a screen provided with convenient entrances and exits and leading to dressing-rooms and refreshments in the vicinity, a roof against inclement weather, the warmth of a fire and the incandescent magic of candlelight. His fee, moreover, was guaranteed, or could at least be secured by controlled admission to the hall. In the open air everything was against him—the hazards of the weather, the makeshift character of stage, auditorium and changing-room, and the perennial disinclination of casual spectators to pay for the show if they could escape without doing so. The single advantage of the open-air theatre—and it was a compelling one as the organizing committees of amateur Miracle Cycles and Saint Plays knew well—was the size of the audience that could be accommodated. It was the lure of this prize which, late in the sixteenth century, persuaded professional companies to simulate the conditions of the hall in arenas open to the sky (but so constructed as to control admission and secure a financial contribution from every spectator in advance) to which they gave the name of public playhouses.

The amateur 'player of Interludes' was under no such pressure to secure large public audiences. In choir schools, grammar schools, universities, as at Court or in noble houses, the hall sufficed to accommodate the local community. It is thus in the hall that a succession of choristers and students, throughout the sixteenth century, presented Interludes for the entertainment of their fellows, whether in English, Latin or Greek, written for them by their masters, and frequently devised as much with a view to training them in the felicities of rhetoric and the techniques of oratory as to providing audiences with entertainment. Such was their success that in the latter half of the century William Hunnis,

John Lyly and others felt confident enough to imitate the adult professionals in presenting their Interludes to public audiences by private invitation. It was in these circumstances that the so-called Private Theatres came to be established in halls at St Pauls, Blackfriars and Whitefriars.

Interludes invariably sought to point a moral. The method, however, could be serious or farcical, the difference depending as much on the sort of audiences whose attention the actors sought to secure as on the status of the actors themselves. Religious subject-matter was as legitimate as source-material as secular life, at least until the Reformation. With that change, both in Germany and in England, the Moral Interlude became a weapon of propagandist polemic that was destined to shake the whole fabric of theatrical *ludi* that had been so laboriously built up over some six hundred years of consistently expanding experiment and community enterprise.

After Martin Luther had nailed his ninety-five principles to the door of the castle church in Wittenberg in 1517 and Henry VIII had married Ann Boleyn in 1533 without having secured Pope Clement VII's consent, religion in North-Western Europe became inseparable from politics: the drama, as a child of the Roman Catholic Church, was automatically sucked into this whirlpool of national and international strife with no hope of extricating itself until after the political conflict had been settled.

In England papal claims to authority over the audience were jettisoned shortly after the break with Rome. With the dissolution of the monasteries, the severe curtailment of the number of Calendar holidays, and the abolition of the Feast of Corpus Christi (1548), drama as it had been known in England for the past century or more was thrown into so chaotic a state as to require statutory legislation to control it from a Parliament nervous lest partisan riots among spectators at a play might spark off more serious uprisings. At the heart of this controversy lie the plays of John Bale (see Introduction to *The Temptation of Our Lord*, pp. 127–30 below). Not for him the calm exposition of Roman Catholic doctrine that characterizes the work of the anonymous author of *Mankind* (*c.* 1470), for all the savagery of its attack on contemporary manners, or the simple retailing of biblical narrative that satisfied the author of *The Conversion of St Paul* (*c.* 1500) and his company of actors: nor could he content himself with the gentle, humanist approach to social criticism that informs Medwall's *Fulgens and Lucres* (1497), where an earthly father, Fulgens, is substituted for God, and where his daughter, Lucres, exercises his gift of free will in her choice between men of vicious and virtuous character as her future husband.

For Bale the Vices must appear on the stage in the dress of the Roman Catholic Church hierarchy, the Virtues as figures that are recognizable as champions of reform in Church and State. The new polarities around which this drama is structured are the sovereign in the role formerly occupied by God the Father, and the Pope, now cast as Antichrist: at the centre is the body politic or Common-wealth, replacing Mankind and Everyman of earlier Moralities. Bale was not wholly original in endowing the drama with this new freedom, since it had already been steered in this direction during the first three decades of the sixteenth century by John Skelton in *Magnificence*, by John Redford in *Wit and Science*, and by John Heywood in many Interludes; but none of them had adopted so radical a standpoint, or urged it in such intemperate language as Bale chose to do when aligning himself between 1535 and 1540 with Archbishop Cranmer and Lord Chancellor Cromwell as an advocate of revolution.

Thus, in the opening scene of *Kyng Johan*, Widow England complains to the king about the avarice of the clergy:

> Nay, bastards they are, unnatural, by the rood!
> Since their beginning they were never good to me.
> The wild boar of Rome—God let him never to thee—
> Like pigs they follow, in fantasies, dreams and lies,
> And ever are fed with his vile ceremonies.
>
> . . . .
>
> K. *John*. By the boar of Rome I trow thou meanest the Pope?
> *England*. I mean none other but him. God give him a rope!
> K. *John*. And why dost thou thus compare him to a swine?
> *England*. For that he and his to such beastliness incline!
> They forsake God's word, which is most pure and clean,
> And unto the laws of sinful men they lean.
> Like as the vile swine the most vile meats desire
> And hath great pleasure to wallow themselves in mire,
> So hath this wild boar, with his Church Universal—
> His sow with her pigs and monsters bestial—
> Delight in men's dross and covetous lucre all.

(Lines 69–85)

In *The Temptation of Our Lord*, the example of Bale's work chosen for inclusion in this book, his language may be more temperate, but when Satan seeks a disguise for himself it is a monk's habit that he chooses (see p. 129 below). From this time forward makers of Interludes had a straight choice; to match and better Bale as a religious and political propagandist, or to retreat sharply from controversy towards the safer territory of traditional, social farce enriched by such borrowings as the authors had learning enough to draw from Roman, Italian, French or Flemish example: even so such borrowings, except in an academic environ-ment, were strictly controlled and restricted by the actors, whose primary interest lay in ensuring that the popular audiences on

[xi]

whom they depended for their livelihood were entertained and not bored.

Polemical drama, however, became ever more dangerous and difficult to follow as the sixteenth century advanced, partly because of the shifting religious persuasions of successive sovereigns and governments, and partly because of the rapid encroachment of an official censorship imposed on all plays before they were performed or printed.[1] It is on this account that so few plays in this *genre* escaped destruction. Only one play of specifically anti-Protestant polemic survives, the anonymous *Respublica* (*c.* 1533), sometimes attributed to Nicholas Udal, the acknowledged author of *Ralph Doister Roister*: this attacks the hypocrisy of the self-styled 'reformers', accusing them of confiscating Church property out of envy and avarice, and of feeding their own pride and ambition in the name of truth.

From the period 1540 to 1560 I have included one play, *Nice Wanton*, *c.* 1550, which clearly reflects its Protestant authorship (see pp. 143–5 below), but which derives its lasting vitality from its humorous situations and lively character drawing; nevertheless it was intended as a serious play in its time, as the criticism of parents in the upbringing of their children is firmly directed at the sentimentality and permissiveness of an older generation who have failed to advance with the times and embrace the sterner disciplines of the new religion.

Notwithstanding these changes of emphasis, however, the basic patterns of dramatic structure and stage conventions remained reactionary during the first decades of the reign of Elizabeth I, as may be judged from *The Marriage Between Wit and Wisdom* (*c.* 1575). Its author, Francis Merbury, was a graduate of Cambridge University: yet although this play was being written when Shakespeare was already a boy of about twelve, Merbury was content to borrow heavily from at least three other earlier plays (see Introduction pp. 163–6 below), redacting them into a new construct along the same lines and with the same efficacy as the authors of mystery cycles and moralities a century earlier. No one can study this play, therefore, without realizing how directly the traditions of medieval composition for the stage were transmitted to actors and dramatists of the Elizabethan and Jacobean era, including the much vaunted 'University Wits'.

Interludes of the Tudor era, for those who are willing to view them within this framework of a rich and continuously developing tradition, also reveal a subtle shift in moral, social and aesthetic values that reflects the changes induced in English society by the shift from Roman Catholic to Protestant approaches to life itself. At the centre of these shifts is the attitude adopted to free will. The

---

[1] On the progress of the censorship see G. Wickham, *Early English Stages*, Vol. II (Pt 1), Chapter 2.

steady growth of Hebraic values as expressed in the Old Testament on the one hand, and of interest in the teaching of St Paul on the other, serves to displace Covetousness from its former undisputed position as chief vice and to set up Sloth, or Idleness, in its place. This change in moral values, so clearly expressed in the cast lists and dialogues of Tudor Interludes, corresponds with the thoughts and desires of a society already committing itself to the philosophic tenets of capitalism, and about to commit itself to those of a new imperialism in imitation of the former *Pax Romana*; for not only had the physical centre of the new religion self-evidently shifted from Rome to London, but a new Deborah had been sent with Jehovah's blessing to reside there.

Where the staging of Interludes is concerned there is no reason to believe that the layout of the hall in the fourteenth or fifteenth centuries differed substantially from that for other indoor revels. With the dais occupied by the high table accommodating the master of the household and his guests, the players used the other end of the hall adjacent to the screen (with the minstrels in the gallery above it) for their play. The play-place was flanked with tables so that space was at a premium and contact with the audience extremely intimate. In essence the conditions resembled those for cabaret in restaurants today. Scenic units of the kind familiar in the theatres of worship, tournaments, civic pageants and Disguisings—ship, castle, pavilion, mountain, cave, arbour or clouds—were available to identify locality should this be necessary: but it is to be doubted, if the texts of Interludes surviving from the closing years of the fifteenth century and the early decades of the sixteenth are a fair guide, whether anything as elaborate as that was called for. A painted cloth, hanging on or near the screen, supplemented by portable stage properties—chairs, tables, stools and so on—could normally meet the simple requirements of such plays, and all these items were readily transportable to other places when the company took to the road.

Since actors were required to play two or three different roles in most Interludes, costume was simple, making quick changes as easy to accomplish as to identify. The style of costume was normally that of contemporary fashion, making it possible for actors, on occasion, to appear to be members of the audience. A case in point occurs with the two servants A and B in Medwall's *Fulgens and Lucres* where the author uses this confusion of identity to considerable comic effect. Nevertheless costume was carefully controlled not only to ensure swift identification of character but to figure in outward and visible manner the dominant features of the character's inner identity. In this way the makers of Interludes succeeded in forging a subtle instrument to contrast mask and face, physical appearance and spiritual reality. Notable cases of this technique are to be found in Redford's *Wit and Science* and Bale's

Three Laws. Abstract personifications of Virtues and Vices were of course standardized and instantly recognizable from constant repetition in tapestry, stained glass and frescoes: thus Justice carried her sword and balances and was normally dressed in red, while Truth was dressed in white and carried a book. In this respect stage conventions had not advanced materially on those first adopted in liturgical music-drama. Variety was provided by word-games, physical combats and songs and dances. Actors, uncertain of their reception at the hands of an audience in festive mood, defended themselves with apologetic prologues and epilogues: given the proximity of the spectators and the strictly subservient nature of the player in relation to his employer this is understandable, and indeed it would have been extraordinary if frequent *ad lib* exchanges were not a common occurrence in the course of performances which relied so heavily upon direct address with its many rhetorical questions and asides.

This technique is carried to its ultimate extreme in the outrageous collection of money from the audience by means of blackmail, executed by Now-a-Days, Nought and New Guise in *Mankind*, and in the astonishingly rapid changes of identity undertaken by 'Idleness' in *The Marriage Between Wit and Wisdom*.

The player of Interludes thus had to be quick-witted, skilled in repartee and a versatile mimic, singer, dancer and acrobat. As a household servant society expected him to respect his station in the social hierarchy; yet his profession often required him to mimic and sometimes to parody the manners and behaviour of his social superiors. As a critic of grasping merchants, pretentious lawyers and pedants, and corrupt clerics, he endeared himself to their victims, yet was feared by the objects of his ridicule. Possessed of the financial means to secure a measure of personal freedom and mobility in strictly regulated and largely static communities, he was at once admired and envied.

Despite the growing interference of successive governments in their way of life, and the attempts of the more extreme Protestants in Elizabethan England to destroy it altogether, they succeeded, thanks to Court patronage, in refining their craft, winning larger audiences, and raising sufficient capital funds to acquire leases of land and to build theatres they could call their own. It was thus to the makers and players of Interludes that Edward Alleyn, James and Richard Burbage, Christopher Marlowe and William Shakespeare owed the foundations on which they built their own careers.

Note on the Texts

In editing the texts included in this volume, I have followed the manuscript or, in cases where that has not survived, the first printed text, glossing words or phrases not readily intelligible today with a modern equivalent in the right-hand margin. Occasionally, in cases where a word or phrase is so archaic or obviously mistaken as to deny meaning to a larger phrase or whole sentence, I have replaced it in the text with a modern translation in italic type and have placed the original word against the letters MS or Q in the margin. Thus,

to be a man's (*mate*) by way of marriage.   Q. *fere*

A particular problem arises with 'ye' and 'you' in *Fulgens and Lucres* and, to a lesser extent, in *The Conversion of Saint Paul*. The niceties of distinction in personal address between social superiors and inferiors as characterized by the use of 'thee', 'thou', 'ye' and 'you' that had been strictly observed in Lydgate's lifetime were becoming blurred by the end of the fifteenth century. Since neither Medwall nor the author of *Saint Paul* is consistent in his use of these courtesies, 'ye' has been modernized to 'you' throughout— a decision that makes inevitable some loss of flavour in the idiom of the original text.

Latin quotations in the text are printed as they occur. The English translation follows immediately. In those rare cases where a scribe or compositor appears to have left out a word, I have printed it in italic type within brackets to call attention to the editorial departure from the Text. Thus,

I thank you sir with all (*my*) heart.

Where stage directions are concerned, I have eliminated all those inserted by earlier editors which do not occur in the original manuscript or first Quarto, replacing those which seem essential either by directions in italic type and placed in brackets for easy recognition or, in cases of greater ambiguity, by supplying an explanatory footnote to help the actor and director in rehearsal. Stage directions that do appear in the original appear in this edition in italic type with no brackets round them: in the case of directions in Latin, the English translation appears beside them.

In the Appendix, rather than attempt to gloss an ancient Middle English text, I have supplied a free, line-by-line translation of *The Interlude of the Student and the Girl* in parallel with the text itself. The two Lydgate texts have been left to speak for themselves, with normal glosses for archaic words placed in the margin.

Department of Drama,   Glynne Wickham
University of Bristol, 1975

FURTHER READING

General: Historical development and critical commentary

Sir Edward Chambers, *The Mediaeval Stage*, 1903, vol. ii, chs 24 and 25; Ian Maxwell, *French Farce and John Heywood*, 1946; Bernard Spivack, *Shakespeare and the Allegory of Evil*, N.Y., 1950; T. W. Craik, *The Tudor Interlude*, 1958; David Bevington, *From Mankind to Marlowe*, 1962; Muriel Bradbrook, *The Rise of the Common Player*, 1962; A. Harbage & S. Schoenbaum, *Annals of English Drama*, *975–1700*, 1964; F. P. Wilson and G. K. Hunter, 'The English Drama, 1485–1585', *Oxford History of English Literature*, 1969; Glynne Wickham, *The Medieval Theatre*, 1974; reprint 1986; William Tydeman, *The Theatre in the Middle Ages*, 1978

Play Texts

The most recent and fullest bibliography of all English Interludes (manuscripts and printed editions) is in Glynne Wickham, *Early English Stages*, vol. iii (1981), pp. 323–335.

Subsequent editions of individual plays and groups of plays include:

Three Tudor Classical Interludes, (*Thersites*; *Jacke Jugeler* and *Horestes*) ed. Marie Axton for D. S. Brewer, Cambridge, 1982.

Two Tudor Interludes (*Youth*; *Hick Scorner*) ed. Ian Lancashire for The Revels Plays, Manchester/Johns Hopkins, 1980.

Three Rastell Plays (*The Four Elements*; *Calisto and Melebea* and *Gentleness and Nobility*) ed. Richard Axton for D. S. Brewer, Cambridge, 1979.

MANKIND

After some three centuries of virtual oblivion, and two more in which this Interlude has varied in critical esteem between grudging acknowledgment of its existence and outright dismissal of any literary or dramatic merit pertaining to it, *Mankind* has unexpectedly been revived in two productions in recent years—one in Toronto in 1966, the other in Bristol in 1971 [1]—and on both occasions it has astonished its audiences by its theatrical vitality and dramatic power. These two productions, in exposing earlier criticism of the play as arid and uncomprehending, have not as yet served to re-establish it as a text worthy of serious study. Nevertheless Mark Eccles, in re-editing the play in 1969 for the Early English Text Society with a helpful introduction, and Paula Neuss, by contributing a highly original essay on the play's dramatic imagery to *Stratford-Upon-Avon Studies 16* (*Medieval Drama*), have already done much between them to square the account with the past, and to make it possible to approach the text with new eyes.

In preparing this edition, it is my hope that I can advance this process a little further by providing a text that is both more readily accessible and self-evidently actable than its predecessors. In this attempt I have had the advantage of being able to work from the Folger Facsimile text, edited by David Bevington in 1972 with facing transcripts. This edition owes its name to the fact that the surviving manuscript is now in the Folger Library in Washington, D.C. (MS V a.354), where it has rested since it was bought at auction in London in 1936. It is bound up with two other Morality Plays, *The Castle of Perseverance* and *Wisdom*, in a single volume known as 'The Macro Plays': this name is derived from the surname of the man who owned these MSS in the eighteenth century, the Rev. Cox Macro, a bibliophile of Bury St Edmunds in Suffolk. This knowledge, together with the names of villages in Cambridgeshire and Norfolk listed by New Guise and Nought in lines 505–15, commits the play firmly to East Anglia. The East Midland dialect in which much of the dialogue is cast confirms this attribution: composition can be dated from the dialogue between 1465 and 1470.

[1] Performed by students of the University of Toronto and the Bristol Old Vic Theatre School respectively.

The play possesses affinities with Lydgate's *The Assembly of the Gods*, but is principally derived from 'The Book of Job' and the New Testament account of the Last Judgement. What Mercy says to the audience in the Prologue advances the moral burden of this Interlude in lofty but uncompromising language.

> Mercy is my name that mourneth for your offence.
> Divert not yourself in time of temptation,
> That ye may be acceptable to God at your going hence.
> . . . .
>
> For, surely, there shall be a strict examination:
> The corn shall be saved: the chaff shall be burnt.

Starting from these sources the anonymous author has chosen, in the manner of Dominican and Franciscan preachers of the fifteenth century, to allegorize upon these materials and provide his audience with vivid, concrete stage pictures of the abstract doctrinal concepts that he wished to expound. Two ideas take precedence: the first is the efforts that Lucifer will make to exploit the discrepancies between mankind's spiritual needs and bodily desires in order to bring the former into subjection to the latter: the second is to illustrate that it is by both deeds and words that mankind will be judged and ultimately committed at Doomsday to everlasting damnation or salvation. Words are regarded by the author to be of at least equal importance with deeds as tangible tokens of an individual's state of mind. The language given to all the characters, and its variations as the Interlude proceeds, are thus just as clear a guide to the development of the moral argument as any of their actions.

Critics therefore in the past, who have been so shocked by the obscenity of much of the dialogue as to expurgate it when committing it to print, or who (lacking that degree of conviction) have deflected readers away from the text by describing it as 'for the most part admittedly and unrelievedly dull', have only succeeded in confessing their own failure to come to terms with the author's original intentions and methods.

Not having directed the play myself, I can make no pretensions to being a final arbiter upon its meaning; but, viewing it as a script for performance in a medieval banquet hall or in a provincial inn, it is obvious that the language with which the author has chosen to endow his characters supports the morals to be drawn from their actions: in short, the latter, as figurative and visible extensions of the former, manifest a logical development by the clerical author of three fundamental points of Roman Catholic doctrine. The first is that Sloth, or Idleness (cf. *Wit and Wisdom*, pp. 164–5 below), is a deadly sin and can bring man's soul to damnation on Judgement Day: the second is that man can readily be seduced into this state of being by failure to discipline his speech: the third is that the sinner who repents is assured of Mercy. To this end the protagonist, Mankind, is given two distinct kinds of language—that which he uses in conversation with Mercy and while he is in control of himself, both at the start and at the end of the play, and that which he employs once he has succumbed to the wiles of Titivillus. This is only the more strongly reinforced by the author's choice of Titivillus as the particular devil used by Lucifer to break Mankind's will power and to bring him into the clutches of Mischief and the other vices. As anyone familiar with the Wakefield Cycle will recognize, Titivillus is a devil armed by Satan with a cloak of invisibility, a net and a satchel to help him in the specific task of collecting men's sinful thoughts and utterances to be stored against them and counted on the Day of Judgement. The author of *Mankind* depicts Titivillus in precisely this guise and equips him with four agents—Mischief, New Guise, Now-a-Days and Nought—whose collective task it is to make Mankind translate the seriousness of his thoughts and the sobriety of his speech into ideas as dissolute and language as obscene as their own. Once they have achieved this they can bring Mankind into a state of 'despair' leading to suicide as effectively as 'Worldly Shame' in *Nice Wanton* ensnares Xantippe (see pp. 158–61 below) with the same objective. Thus Devil, World and Flesh work in consort to corrupt and destroy human beings.

In order to equate his abstract protagonist, Mankind, with human beings at large, the author used several figurative analogues to anchor him firmly both in time past and time present. By depicting him with his spade, his allotment plot and his corn, he conjured up for medieval audiences the figures of Adam and Cain: the significance of these familiar biblical images is then further reinforced by the constant harping in the dialogue on the idea that all earthly life is a succession of tests, like those experienced by Job, designed to fortify the soul and bring it to salvation. Thus,

> God will prove you soon: and, if that ye be constant,
> Of his bliss perpetual ye shall be partner.

This concept, as transferred to the stage, reaches forward to the testing of Angelo in *Measure for Measure*. At the same time the author takes great care to involve his audience directly in the play by making them participate in the very actions which are to undo Mankind. First, he destroys the barriers between play and real life, actor and audience, by making his chief Vice, Mischief (and later Now-a-Days in the role of a carol singer), enter from among the audience, thus endowing the actor/character with the same, ambiguous double image that Medwall gives to the two servants A and B in *Fulgens and Lucres* (see pp. 41–3 below): next, he uses the device of community singing to make his audience foul their lips with

[3]

the same obscene parody of sacred music that he employs to reveal the loutish degradation of Nought, New Guise and Now-a-Days.

> Now, I pray all yeomanry, that is here,
> To sing with us a merry cheer.

Thirdly, he makes his audience into accomplices in blackmail and then employs them as the Devil's personal financiers when the Vices refuse to make Titivillus materialize without cash in advance.

> We shall gather money unto;
> Else there shall no man see him.

The dramatic skill of this device is only the more striking because of the exploitation implicit in it of the proverbial invisibility of Titivillus.

There can be no question then but that the author of *Mankind* knew precisely what he was doing both as a theologian and as a dramatist. Doctrine, dialogue and stage action advance hand in hand with studied consistency to illustrate in a swift succession of vivid, and frequently shocking, theatrical tableaux the Church's teaching that it is by a man's works and his words that he shall be known and judged. An obvious example of this technique is the stage direction

> Here Titivillus goes out with the spade.

that follows immediately upon Mankind's decision to quit physical work: another is the progressive shortening of Mankind's coat as a visible symbol of the degeneration in Mankind's speech and character. Constant vigilance, as Mercy insistently repeats to Mankind, is the only protection, under God's Grace, against the vicious fancies which idleness generates: nowhere do such dangerous thoughts find a more fertile soil for translation into deeds than in a tavern:

> Distemper not your brain with strong ale nor with wine!

But once Mankind has abandoned his will to work, it is to the tavern that he goes.

> I will haste me to the ale-house
> And speak with New Guise, Now-a-Days and Nought.

His purpose there is to find a whore; the cash to pay the bills is to be got by robbing a church.

This scenic image of the tavern as the Devil's kitchen figures in Interlude after Interlude throughout the sixteenth century and still possessed sufficient theatrical vitality at the close of it for Shakespeare to seize on the Boar's Head in Eastcheap as the proper house for Falstaff and as the appropriate environment for the testing of the character of Prince Hal in the two parts of *Henry IV*.

[4]

Another scenic image of importance is that which the author uses to introduce the three Vices, New Guise, Now-a-Days and Nought. In my view this is a deliberate parody of a bearward and his dancing bear. New Guise, escorted by a piper, thus enters in the role of the bearward and Nought in that of the bear: Now-a-Days is employed by New Guise to prod or whip Nought into giving an amusing performance. A picture of just such a scene—musician with pipes, trainer with whip, a third man and a bear at the end of a rope—is printed by Joseph Strutt in *Sports and Pastimes of the People of England* (London, 1810), Plate XXII. I therefore think it likely that in performance Nought entered dressed up in a panto-mime bearskin with a detachable head. This image suffices to equate the Vices at the outset with loutish thugs whose spiritual kinship lies with the lower animals rather than civilized men: this accords with Nought's fouling of himself with his own excrement shortly before his final exit.

Parody is again used to point a moral in the outrageous Court scene presided over by Mischief in the role of judge in which Mankind is sentenced to those very things that are most likely to damn him at the final Judgement: this too finds its parallel in the mock trial scenes in the Boar's Head Tavern in *Henry IV* Part 1, Act II, scene iv.

The overall setting for this remarkable sequence of scenic images, however, is quite simply the Hall of a Manor House, or possibly a Priory, or alternatively a Guildhall or the dining-room of an hotel or inn. The *platea*, place or acting area unifies the whole action which requires nothing in the way of physical scenery, the locations being clearly identified by the dialogue and some simple stage properties. The play could thus readily be taken on tour by the normal professional company of six players, and with the part of Titivillus being doubled by the actor playing Mercy. A raised stage was not normal in England at this date, and there is nothing in the text to suggest that one is needed: the hall screen, whether with one door or two, separated the acting area in the hall from the actors' dressing-room in the adjacent kitchen area, and all exits and entrances are deliberately made through the audience, that is through 'the sovereigns' that sit and 'the brethren' that stand. It is thus a very intimate setting, and the relationship with the audience close enough for actual individuals of their acquaintance to be named by New Guise and Now-a-Days in the horse-stealing scene.

Mankind, then, is a remarkable play designed by its author to shock audiences out of lethargy and complacence. It can still do so in performance, *provided* that the director recognizes that it is a serious tragicomedy and not a quaint and bawdy farce; that he will trust his author and refrain from expurgating the text because of its apparent obscenity, and from ruthless cutting of those parts of it that are not comic for fear that they will be found unintelligible and dull by a modern audience.

EDITIONS

J. M. MANLY, *Specimens of the Pre-Shakespearean Drama* 1, 1897;

A. BRANDL, *Quellen des weltlichen Dramas in England vor Shakespeare*, in *Quellen und Forschungen* lxxx, Strassburg, 1898;

F. J. FURNIVALL & A. W. POLLARD, *The Macro Plays* for the Early English Text Society, 1904: reprinted 1924;

J. S. FARMER, *The Tudor Facsimile Texts*, 1907; Amersham, 1914;

J. S. FARMER, *Lost Tudor Plays*, 1907: reprinted 1966;

J. Q. ADAMS, *Chief Pre-Shakespearean Dramas*, Boston, 1924;

MARK ECCLES, *The Macro Plays*, for E.E.T.S., 1969;

DAVID BEVINGTON, *Folger Facsimiles: The Macro Plays*, 1972.

MODERN COMMENTARIES

SISTER M. P. COOGAN, *An Interpretation of the Moral Play*, '*Mankind*', Washington, 1947;

DONALD C. BAKER, 'The Date of *Mankind*', Philological Quarterly, xlii (1963) 90–1;

MARK ECCLES, 'Introduction', *The Macro Plays* for E.E.T.S., 1969;

PAULA NEUSS, 'Active and Idle Language: Dramatic Images in *Mankind*', *Stratford-upon-Avon Studies 16 (Medieval Drama)*, ed. Neville Denny, 1973.

MANKIND
c. 1470

(*The Names of the Players*)
Mercy   New Guise
Mankind   Nought
Mischief   Now-a-Days
            Titivillus

(*Enter Mercy*)

Mercy. The very Founder and Beginner of our first creation,
   Among us sinful wretches He oweth to be magnified;
   That, for our disobedience, He had none indignation
   To send His own Son to be torn and crucified.
5 Our obsequious service to Him should be applied:
   Where He was Lord of all, and made all thing of nought,
   For the sinful sinner, to have him revived,
   And, for his redemption, set His own Son at nought.
   That may be said and verified: Mankind was dear bought.
10 By the piteous death of Jesu he had his remedy;
   He was purged of his default—that wretchedly had wrought—
   By his glorious passion, that blessed lavatory.   *purifier*
   O sovereigns! I beseech you your conditions to rectify;
   And, with humility and reverence, to have a
       remotion   *to return*
15 To this blessed Prince, that our nature doth glorify;
   That ye may be participable of His retribution.   *partake of*
   I have be(en) the very mean for your restitution
   Mercy is my name, that mourneth for your offence.
   Divert not yourself in time of temptation.
20 That ye may be acceptable to God at your going hence:
   The great mercy of God, that is of most pre-eminence,
   By meditation of Our Lady, that is ever abundant
   To the sinful creature that will repent his negligence:
   I pray God, at your most need, that Mercy be your defendant.
25 In good works I advise you, sovercigns, to be perseverant;
   To purify your souls that they be not corrupt:
   For your ghostly enemy will make his avaunt,   *boast*
   Your good conditions if he may interrupt.

[7]

O! ye sovereigns that sit, and ye brothern that stand right up,
30   Pryke not your felicities in things transitory!   *fasten*
Behold not the earth, but hold your eye up!
See how the head the members daily do magnify.
Who is the head? forsooth! I shall you certify:
I mean our Saviour that was likened to a lamb.
35   And His saints be the members, that daily he doth satisfy
With the precious river that runneth from his womb. *stomach*
There is none such food by water, nor by land;
So precious, so glorious, so needful to our intent;
For it hath dissolved Mankind from the bitter bond
40   Of the mortal enemy, that venomous serpent: *Lucifer*
From the which, God preserve you all at the last judgment!
For, sickerly, there shall be a streyt   *surely; strict*
   examination:
The corn shall be saved; the chaff shall be brent—
I beseech you heartily have this premeditation.

(*Enter Mischief*)

45   *Mischief.*   I beseech you heartily leave your calc[*ul*]ation!
Leave your chaff! leave your corn! leave your dalliation!
Your wit is little; your head is mickle; ye are full   *large*
   of predication!   *dogma*
But, sir! I pray (*you*) this question to clarify:
Mish, mash! Driff, draff!
50   Some was corn and some was chaff:
My dame said my name was Raff;
Unshut your lock and take an halfpenny!

Mercy.   Why come ye hither, brother? ye were not desired.

Mischief.   For a winter corn thresher, sir, I have hired.
55   And ye said: the corn should be saved and the chaff should
   be fired;
And he proveth nay, as it showeth by this verse:
'Corn serveth breadibus, chaff horsibus, straw firibusque.'
This is as much to say, to your lewd understanding,
As: the corn shall serve to bread at the next baking:
   'Chaff horsibus, et reliqu(*i*)d,'
60   The chaff to horse shall be good provender;
When a man is for-cold the straw may be brent;
And so forth, etc.

Mercy.   Avoid, good brother! ye been culpable
To interrupt thus my talking delectable.   *pleasantries*
65   *Mischief.*   Sir! I have neither horse nor saddle;
Therefore, I may not ride.

52 Said as he stuffs a coin into his mouth.

[8]

Mercy.   Hie you forth on foot, brother! in God's name!

Mischief.   I say, sir! I am come hither to make you
    game;   *sport, pastime*
    Yet, bade ye me not go out in the devil's name,
70   And I will abide.

[*A leaf of the manuscript has probably been lost at this point. The text commences again with the entry of New Guise, Nought and Now-a-Days with a band of minstrels*]

New Guise.   And ho, minstrels! play the common
    trace;   *dance steps*
    Lay on with thy bales till his belly brest! *stick, whip; bursts*

Nought.   I put case I break my neck—how than?   *suppose*

New Guise.   I give no force, by saint Anne!   *I don't care*

75 *Now-a-Days.*   Leap about lively! thou art a valiant man;
    Let us be merry while we be here!

Nought.   Shall I break my neck to show you sport?

Now-a-Days.   Therefore, ever beware of thy report!

Nought.   I beshrew you all! here is a shrewd sort;
80   Have thereat then, with a merry cheer!

              Here they dance. Mercy saith

Mercy.   Do way! do way this revel, sirs! do way!   *Stop!*

Now-a-Days.   Do way, good Adam? do way?
    This is no part of thy play.

Nought.   Yes, marry! I pray you; for I love not this revelling;
85   Come forth, good father! I you pray;
    By a little ye may assay.
    Anon, off with your clothes! if ye will pray.
    Go to! I have had a pretty scottling.   *scampering*

Mercy.   Nay, brother! I will not dance.

90 *New Guise.*   If ye will, sir! My brother will make *Yes, you will!*
    you to prance.

Now-a-Days.   With all my heart, sir! if I may you avance;
    Ye may assay by a little trace.   *a few steps*

Nought.   Yea, sir! will ye do well?
    Trace not with them, by my counsel!   *Dance*
95   For I have traced somewhat too fell;   *violently*

70 sd On this entrance and the possible parody of a bearward and his dancing bear in the dialogue that follows, see Introduction, p. 5 above.
86 Try a little yourself.

I reckon it is a narrow space.
But, sir! I trow, of us three I heard you speak.

New Guise.   Christ's curse have ye, therefore! for I was in sleep.

Now-a-Days.   A(*nd*) I had the cup in my hand, ready to go to
meat—
100   Therefore, sir! curtly, greet you well!   *in brief*

Mercy.   Few words! few, and well set!

New Guise.   Sir! it is the new guise and the new jet.   *fashion*
Many words and shortly set—
This is the new guise, every deal.

105   *Mercy.*   Lady, help! how wretches delight in their sinful ways!

Now-a-Days.   Say no(*ugh*)t against the new guise now-a-days!
Thou shall find us sh(*r*)ews at all assays:
Beware! ye may soon lick a buffet.   *taste*

Mercy.   He was well occupied that brought you hither!

110   *Nought.*   I heard you call New Guise, Now-a-Days, Nought:
all these three together.
If ye say that I lie, I shall make you to slither:
Lo, take you here a trepitt!   *trip, tumble*

Mercy.   Say me your names! I know you not.

New Guise (Now-a-Days and Nought, in turn) New Guise, I!
Now-a-Days, (I)! I, Nought!

115   *Mercy.*   By Jesu Christ! that me dear bought;
Ye betray many men.

New Guise.   Betray? nay, nay, sir! nay, nay!
We make them both fresh and gay!
But, of your name, sir, I you pray
120   That we may you ken.

Mercy.   Mercy is my name and my denomination.
I conceive ye have but a little force in my   *hardly know me*
communication.

New Guise.   Ay, ay! your body is full of English Latin.
I am afraid it will burst!
125   'I curse you!' said the butcher unto me   MS. *Pravote!*
When I stole a leg of mutton!
You are a strong, cunning priest!

Now-a-Days.   I pray you heartily, worshipful clerk!
To have this English made in Latin:
130   'I have eaten a dishful of curds,
And I have shitten your mouth full of turds.'
Now, open your satchel with Latin words,
And say me this, in clerical manner!

[10]

Also, I have a wife; her name is Rachel;
135   Betwixt her and me was a great battle;
And fain of you I would hear tell   *gladly*
Who was the most master.

Nought.   Thy wife, Rachel, I dare lay twenty lice!

Now-a-Days.   Who spake to thee? fool! thou art not wise;
140   Go and do that longeth to thine office: *belongs*
Osculare fundamentum!   *Kiss his arse!*

Nought.   Lo, master! lo, here is a pardon belly-meet;
It is granted of Pope Pockett:
If ye will put your nose in his wife's socket,
145   Ye shall have forty days of pardon!   *less in Purgatory*

Mercy.   This idle language ye shall repent!
Out of this place I would ye went!

New Guise.   Go we hence all three, with one assent;
My father is irk of our eloquence;   *Mercy; weary*
150   Therefore, I will no longer tarry.
God bring you, master, and blessed Mary
To the number of the demonical frayry—   *friary*

Now-a-Days.   Come wind! come rain!
Though I come never again;
155   The devil put out both your eyne!
Fellows! go we hence tight!   *quickly*

Nought.   Go we hence, a devil way!
Here is the door; here is the way!
Farewell, gentle Geoffrey!
160   I pray God give you good night!

                [*They go out together, singing*

Mercy.   Thanked be God! we have a fair deliverance
Of these three unthrifty guests!
They know full little what is their ordinance.   *destiny*
I [*will*] prove by reason they be worse than beasts:
165   A beast doth after his natural institution;
Ye may conceive, by their disport and behaviour,
Their joy and delight is in derision
Of their own Christ, to His dishonour.
This condition of living, it is prejudicial;

---

142 *belly-meet:* to satisfy the stomach. This verse is cast in the language of
     Reformation polemic that was to be used so extensively by John Bale
     in his plays in the 1530s; see p. xi above.
152 To join the devils in Hell.
159 An alliterative insult.

170   Beware thereof! it is worse than any felony or treason.
       How may it be excused before the Judge of (us) all
       When, for every idle word, we must yield a reason?
       They have great ease; therefore, they will take no thought;
       But how then, when the angel of heaven shall blow the
          trump,
175   And say to the transgressors that wickedly have wrought:
       'Come forth unto your Judge, and yield your account'?
       Then shall I, Mercy, begin sore to weep;
       Neither comfort nor counsel, there shall none be had;
       But, such as they have sown, such shall they reap;
180   They be wanton now; but, then, shall they be sad.
       The good new guise, now-a-days, I will not disallow;   *blame*
       I discommend the vicious guise—I pray have me excused—
       I need not to speak of it; your reason will tell it you:
       Take that is to be taken, and leave that is to be refused!

(Enter Mankind)

185   *Mankind.*   Of the earth and of the clay we have our propagation;
       By the providence of God thus we be derivate,   *derived*
       To whose mercy I recommend this whole congregation.
       I hope unto His bliss ye be all predestinate:
       Every man, for his degree, I trust shall be participate;
190   If we will mortify our carnal condition,
       And our voluntary desires—that ever be
          pervertionate—
                           contrary, perverse
       To renounce these and yield us under God's provision.
       My name is Mankind. I have my composition
       Of a body and of a soul, of condition contrary.
195   Betwixt the twain is a great division:
       He that should be subject, now he hath the victory.
       This is to me a lamentable story:
       To see my flesh, of my soul to have governance;
       Where the good wife is master, the goodman may be sorry.
200   I may both sigh and sob; this is a piteous remembrance.
       O, thou my soul! so subtle in thy substance,
       Alas! what was thy fortune and thy chance
       To be associate with my flesh, that stinking dunghill?
       Lady, help! Sovereigns! it doth my soul   *worthy spectators*
          much ill
205   To see the flesh prosperous, and the soul trodden under
       foot.

---

182 This obscure passage, freely translated, means, 'I don't blame either
      fashion or novelty in themselves, only the abuse of them.'
199 This proverb forms the basis of Lydgate's *Mumming at Hertford* q.v.,
      pp. 204 ff. below.

I shall go to yonder man; and assay him I will;   *seek his help*
I trust of ghostly solace he will be my boot.   *remedy*

(*Mankind approaches Mercy*)

All hail, seemly father! ye be welcome to this house;
Of the very wisdom ye have participation.
210 My body with my soul is ever querulous;   *in argument*
I pray you, for Saint Charity! of your supportation.
I beseech you, heartily, of your ghostly comfort;
I am unsteadfast in living; my name is Mankind;
My ghostly enemy, the Devil, will have a great disport,
215 In sinful guiding if he may see me end.

Mercy.   Christ send you good comfort! ye be welcome, my friend!
Stand up on your feet! I pray you, arise!
My name is Mercy; ye be to me full hend: *goodlooking, gracious*
To eschew vice I will you advise.

220 *Mankind.*   O, Mercy! of all grace and virtue ye are the well:
I have heard tell, of right-worshipful clerks,
Ye be approximate to God and near of his counsel;
He hath institute you above all His works—   *placed*
Oh! your lovely words to my soul are sweeter than honey.

225 *Mercy.*   The temptation of the flesh ye must resist, like a man;
For, there is ever a battle betwixt the soul and the body:
Vita hominis est milicia super terram.
Oppress your ghostly enemy, and be Christ's own knight;
Be never a coward again(*st*) your adversary;
230 If ye will be crowned, ye must needs fight!
Intend well; and God will be to you adjutory!
Remember, my friend! the time of continuance;
So, help me God! it is but a cherry-time.   *short-season*
Spend it well! serve God with heart's affiance!
235 Distemper not your brain with good ale, nor with wine!
Measure is treasure; I forbid you not the use;
Measure yourself ever! Beware of excess!
The superfluous guise, I will that ye refuse:
When nature is sufficed, anon that ye cease.
240 If a man have a horse, and keep him not too high,
He may then rule him at his own desire;
If he be fed over well, he will disobey;
And, in hap, cast his master in the mire.   *may well*

(*Re-enter New Guise: he stands apart, out of sight of Mankind*)

New Guise.   Ye say true, sir! ye are no faitour;   *deceiver*
245 I have fed my wife so well till she is my master.

[13]

I have a great wound on my head! lo! and thereon lieth a
    plaster;
And another—where I piss my peson   *codpiece*
And my wife were your horse, she would you all
    to-banne.   *blame*
Ye feed your horse in measure; ye are a wise man!
250   I trow and ye were the king's palfry-man,   *groom*
A good horse should be gesumme.   *scarce*

Mankind. Where speaks this fellow? Will he not come near?

Mercy. All too soon, my brother, I fear me, for you!
He was here right now—by Him that bought me dear!—
255   With other of his fellows; they can much sorrow.   *cause*
They will be here right soon, if I out depart.
Think on my doctrine! it shall be your defence;
Learn while I am here! set my words in heart!
Within a short space I must needs hence.

(Now-a-Days and Nought return)

260   *Now-a-Days (to Mercy).* The sooner the liever; and that *better*
    be even anon!
I trow your name is Do-little—ye be so long from home;
If ye would go hence we shall come, everyone,
Mo than a good sort!
Ye have leave, I dare well say!
265   When ye will, go forth your way!—
Men have little dainty of your play   *pleasure in*
Because ye make no sport.

Nought. Your pottage shall be for-cold, sir! when will ye go
    dine?
I have seen a man lost twenty nobles in as little time;
270   Yet it was not I, by saint Quintin!
For I was never worth a pot full a'worts sithen I   *vegetables*
    was born.
My name is Nought; I love well to make merry;
I have be sithen with the common tapster of Bury.   *meantime*
275   I played so long the fool that I am even very weary:
Yet shall I be there again, to-morrow.

(They go out)

Mercy. I have much care for you, my own friend!   *worry*
Your enemies will be here anon; they make their
    avaunt.   *boast*
Think well in your heart—your name is Mankind—
Be not unkind to God, I pray you! be his servant!

268 Your soup will get cold.
270 *by saint Quintin:* the hypocrite's oath.

[14]

280   Be steadfast in condition! see ye be not variant!
      Lose not, through folly, that is bought so dear.
      God will prove you soon; and, if that ye be constant,
      Of His bliss perpetual ye shall be partner.
      Ye may not have your intent at your first desire;
285   See the great patience of Job in tribulation:
      Like as the smith trieth iron in the fire,
      So was he tried by God's visitation.
      He was of your nature, and of your fragility:
      Follow the steps of him, my own sweet son!
290   And say, as he said, in your trouble and adversity:
      *Dominus dedit, Dominus abstulit, sicut sibi placuit; sit nomen
        Domini benedictum.*
      (*The Lord giveth and the Lord taketh away as he pleases;
        blessed be the name of the Lord.*)
      Moreover, in special, I give you in charge:
      Beware of New Guise, Now-a-Days and Nought!
      Nice in their array, in language they be large;
295   To pervert your conditions all their means shall be sought.
      Good son! intermix not yourself in their company!
      They heard not a mass this twelvemonth, I dare well say;
      Give them none audience! they will tell you many a lie;
      Do truly your labour, and keep your holyday!
300   Beware of Titivillus—for he leseth no way,   *never lets go*
      That goeth invisible and will not be seen;
      He will rond in your ear, and cast a net before your eyne;
      He is worst of them all: God let him never thene!   *thrive*
      If ye displease God, ask mercy anon;   *at once*
305   Else Mischief will be ready to brace you in his bridle.
      Kiss me now, my dear darling! God shie(l)d you
        from your fone!   *enemies*
      Do truly your labour, and be never idle!
      The blessing of God be with you, and with all these
        worshipful men!   *the audience*

      (*Exit Mercy*)

   Mankind.   Amen! for saint Charity, Amen!
310   Now, blessed be Jesu! my soul is well satiate
      With the mellifluous doctrine of this worshipful man.
      The rebellion of my flesh, now it is superate,
      Thanking be (*to*) God, of the conning that I ken.
      Here will I sit, and tittle in this paper   *write down*
315   The incomparable estate of my promotion.
      Worshipful Sovereigns! I have written here

294 On the significance of the word 'nice', see Introduction to *Nice Wanton*.
302 *rond in your ear*: speak privately, whisper.
313 The knowledge that I know.

[15]

The glorious remembrance of my noble condition,
To have remo(r)se and memory of myself: thus written it is
To defend me from all superstitious charms:
320 *Memento, homo, quod cinis es, et in cinerem reverteris,*
 (*Remember, Mankind, that from dust you came and to dust you
  will return.*)
Lo! I bear on my breast the badge of mine arms.

         (*He hangs the paper round his neck*)

   (*New Guise enters, but remains in the background*)

New Guise. The weather is cold; God send us good fires!
 Cum sancto sanctus eris, et cum perverso, perverteris.
 Ecce quam bonum et quam jocundum, quod the devil to the friars,
325 *Habitare fratres in unum.*

Mankind. I hear a fellow speak; with him I will not
 mell.   *mix*
 This earth with my spade I shall assay to delve;
 To eschew idleness I do that mine own self;
 I pray God send it His fusion!   *abundance*

    (*Enter Now-a-Days and Nought*)

330 *Now-a-Days.* Make room, sirs, for we have be long!
 We will come give you a Christmas song.

Nought. Now, I pray all the yeomanry that is here,
 To sing with us a merry cheer:

           (*Nought sings*)

 It is written with a coal, it is written with a coal—

335 *New Guise & Now-a-Days.* *It is written with a coal, it is
 written,* etc.

Nought. *He that shitteth with his hole, he that shitteth with his
 hole—*

New Guise & Now-a-Days. *He that shitteth with his hole,* etc.

Nought. *But he wipe his arse clean, but he,* etc.—

New Guise & Now-a-Days. *But he wipe his arse clean, but he,* etc.

340 *Nought.* *On his breech it shall be seen, on his breech,* etc.

New Guise & Now-a-Days. *On his breech it shall be seen, on his
 breech,* etc.

Cantant Omnes. *Holyke, holyke, holyke! holyke, holyke, holyke!*

New Guise. Hey, Mankind! God speed you with your spade!
 I shall tell you of a marriage:

334 f. Nought's objective is to involve the audience by making them participate in this obscene parody of a carol: in performance it should be sung
 as a 'round', or as a parody of a 'motet with burden'.

[16]

345   I would your mouth and his arse, that this made,

      Were married junctly together!   *jointly*

Mankind.   Hie you hence, fellows! with

      breding;   *reproach, for shame*

      Leave your derision and your japing!

      I must needs labour; it is my living.

350   *Now-a-Days.*   What, sir! we came but late hither—

      Shall all this corn grow here

      That ye shall have the next year?

      If it be so, corn had need be dear!

      Else ye shall have a poor life.

355   *Nought.*   Alas, good father! this labour fretteth you to the bone;

      But, for your crop I take great moan;

      Ye shall never spend it alone—

      I shall assay to get you a wife.

      How many acres suppose ye here, by estimation?

360   *New Guise.*   Hey! how ye turn the earth up and down!

      I have be(*en*), in my days, in many (*a*) good town,

      Yet saw I never such another tilling!

Mankind.   Why stand ye idle! it is pity that ye were born!

Now-a-Days.   We shall bargain with you; and neither mock nor

      scorn—

365   Take a good cart in harvest, and load it with your corn,

      And what shall we give you for the leaving?

Nought.   He is a good, stark labourer; he would fain   *sturdy*

      do well—

      He hath met with the good man Mercy in a

      shroud sell: *shady nook*

      For all this, he may have many a hungry meal.   *unlucky time*

370   Yet will ye see, he is politic:

      Here shall be good corn; he may not miss it;

      If he will have rain, he may overpiss it;

      And if he will have compos(*t*) he may overbliss it

      A little, with his arse-lick!   *wipe*

375   *Mankind.*   Go and do your labour! God let you

      never thee!   *prosper*

      Or, with my spade, I shall you ding, by the holy   *knock*

      Trinity!

      Have ye none other man to mock, but ever me?

      Ye would have me of your set?

      Hie you forth lively! for hence I will you driffe!   *chase*

      (*Mankind hits out at them with his spade*)

351–2 'this' refers to the small area of ground being dug by Mankind. The
      couplet is thus satirical in intention and sets the tone for the mockery
      that follows.

380 *New Guise.* Alas, my jewels! I shall be   *testicles*
    shent of my wife!   *punished*

    Now-a-Days. Alas! and I am like never for to thrive;
    I have such a buffet!

    Mankind. Hence, I say, New Guise, Now-a-Days, and Nought!
    It was said beforn: all the means shall be sought

385   To pervert my conditions and bring me to nought—
    Hence, thieves! ye have made many a leasing!   *lie, slander*

    Nought. Marred I was for cold, but now am I warm!
    Ye are evil advised, sir! for ye have done harm.
    By Cock's body sacred! I have such a   *By the Sacrament*
        pain in my arm

390   I may not change a man a farthing!

    Mankind. Now, I thank God, kneeling on my knee:
    Blessed be His name! He is of high degree.
    By the aid of his grace, that He hath sent me,
    Three of mine enemies I have put to flight;

                                  (shows his spade)

395   Yet this instrument, sovereigns! is not made to defend—
    David saith: *Nec in hasta, nec in gladio, saluat Dominus.*
    (Neither in the spear nor in the sword does the Lord rejoice.)

    Nought. No, marry! I beshrew you! it is in *spadibus*!
    Therefore, Christ's curse come on your *headibus*,
    To send you less might!

                                  (They go out)

400 *Mankind (to the audience.)* I promise you, these fellows will no
        more come here;
    For some of them, certainly, were somewhat too near!
    My father, Mercy, advised me to be of a good cheer,
    And again my enemies manly for to fight.   *against*
    I shall convict them, I hope, every one—

405   Yet I say amiss; I do it not alone—
    With the help of the grace of God I resist my fone.   *foes*
    And their malicious heart(s).
    With my spade I will depart, my worshipful sovereigns!
    And live ever with labour, to correct my insolence.

410   I shall go fet(ch) corn for my land; I pray you of patience;
    Right soon I shall revert.   *return*

                          (He goes out) (Exit)

                      (Enter Mischief)

    Mischief. Alas, alas! that ever I was wrought!
    Alas! the while I *(am)* worse than nought!
    Sithen I was here, by Him that me bought!

[18]

415   I am utterly undone!
       I, Mischief, was here, at the beginning of the game,   *play*
       And argued with Mercy; God give him shame!
       He hath taught Mankind, while I have be vane,
       To fight manly against his fone;
420   For with his spade—that was his weapon—
       New Guise, Now-a-Days, Nought hath (*he*) all to-beaten:
       I have great pity to see them weeping.
       Will ye list? I hear them cry!

         (*New Guise, Now-a-days, and Nought enter*) They moan.

       Alas, alas! come hither! I shall be your borrow.   *protector*
425   Alack, alack! *veni, veni!* Come hither, with sorrow!
       Peace, fair babies! ye shall have a napple to-morrow:
       Why greet you so, why?   *weep*
    New Guise.   Alas, master! alas my privity!

              (*starts to remove his trousers*)

    Mischief.   A! where? alack! fair babe, ba me!   *kiss*
430   Abide! too soon I shall it see!   *Stop!*

    Now-a-Days.   Here, here! see my head, good master!

    Mischief.   Lady, help! silly darling! *veni, veni!*
       I shall help thee of thy pain;
       I shall smite off thy head, and set it on again.

435   *Nought.*   By our Lady, sir! a fair plaster!
       Will ye off with his head? it is a shrewd charm!
       As for me I have none harm;
       I were loath to forbear mine arm.   *amputate*
       Ye play: *in nomine Patris,* chop!

440   *New Guise.*   Ye shall not chop my jewels, and I may!

    Now-a-Days.   Yea, Christ's cross! Will ye smite my head away?
       There were one and one. Out! ye shall not assay—
       I might well be called a fop!   *fool*

    Mischief.   I can chop it off, and make it again.

445   *New Guise.*   I had a shrewd recumbentibus,   *knock-out blow*
       but I feel no pain.

    Now-a-Days.   And my head is all safe and whole again.
       Now, touching the matter of Mankind,
       Let us have an interlection sithen ye be come   (?) *council*
       hither;
       It were good to have an end.

450   *Mischief.*   Ho, ho! a minstrel! know ye any aught?

442 That would be one after another.
444 Possibly parodying the Doctor in the Mummers' Play.

Nought. I can pipe on a Walsingham whistle, I, Nought, Nought.

Mischief. Blow apace! thou shall bring him in with a flute.

(*Titivillus roars from outside*)

Titivillus. I come with my legs under me!

Mischief. Ho! New Guise, Now-a-Days, hark! or I go;   *ere*
455   When our heads were together I spake of 'Si didero'.

New Guise. So! go thy way! we shall gather money unto;
    Else there shall no man him see.   *Titivillus*
    Now ghostly to our purpose, worshipful sovereigns!
    We intend to gather money, if it please your negligence,
460   For a man with a head that is of great omnipotence—

Now-a-Days. Keep your tail! in goodness, I pray you, good brother!—
    He is a worshipful man, sirs, saving your reverence!
    He loveth no groats, nor pence of two pence;   *worth*
    Give us red royals if ye will see his abominable presence!

465 *New Guise.* Not so! ye that mow not pay the tone, pay the tother—
    At the good man of this house first we will assay!   *our host*
    God bless you, master! ye say us ill, yet ye will not say nay.
    Let us go by and by, and do them pay!
    Ye pay all alike? well mu(*s*)t ye fare!

470 *Nought.* I say, New Guise, Now-a-Days!
    Estis vos pecuniatus? (*Are you in the money?*)
    I have cried a fair while, I beshrew your patus!

Now-a-Days. *Ita vere magister*; come forth now
    your gatus!   *That's true, master; ways*
    He is a goodly man, sirs! make space and beware!

(*Enter Titivillus dressed devilwise, net in hand*)

475 *Titivillus.* *Ego sum dominantium dominus,* and
    my name is Titivillus!   *I am Lord of Lords*
    Ye that have good horses, to you I say, *Caveatis!*   *Beware!*
    Here is an able fellowship to trise him out at your   *snatch*
    gates.

              Loquitur ad New Guise   *Speaks to*

    Ego probo sic : sir New Guise, lend me a
    penny!   *I like that, agreed*

---

455 'Si didero': a popular song: one good turn deserves another.
461 *Keep your tail*: tally, i.e. count the cash.
464 *red royals*: gold coins wc h 50p.

New Guise.   I have a great purse, sir! but I have no money!
480   By the mass! I fail two farthings of an half-penny;
        Yet had I ten pounds this night that was.

Titivillus (loquitur ad Now-a-Days).   What is in thy purse?
        thou art a stout fellow!

Now-a-Days.   The devil have thee (*paid*)! I am a   MS. *qwytt*
        clean gentleman   *penniless*
        I pray God I be never worse stored than I am!
485   It shall be otherwise, I hope, or this night pass.

Titivillus (loquitur ad Nought).   Hark now, I say! thou hast many
        a penny?

Nought.   *Non nobis, Domine, non nobis:* by saint
        Denis!   *Not to us, O Lord, not to us*
        The devil may dance in my purse for any penny;
        It is as clean as a bird's arse.

490   *Titivillus (to the audience).*   Now I say, yet again, *Caveatis!*
        Here is an able fellowship to trise them out of your   *snatch*
        gates.
        Now, I say, New Guise, Now-a-Days, and Nought,
        Go and search the country, anon, that be sought!
        Some here, some there—what if ye may catch aught—
495   If ye fail of horse, take what ye may else!

New Guise.   Then speak to Mankind for the recumbentibus of
        my jewels!   *beating my testicles*

Now-a-Days.   Remember my broken head in the worship of the
        five vowels!

Nought.   Yes, good sir! and the sciatica in my arm—

Titivillus.   I know full well what Mankind did to you;
500   Mischief hat(*h*) informed (*me*) of all the matters through;
        I shall venge your quarrel, I make God a vow!
        Forth! and espy where ye may do harm!
        Take W(*illiam*) Fide if ye will have any mo—
        I say, New Guise! Whither art thou advised to go?   *resolved*

505   *New Guise.*   First, I shall begin at m(*aster*) Huntington of
        Sawston;
        From thence I shall go to William Thurlay of Hauxton,
        And so, forth to Pycharde of Trumpington:
        I will keep me to these three.

Now-a-Days.   I shall go to William Baker of Walton;
510   To Richard Bollman of Gayton;

505 f The men named in these verses lived in fenland villages and were
known to actors and audience alike. *Pycharde* is a surname.

[21]

I shall spare Master Wood of Fulbourn:
He is a *noli-me-tangere*!

Nought.   I shall go to William Patrick of Massingham;
I shall spare Master Allington of Bottisham,
515   And Hammond of Swaffham,
For dread of *In manus tuas . . . queck*!   *hanging*
Fellows, come forth! and go we hence together!

New Guise.   Sith we shall go, let us see well where and whither;
If we may be take, we come no more hither;
520   Let us con well our neck-verse that we have not a check.

Titivillus.   Go your way—a devil way—go your way, all!
I bless you with my left hand: foul you befall!
Come again, I warn, as soon as I you call,
A(*nd*) bring your advantage into this
    place!   *whatever you steal*

(They go out and leave Titivillus)

525   To speak with Mankind I will tarry here this tide,
And assay his good purpose for to set aside;
The good man, Mercy, shall no longer be his guide:
I shall make him to dance another trace!
Ever I go invisible—it is my jet—
530   And before his eye, thus, I will hang my net
To blench his sight; I hope to have his foot met.   *measure*
To irk him of his labour I shall make a frame: *device*
This board shall be hid under the earth, privily;

(He buries it)

His spade shall enter, I hope, unreadily.
535   By then he hath assayed he shall be very angry,
And lose his patience, pain of shame!   *on penalty*
I shall menge his corn with drawk and with
    darnel;   *mix; weeds*
It shall not be like to sow nor to sell—
Yonder he cometh: I pray of counsell;
540   He shall ween grace were wane.   *think; lacking*

(Enter Mankind)

Mankind.   Now, God of His mercy, send us of His
    sonde!   *blessing*
I have brought seed here to sow with my lond;
While I over-delve it, here it shall stond.
In nomine Patris, et Filii, et Spiritus Sancti!

---

512 Someone not to be entangled with.
520 The neck-verse was the third verse of Psalm 50; a protection against
        hanging for a man who could recite it correctly.
522 *my left hand:* the hand of the thief and hypocrite.
535 When he tries to dig.

545   (*He blesses the spade and seed*) now I will begin.
This land is so hard, it maketh unlusty and
     irk;   *weak and weary*
I shall sow my corn at winter, and let God work.
Alas! my corn is lost: here is a foul work!
I see well, by tilling, little shall I win:
550   Here I give up my spade, for now and for ever.

              (*Here Titivillus goes out with the spade*)

To occupy my body, I will not put my endeavour:
I will hear my evensong here or I dissever.   *depart*
This place I assign as for my kirk;
Here, in my kirk, I kneel on my knees:
555   *Pater noster, qui es in celis—*   *Our Father, etc.*

                (*Enter Titivillus*)

Titivillus.   I promise you I have no lead on my heels;
I am here again to make this fellow irk.   *tired*
Whist! peace! I shall go to his ear and tittle therein— *whisper*

                (*Goes to Mankind*)

A short prayer thirleth heaven—of thy   *pierces*
     prayer blin!   *stop*
560   Thou art holier than ever was any of thy kin:
Arise, and avent thee! nature compels!   *empty your bowels*

Mankind (*to the audience*).   I will into thi(s) yard, sovereigns!
     and come again soon;
For dread of the colic, and eke of the stone,
I will go do that needs must be done;
565   My beads shall be here for whomsoever will else.   *else wants*

      (*Mankind goes out leaving his rosary behind*)

Titivillus.   Mankind was busy in his prayer, yet I did him arise;
He is conveyed, by Christ! from his divine service.
Whither is he? trow ye? I-wis! I am wonder-wise   *Indeed!*
I have sent him forth to shit lesings.   *lies*
570   If ye have any silver, in hap pure brass,   *that is actually* . . .
Take a little pow(d)er of Paris and cast over his face;
And even in the owl-flight let him
     pass—   *it will pass for silver*
Titivillus can learn you many pretty things!
I trow Mankind will come again soon,
575   Or else, I fear me, evensong will be done:

541–8 On the stage the abruptness of this change is not so obvious as it is
    in reading since Titivillus, whom Mankind cannot see, extends the
    incident in part by his constant harassment with his net of Mankind's
    efforts to turn the soil, and in part by the theft of the corn seed.
551 I will stop working.

[23]

His beads shall be triced aside, and that anon.   *snatched, tossed*

Ye shall (*see*) a good sport if ye will abide—

Mankind cometh again! well fare he!

I shall answer him *ad omnia quare*   *on all counts*

580   There shall he set abroach a clerical matter;   *If he starts to discuss*

I hope of his purpose to set him aside.

(Re-enter Mankind)

Mankind.   Evensong hath be(*en*) in the saying, I trow, a fair while;

I am irk of it; it is too long by one mile.   *tired*

Do way! I will no more so oft over the church stile;

585   Be as be may, I shall do another.   *something else*

Of labour and prayer, I am near irk of both;

I will no more of it though Mercy be wroth.

My head is very heavy, I tell you, forsooth!

I shall sleep full my belly, and he were my brother.

(Mankind sleeps and snores)

590 *Titivillus.*   And ever ye did, for me keep now your silence!

Not a word! I charge you, pain of forty pence!

A pr(*et*)ty game shall be showed you or ye go hence.

Ye may hear him snore; he is sad a-sleep.   *sound*

Whist! peace! the devil is dead! I shall go rond in his ear: *whisper*

595   Alas, Mankind, alas! Mercy (*has*) stolen a mare;

He is run away from his master, there wot no man where;

Moreover, he stale both a horse and a nete!   *cow*

But yet, I heard say, he brake his neck as he rode in France;

But I think he rideth on the gallows, to learn to the dance,

600   Because of his theft: that is his governance.

Trust no more on him; he is a marred man!

Mickle sorrow with thy spade beforn thou hast wrought;   *hitherto*

Arise, and ask mercy of New Guise, Now-a-Days, and Nought!

They come! Advise thee for the best; let their good will be sought;

605   And thy own wife brethel, and take thee a leman!   *deceive*   *whore*

Farewell, everyone! for I have done my game;

For I have brought Mankind to mischief and to shame.

(Titivillus goes out)

Mankind (*waking up*).   Whoop! ho! Mercy hath broken his neckerchief, a vows!   *he declares*

[24]

Or he hangeth by the neck high up on the gallows.
610 Adieu, fair masters! I will haste me to the ale-house,
And speak with New Guise, Now-a-Days, and Nought:
A(*nd*) get me a leman with a smattering face. *kissable*

(*Enter New Guise through the audience*)

New Guise. Make space! for Cock's body sacred, make space!
Aha! well overrun! God give him evil grace! *overtaken*
615 We were near Saint Patrick's way, by Him that me bought!
I was twitched by the neck; the game was begun;
A grace was the halter brast asunder— *Mercifully; burst*
Ecce signum!— *Behold the mark*
The half is about my neck: we had a
near run! *narrow escape*
'Beware!' quod the good wife when she smote off her
husband's head—'beware!'
620 Mischief is a convict, for he could his
neck-verse— *recite the text*
My body gave a swing when I hung upon the casse. *gibbet*
Alas! who will hang such a likely man, and a fierce,
For stealing of an horse? I pray God give him care!
Do way this halter! what (*the*) devil doth *Do away with*
Mankind here? with sorrow!—
625 Alas, how my neck is sore, I make avow!

Mankind. Ye be welcome, New Guise! Sir! what cheer with
you?

New Guise. Well, sir! I have no cause to mourn.

Mankind. What was there about your neck? so God you amend!

New Guise. In faith! saint Audrey's holy bend; *neckband*
630 I have a little disease, as it please God to send, *discomfort*
With a running ringworm.

(*Enter Now-a-Days from the audience*)

Now-a-Days. Stand, aroom! I pray thee, brother mine!
I have laboured all this night; when shall we go dine?
A church, here beside, shall pay for ale, bread, and wine;
635 Lo! here is stuff will serve.

New Guise. Now, by the holy Mary! thou art better merchant
than I!

(*Enter Nought through the audience*)

Nought. Avaunt, knaves! let me go by!
I can not geet, and I should starve. *get money; even if*

(*Enter Mischief*)

Mischief. Here cometh a man of arms; why stand ye so still?
640 Of murder and manslaughter I have my belly fill.

[25]

Now-a-Days. What, Mischief! have ye been in prison? and it
    be your will,
    Meseemeth ye have sco(*u*)red a pair of fetters.

Mischief. I was chained by the arms; lo! I have them here.
    The chains I brast asunder and killed the jailor;

645   Yea, and his fair wife halsed in a corner: *assaulted*
    A! how sweetly I kissed that sweet mouth of hers!
    When I had do, I was mine own bottler;   *finished*
    I brought away with me both dish and doubler.   *plate*
    Here is enou(*gh*) for me: be of good cheer!

650   Yet, well fare the new che(*vi*)sance!   *way to raise cash*

Mankind. I ask mercy of New Guise, Now-a-Days and Nought;
    Once, with my spade, I remember that I fought;
    I will make you amends if I hurt you aught,
    Or did any grievance.

655 *New Guise.* What a devil liketh thee to be of this disposition?

Mankind. I dreamed Mercy was hang(*ed*): this was my vision;
    And that, to you three, I should have recourse
      and remotion.   *inclination*
    Now, I pray you, heartily, of your good will;
    I cry you mercy of all that I did amiss!

660 *Now-a-Days (aside).* I say, New Guise, Nought!
    Titivillus made all this;   *achieved*
    As siker as God is in heaven, so it is!   *sure*

Nought (to Mankind). Stand up on your feet! why stand ye
    so still?

New Guise. Master Mischief! we will you exhort,
    Mankind's name, in your book, for to report.

665 *Mischief.* I will not so! I will set a court—
    Now-a-Days, make proclamation!
    Ah! do it (*in*) *forma juris dasarde*!   *blockhead*

      (*He seats himself as if he were the Manor Court Judge*)

Now-a-Days. Oyez! oyez! oyez!
    All manner of men, and common women,
670   To the Court of Mischief either come or send;
    Mankind shall return, he is one of our men!

Mischief. Nought! come forth! thou shall
    be steward.   *Clerk of the Court*

New Guise. Master Mischief! his side-gown may
    be tolled   *lopped, cut short*
    He may have a jacket thereof, and money told.   *counted*

      (*He strips him of his coat*)

673 *side-gown :* long, old-fashioned coat.

[26]

[*Nought writes*

675 *Mankind.*   I will do for the best, so I have no cold.
      Hold! I pray you, and take it with you.
      And let me have it again in any wise.

New Guise.   I promise you a fresh jacket after the
      new guise.   *cut in half*

Mankind.   Go! and do that longeth to your office;
680   A(*nd*) spare that ye may!

                          (*New Guise goes out with the coat*)

Nought.   Hold, Master Mischief, and read this!

                          (*He hands him his notebook*)

Mischief.   Here is *blottibus in blottis,*
      Blottorum blottibus istis :
      I beshrew your ears! a fair hand!   *good handwriting*
685 *Now-a-Days.*   Yea! it is a good running fist;
      Such a hand may not be missed!

                                      (*Goes out*)

Nought.   I should have done better, had I wist.

Mischief.   Take heed, sirs, it stand you on hand!
      Curia tenta generalis,   *Manor Court Roll*
690   In a place—where good ale is!—
      Anno regni regitalis.
      Edwardi nullateni,
      On yestern-day in Febru'ry—the year passeth fully—
      As Nought hath written—here is our Tulli,   *Cicero*
695   *Anno regni regis nulli.*

Now-a-Days.   What ho, New Guise! thou makest much
      tarrying;
      That jacket shall not be worth a farthing.

(*Re-enter New Guise with the coat cut down to a short jacket*)

New Guise.   Out of my way, sirs! for dread of fighting!
      Lo! here is a feat tail, light to leap about!
700 *Nought.*   It is not shapen worth a morsel of bread;
      There is too much cloth; it weighs as any lead.
      I shall go and mend it; else I will lose my head—
      Make space, sirs! let me go out!

                          (*Nought snatches the coat and goes out*)

689 Nought's Latin is so illiterate that what he has written down is a parody
      of the Court's procedures. The comparison with Cicero is thus sarcastic.
699 *feat tail :* fashionably cut garment.

[27]

Mischief.   Mankind, come hither! God send you the gout!
705   Ye shall go to all the good fellows in the country about;
    Unto the good-wife when the good-man is out—
    'I will,' say ye!

Mankind.   I will, sir!

New Guise.   There arn' but six deadly sins; lechery   *are only*
    is none;
710   As it may be verified by us brethels everyone.   *deceivers*
    Ye shall go rob, steal, and kill, as fast as ye may gone—
    'I will,' say ye!

Mankind.   I will, sir!

Now-a-Days.   On Sundays, on the morrow, early betime,
715   Ye shall with us to the ale-house early, to go dine;
    And forbear mass and matins, hours and prime—
    'I will,' say ye!
Mankind.   I will, sir!

Mischief.   Ye must have by your side a long da-pacem,   *dagger*
720   As true men ride by the way, for to unbrace them;
    Take their money, cut their throats; thus over-face them—
    'I will,' say ye!

Mankind.   I will, sir!

(*Re-enter Nought with the coat now cut down to the size of a fencing jacket*)

Nought.   Here is a jolly jacket (*he puts it on Mankind*)—
    How say ye?

725 *New Guise.*   It is a good jake of fence for a man's body—
    Hi, dog! hi! whoop, ho! go your way lightly!
    Ye are well made for to ren!

Mischief.   Tidings! tidings! I have espied one!
    Hence with your stuff! fast we were gone!
730   I beshrew the last shall come to his home!   *curse*
Dicant Omnes.   Amen!   *They say together*

(*Enter Mercy*)

Mercy.   What ho, Mankind! flee that fellowship, I you pray!

Mankind (*to Mercy*).   I shall speak with thee another time;
    to-morn or the next day.
(*To the others and to the audience.*)   We shall go forth
    together to keep my father's year-day: *celebrate; deathday*
735   A tapster! a tapster! stow, statt, stow!   *Ho, woman! Ho!*

725 Lit. *jake:* leather jacket; *fence:* defence. The wardrobe should thus provide a leather surcoat of the kind worn by a foot-soldier of the time.

Mischief.   A mischief go with (*thee*)! here I have a foul fall.
   Hence! away from me! or I shall beshit you all!

New Guise.   What ho, ostler! ostler, lend us a foot-ball!
   Whoop! anow, anow, anow!   *enough*

                                              (*They go out*)

740 *Mercy.*   My mind is dispersed; my body trembleth as the
            aspen leaf;
         The tears should trickle down by my cheeks,
            were not your reverence!   *barring your presence*
         It were to me solace, the cruel visitation of death.
         Without rude behaviour I can(*not*) express this inconvenience:
         Weeping, sighing, and sobbing, were my sufficience;
745   All natural nutriment, to me, as carene,   *carrion*
            is odible;   *hateful*
         My inward affliction yieldeth me tedious unto your presence;
         I cannot bear it evenly that Mankind
            is so flexible.
         Man unkind, wherever thou be! for all this world was not
            apprehensible   *could not conceive how*
         To discharge thine original offence, thraldom and captivity,
750   Till God's own well-beloved Son was obedient
            and passible: *able to suffer*
         Every drop of His blood was shed to purge thine iniquity.
         I discommend and disallow this often mutability!
         To every creature thou art dispectuous and odible—
         Why art thou so uncurtess, so inconsiderate? alas,   *unkind*
            woe is me!
755   As the vane that turneth with the wind, so thou art
            convertible!
         In trust is treason; thy promise is not credible;
         Thy perversious ingratitude I cannot rehearse;
         To God and to all the holy court of heaven thou art despicable
         As a noble versifier maketh mention in his verse:
760   ' *Lex et natura, Christus et omnia jura*
         (*Law and nature, Christ and all justice*)
         Damnant ingratum; lugent eum fore natum.'
         (*Condemn the ungrateful: it were better he was not born.*)
         O, good Lady, and Mother of Mercy! have pity and compassion
         Of the wretchedness of Mankind, that is so wanton and so
            frail!
         Let mercy exceed justice, dear Mother! admit this suppli-
            cation!
765   Equity to be laid on party, and mercy to prevail!   *aside*

---

736 These remarks make sense if, in performance, Mischief jumps or falls
     down from the Judge's makeshift throne in his haste to get away.

Too sensual living is reprovable, that is now-a-days,
As by the comprehence of this matter it may be   *contents*
   specified.
New Guise, Now-a-Days, Nought, with their
   allectuous ways   *beguiling*
They have perverted Mankind, my sweet son, I have well
   espied.
770   A! with these cursed caitiffs, and I may, he shall not long
   endure;
   I, Mercy, his father ghostly, will proceed forth and do my
   property.
   Lady, help! this manner of living is a detestable pleasure;
   Vanitas vanitatum : all is but a vanity!
   Mercy shall never be convict of his uncurtess condition;
775   With weeping tears, by night and by day, I will go and never
   cease.
   Shall I not find him? Yes, I hope. Now, God be my protection!
   My predelict son! where be ye? Mankind!   *dearly beloved*
   Ubi es?

(*Mischief re-enters with his companions*)

Mischief.   My prepotent father! when ye   *especially powerful*
   sup, sup out your mess!   *ration*
   Ye are all to-gloried in your terms; ye make many a lesse.   *lie*
780   Will ye hear? he cryeth ever 'Mankind, *Ubi es?*'

New Guise.   Hic, hic, hic, hic! hic, hic, hic! hic, hic!
   That is to say: here! here! here! nigh dead in the creek.
   If ye will have him, go and seek, seek, seek!
   Seek not over long, for losing of your mind!

785   *Now-a-Days.*   If ye will have Mankind—ho, *domine, domine*
   domine!—
   Ye must speak to the shrive for a *cepe coppus;*   *sheriff; writ*
   Else ye must be fain to return with *non est inventus.*
   How say ye, sir? my bolt is shot!

Nought.   I am doing of my needings; beware   *relieving nature*
   how ye shoot!
790   Fie, fie, fie! I have foul arrayed my foot!
   Be wise for shooting with your tackles, for,   *weapons*
   God wot!
   My foot is foully over-shit.

Mischief.   A parlement! a parlement! come forth, Nought,
   behind!

786 Lit. 'You must ask the Sheriff for a writ of habeas corpus: otherwise he
   will have to tell you that no such person exists within his jurisdiction.'

A counsel belive! I am afeared Mercy will him find.   *at once*
795 How say ye? and what say ye? how shall we do with
    Mankind?

New Guise. Tush, a fly's wing! will ye do well?
He weeneth Mercy were hung for stealing of a mare. *believes*
Mischief! go say to him that Mercy seeketh everywhere;
He will hang himself, I undertake, for fear.

800 *Mischief.* I assent thereto; it is wittily said, and well.

Now-a-Days. I whip it in thy coat! anon it were done!
Now, saint Gabriel's mother save the clothes
   of thy shoon!   *preserve the clouts of your shoes*
All the books in the world, if they had be undone,
Could not a counselled us bet.   *better*

(*Here Mischief goes out. Meeting Mankind as he is
going out, he salutes him*)

805 *Mischief.* Ho, Mankind! Come and speak with Mercy; he is
    here, fast-by!

Mankind. A rope! a rope! a rope! I am not worthy.

Mischief. Anon, anon, anon! I have it here ready;
With a tree also that I have get.
Hold the tree, Now-a-Days! Nought! take heed and be wise!

(*They bring in the tree shaped like a gibbet*)

810 *New Guise.* Lo, Mankind! do as I do! this is thy new guise;
Give the rope just to thy neck: this is mine advice.

Mischief. Help thyself, Nought! lo, Mercy is here!
He scareth us with a bales: we may no longer tarry. *whip*

New Guise. Queck, queck, queck! alas my throat! I beshrew
    you, marry!
815 A Mercy! Christ's copped curse go with you, *multiple*
    and saint Davy!
Alas, my weasand! ye were somewhat too near! *throat*

(*All but Mercy and Mankind go out*)

Mercy. Arise, my precious redempt son! ye be to me full dear.
He is so timorous; meseemeth his vital spirit doth expire.

Mankind. Alas! I have be(en) so bestially disposed; I dare not
    appear;
820 To see your solacious face, I am not worthy to desire.

801 (?) I agree! Do it now.
807 cf. *Nice Wanton*, p. 159 below, where Worldly Shame offers Xantippe a
    knife.
814 *Queck, queck, queck*: gasps of strangulation.

Mercy. Your criminous complaint woundeth my   *contrite*
      heart as a lance.
   Dispose yourself meekly to ask mercy, and I will assent.
   Yield me neither gold nor treasure, but your humble obeisance,
   The voluntary subjection of your heart, and I am content.

825 *Mankind*. What! ask mercy yet once again? alas! it were a wild
      petition.
   Ever to offend, and ever to ask mercy—that is a puerility.
   It is so abominable to rehearse my worst transgression;
   I am not worthy to have mercy, by no possibility.

Mercy. O, Mankind! my sing(*u*)ler solace! this is a lamentable
      excuse!
830   The dolorous fears of my heart, how they begin to amount!
   O, blessed Jesu! help thou this sinful sinner to reduce! *reclaim*
   Nam haec est mutatio, dexterae Excelsi ; vertit Impios, et non sunt.
   Arise! and ask mercy, Mankind! and be associate to me.
   Thy death shall be my heaviness; alas! 'tis pity it should be thus.
835   Thy obstinacy will exclude thee from the glorious perpetuity.
   Yet for my love, ope thy lips and say, *Miserere mei, Deus!*
                          (*Pity me, O Lord*)

Mankind. The egal justice of God will not permit such   *fair*
      a sinful wretch
   To be revived and restored again; it were impossible.

Mercy. The justice of God will as I will, as Himself
      doth precise: (?) *preach*
840   *Nolo mortem peccatoris, inquit,* if he will be
      reducible.   *reclaimable*
   (*I do not desire the death of the sinner saith the Lord*)

Mankind. Then, mercy, good Mercy! what is a man without
      mercy?
   Little is our part of paradise were mercy ne where.
   Good Mercy! excuse the inevitable objection of my   *attack*
      ghostly enemy;
   The proverb saith: the truth tryeth thyself. Alas! I have much
      care!

845 *Mercy*. God will not make you privy unto His last judgment:
   Justice and equity shall be fortified, I will not deny;
   Truth may not so cruelly proceed in his straight argument
   But that mercy shall rule the matter, without controversy.
   Arise now, and go with me in this deambulatory.   *cloister*
850   Incline your capacity; my doctrine is convenient.
   Sin not in hope of mercy; that is a crime notory;
   To trust overmuch in a prince, it is not expedient.
   In hope, when ye sin, ye think to have mercy—beware of that
      adventure!

[32]

The good Lord said to the lecherous woman of Canaan—
855 The holy gospel is the authority, as we read in Scripture—
'*Vade! et jam amplius noli peccare!*'
Christ preserved this sinful woman taken in
avoutry;   *adultery*
He said to her these words: 'Go, and sin no more!'
So to you; Go, and sin no more! Beware of vain confidence of
mercy!
860 Offend not a prince on trust of his favour! as I said before.
If ye feel yourself trapped in the snares of your ghostly enemy,
Ask mercy anon; beware of the continuance!
While a wound is fresh it is proved curable by surgery;
That, if it proceed over long, it is cause of great grievance.

865 *Mankind.*   To ask mercy and to have—this is a liberal possession:
Shall this expeditious petition ever be allowed, as ye have in-
sight?

Mercy.   In this present life mercy is plenty, till death maketh
his division;
But when ye be go, *usque ad minimum quadrantem*—ye shall
reckon this right.   (*right up to the smallest particle*)
Ask mercy and have, while the body with the soul hath his
annexion;   *union*
870 If ye tarry till your decease, ye may hap of your desire to miss;
Be repentant here; trust not the hour of death; think on this
lesson:
Ecce nunc tempus acceptabile! ecce nunc dies salutis!
(*Behold, now is the accepted time! behold, now is the day of
salvation!*)
All the virtue in the wor(*l*)d, if ye might comprehend,
Your merits were not premiable to the bliss   *cannot earn*
above;
875 Not to the le(*a*)st joy of heaven, of your proper effort to ascend;
With Mercy ye may: I tell ye no fable—Scripture doth prove.

Mankind.   O, Mercy! my suavious solace and singular   *sweet*
recreatory!   *regenerator*
My predelict special! ye are worthy to have my love;
For, without desert and means supplicatory,
880 Ye be compatient to my inexcusable reproof.   *compassionate*
A! it swemmeth my heart to think how unwisely   *grieves*
I have wrought!
Titivillus, that goeth invisible, hung his net before my eye;
And, by his fantastical visions, sedulously sought
By New Guise, Now-a-days, Nought, caused me to obey.

885 *Mercy.*   Mankind! ye were oblivious of my
doctrine monitory;   *monitory teaching*

[33]

I said before: Titivillus would assay you a bront.   *try to attack*
Beware from henceforth of his fables delusory!
The proverb saith: *Jacula prefata minus ledunt.*
(*The blows which are predicted hurt less.*)
Ye have three adversaries—he is master of   *Lucifer*
   them all—
890   That is to say, the Devil, the World, the Flesh, and
   the Fell;   *your own body and skin*
The New Guise, Now-a-Days, and Nought, the world we may
   them call;
And, properly, Titivillus signifieth the fiend of hell;
The Flesh, that is the unclean concupiscence of your body.
These be your three ghostly enemies in whom ye have put
   your confidence;
895   They brought you to Mischief to conclude your temporal
   glory:
As it hath be showed before this worshipful audience.
Remember how ready I was to help you; from such I was not
   dangerous;   *reluctant*
Wherefore, good son! abstain from sin evermore after this!
Ye may both save and spoil your soul, that is so precious:
900   *Libere velle, libere nolle!* God may not deny, Iwis.   *indeed*
(*Freely to will, freely not to will!*)
Beware of Titivillus with his net, and of all his envious will;
Of your sinful delectation that grieveth your ghostly substance:
Your body is your enemy: let him not have his will.
Take your leave when ye will. God send you good
   perseverance!

905   *Mankind.* Sith I shall depart, bless me, father! hence then
   I go—
God send us all plenty of His great mercy!

Mercy. Dominus custodi(a)t te ab omni malo!
(*The Lord protect you from all evil!*)
In nomine Patris, et Filii, et Spiritus Sancti. Amen!
(*In the name of the Father, and the Son and the Holy Spirit.*)

[*Here Mankind goes out*

(EPILOGUE)

Worship(*f*)ul sovereigns! I have do(*ne*) my property;
910   Mankind is delivered by my several patrociny.   *protection*
God preserve him from all wicked captivity;
And send him grace, his sensual conditions to mortify!
Now for His love, that for us received His humanity,
Search your conditions with due examination!
915   Think and remember: the world is but a vanity,

As it is proved daily by diverse transmutation,
Mankind is wretched; he hath sufficient proof;
Therefore, God (*keep*) you all
    per suam misericordiam,   *through His mercy*
That ye may be pleyferis with the angels   *companions in joy*
    above,
920 And have to your portion *vitam eternam*.   *life everlasting*
    Amen!

FINIS

FULGENS AND LUCRES

Although devised for a Cardinal and written by his Chaplain, *Fulgens and Lucres* is far closer both in its subject matter and literary tone to the spirit of Lydgate's *Mumming at Hertford* than to *Mankind* or *Everyman*. In the annals of English drama it assumes a special interest as the first complete and wholly secular Interlude that has survived; but while the narrative is adapted from romance literature—Bonaccorso of Pistoja the Younger's *De Vera Nobilitate* in particular—the burden of it is quite as moral as its overtly religious counterparts. The moral, however, is here social and political, and in keeping with Henry VII's determination to protect the newly established Tudor dynasty by entrusting political power to men who owed everything to him rather than inherited titles and wealth.

Henry Medwall's patron, John Morton, was just such a man. During his early years as a churchman he had supported the Lancastrian cause during the Wars of the Roses; but he had won the respect of the Yorkist King Edward IV and had been rewarded with the bishopric of Ely. On the accession of Richard III he went into exile in Flanders. From there, as a key figure in the reconciliation of the rival Houses of York and Lancaster through the marriage of Henry Tudor to Elizabeth of York, he returned to England and was again rewarded, this time with promotion, as Archbishop and Cardinal, to the See of Canterbury. In this capacity he became the chief officer of the central government at Westminster as Lord President of the Privy Council, residing at Lambeth Palace, controlling the Exchequer and entertaining ambassadors on diplomatic missions. It was in this context—probably during the Christmas season of 1497 when the Flemish and Spanish ambassadors were in London to discuss trade and to start the negotiations that were to lead to the betrothal of Prince Arthur to Catherine of Aragon—that Morton commissioned his chaplain, Henry Medwall, to prepare *Fulgens and Lucres*.

Devised in two self-contained parts, for performance between sections, or courses, of a banquet in the hall of the palace, with wine on the table and a fire in the hearth, the play adapts a disputation in the manner of Cicero and Petrarch to contrast the rival claims of the old aristocracy and the new men of proven ability from the middle class for high office in Tudor England. Like *Sir Gawain and the Green Knight* (*c.* 1365), Medwall's play is loosely structured on a variety of traditional Christmas games and pastimes—songs, wrestling, jousting, mumming and debates—which are then given coherence within a narrative that incorporates them, either progressively or to supply variety or as parodies for dramatic and moral purposes. Medwall is himself explicit about this, describing these devices as,

> Divers toys mingled in the same   (*the main argument*)
> To stir folk to mirth and game
> And to do them solace. II. 22–4.

The core of the play's moral matter is expounded by Gaius Flaminius in the course of the final debate with his rival Publius Cornelius:

> . . . this I wot well
> That both he and I came of Adam and Eve;
> There is no difference that I can tell
> Which maketh one man another to excell
> So much as doth virtue and goodly manner
> And therein I may well with him compare. II. 665–70.

This disposes of the claims of birth and inherited wealth at a stroke, substituting natural ability and personal achievement as the only criteria for respect and promotion. Within this context Lucres, the bride for whose hand the two men are contending, becomes figuratively translated into the personification of the state or Commonwealth, and the debate is enlarged to reveal its full social and political significance. Lucres can thus be regarded as the primogenetrix of a long succession of stage characters ranging through Skelton's 'Poverty' in *Magnificence* via Bale's 'Widow England' in *King Johan* and Sir David Lyndsay's 'Commonwealth' in *Ane Satire of the Three Estates* to the title role in *Respublica*. The host, Cardinal Morton, in the mirror image of the play, becomes clearly associated with Gaius Flaminius, the victor of the debate and bridegroom to Lucres. The cherished image of Christ as bridegroom to His Church is thus skilfully transferred to the Archbishop of Canterbury and Lord President of the Council as bridegroom to the body politic before the ambassadors and assembled guests.

Medwall leads his audience to this conclusion in an entertaining manner that befits the instructions,

> Usher! Get them good wine thereto!
> Fill them of the best!
> Let it be done, or you will be shent!   (*punished*)
> For it is the will and commandment
> Of the master of the feast. I. 1418–22.

[38]

In such an environment a dry debate, no matter how profound the argument or how learned the supporting citations, would quickly induce boredom and lead to the noisy dismissal of the actors. Instead, Medwall first secures the interest of his sophisticated audience with a dramatization of John Tiptoft, Earl of Worcester's translation of Bonaccorso's *De Vera Nobilitate* which Caxton had printed sixteen years earlier in 1481 as a companion piece with his translations of Cicero's *De Amicitia* and *De Senectute*: then he proceeds to prefigure the crucial debate first in a comic parody of a tournament (a device for which precedent exists in *The Castle of Perseverance*) and then within a choreographic interlude of Spanish and Flemish Mummers. Unlike the Lydgate Mummings, no Presenter or explanatory ballad is provided: it is thus to be presumed that the choreographer of this mumming has a free hand within the limits imposed by the debate which it prefigures. Lastly, he counterbalances the risk he has taken in selecting characters from Roman antiquity, that his moral will be ignored or dismissed as only applicable to Roman times, by setting them within the Tudor frame of the two ambiguous servant-actors A and B. F. S. Boas and A. W. Reed in the introduction to their edition of the play (Oxford, 1926) state that 'the consequence of this intermingling of actors and spectators is an imperfect sense of dramatic objectivity'. If from a purely literary standpoint this may be true, it is nonsense in the proper dramatic context of the play in performance where the device is perfectly calculated to foreshorten time and place and admirably realized to secure just that effect. It is the traditional method of the authors of the Miracle Cycles, where anachronisms in names, dress and dialogue are deliberately employed to make scriptural event directly applicable to contemporary life, historical time being regarded as comparatively irrelevant *sub specie aeternitatis*.[1] Moreover, as a dramatic device it ensures audience involvement in the action, and should be compared with the uses made of it in *Mankind* (see pp. 16 and 20 above).

Little is known of Medwall himself. A native of Hampshire, Sussex or Surrey, he was ordained 'Acolyte' in 1490. He does not appear to have taken his calling seriously; for although appointed to a rectory at Balyngham near Calais in 1492 and to another near Norwich in 1493, he took up residence in neither of them and resigned shortly after Cardinal Morton's death in 1500. He was granted permission to travel on the Continent in 1501: thereafter he might as well have died for all we know of him.

During Morton's lifetime, Medwall numbered John and Thomas More and John and William Rastell among his literary acquaintances and seems to have been more closely associated with educational than with religious duties in Morton's household. The

[1] e.g. Sir Pilate, J.P., Caiaphas dressed as a Catholic bishop, Pennine shepherds afraid of Scottish border thieves, etc.

only other play that can be firmly ascribed to him is *Nature*, an allegorical morality in two parts with twenty-two characters that has more in common with *Mankind* than with *Fulgens and Lucres*: it was printed by John Rastell, *c.* 1520.[1]

Fulgens and Lucres was revived by students of the Drama Department of Bristol University in 1964. It was presented in the Reception Room of the University (the dimensions of which are similar to those of a large Tudor Hall) where the audience could be seated at refectory tables and served with refreshments as the text directs. With the High Table at the dais-end of the Hall and two long tables down each side, the central floor space remains free as the acting area. With a musicians' gallery above the screen at the kitchen end of the hall, and with two doors in the screen for servants entering with food and leaving with empty plates, nothing else is needed beyond costumes and appropriate hand properties. If there is no gallery, the musicians can be placed on a small rostrum-stage in a corner apart from the main action; and if there is only one door in the screen, two entrances can easily be created by suspending a false screen, or curtain, advanced some three or four feet forward from the door itself.

The play survives in a single copy of the Quarto printed by John Rastell, *c.* 1520, now in the Huntington Hertford Library at Pasadena, California. A facsimile edition was printed (New York, 1920) by Seymour de Ricci. Six years later F. S. Boas and A. W. Reed published their edition with an Introduction and Notes (O.U.P., 1926) preserving the original spelling and punctuation.

Fifty years have elapsed since then and, with both editions long since out of print, the play has ceased to be readily accessible to students of English or Drama. In preparing this edition, therefore, I have modernized the spelling and punctuation throughout. Occasionally I have modernized a particular word form, but I have preserved the original word in a marginal note prefaced by the letter Q (= quarto) for easy identification: where, however, to have done this would have altered the rhyme-scheme, I have preserved the original, glossing it with modern equivalents in the margin in the normal way.

EDITIONS

J. RASTELL, Quarto, London, *c.* 1520.
S. DE RICCI, Huntington Facsimile, New York, 1920.
F. S. BOAS and A. W. REED, Oxford, 1926.

[1] On Medwall's connection with Eton College see David Blewitt, 'Records of Drama at Winchester and Eton, 1397–1576', *Theatre Notebook*, vol. xxxviii (1984) No. 3, pp. 135–43.

FULGENS AND LUCRES
by Henry Medwall

Characters

Fulgens, a Roman Senator
Publius Cornelius, a Patrician
Gaius Flaminius, a Plebeian
A, a youth, afterwards servant to Gaius Flaminius
B, a youth, afterwards servant to Publius Cornelius
Lucres, daughter to Fulgens
Joan, handmaid (ancilla) to Lucres

Pars Prima (*First Part*)

Intrat A dicens: (*A enters speaking*)

A.   For Goddes will
What mean ye, sirs, to stand so still?
Have not ye eaten and your fill,
And paid nothing therefore?
5   Iwis, sirs, thus dare I say,   *Indeed*
He that shall for the shott pay   *reckoning, bill*
Vouchsafeth that ye largely assay
Such meat as he hath in store.
I trow your dishes be not bare
10   Nor yet ye do the wine spare;
Therefore be merry as ye fare,
Ye are welcome each one
Unto this house without feigning.
But I marvel much of one thing,
15   That after this merry drinking
And good recreation
There is no words among this press,   *throng, crowd*
Non sunt loquele neque sermones
(*There is no speech nor language, where their voice is not heard*)
But, as it were men in sadness,
20   Here ye stand musing—
Whereabout I cannot tell!   *what about*

18 Psalm XIX, v. 3.
20 A line appears to be missing here to complete the triple rhyme with
'tell' and 'damesell'.

[41]

Or some else pretty damesell
For to dance and spring.
Tell me, what calt, is it not so?   *whatever you call it*
25 I am sure here shall be somewhat ado,
And Iwis I will know it or I go
Without I be driven hence.

Intrat B : (Enter B)

B. (*To A*)   Nay, nay! (*Truly*) man, I undertake   Q. *Hardely*
No man will such mastries make   *constraint*
30 And it were but for the manner sake;   *only for custom's sake*
Thou mayest tarry by licence
Among other men and see the play:
I warrant no man will say nay.

A.   I think it well even as ye say,   *just as*
35 That no man will me grieve.   *lay hands on me*
But I pray you tell me that again:
Shall here be a play?

B.   Yea, for certain.

A.   By my troth, therof am I glad and fain   *happy*
And ye will me believe;   *If*
40 Of all the world I love such sport,
It doth me so much pleasure and comfort,
And that causeth me ever to resort
Wher such thing is to do.
I trowe your own selfe be one
45 Of them that shall play.

B.   Nay, I am none,
I trow thou speakest in derision
To lyke me therto.   *compare*

A.   Nay, I mock not, wot ye well,
For I thought verrily by your apparel
50 That ye had been a player.

B.   Nay, never a dell!   *not on your life!*

A.   Then I cry you mercy!
I was to blame lo therefore I say
There is so much nice array
Among these gallants nowaday
55 That a man shall not lightly
Know a player from another man!
But now to the purpose where I began:
I see well here shall be a play then.

56 The social status of the professional actor in medieval and Tudor
England was highly ambiguous. The pretensions of men whose way of
life both relieved them of manual work and enabled them to cross the

  B. Yea, that there shall, doubtless;
60 And I trow ye shall like it well.

  A. It seemeth then that ye can tell
  Somewhat of the matter.

  B.   Yea, I am of counsel: *in the know*
  One told me all the process.   *plot*

  A. And I pray you, what shall it be?

65 *B.* By my faith, as it was told me—
  More than once or twice!—
  As far as I can bear it away,   *remember it*
  All the substance of their play
  Shall proceed this wise.   *way*

70 When the empire of Rome was in such flower
  That all the world was subject to the same,
  Then was there a noble senator,
  And, as I remember, Fulgens was his name,
  Which had a daughter of noble fame;
75 And yet, as th' author saith in very deed,
  Her noble virtue did her fame exceed.

  Albeit there was not one, almost,
  Throughout all the city, young nor old,
  That of her beauty did not boast:
80 And, over that, her vertues manifold
  In such manner wise were praised and told
  That it was thought she lacked nothing
  To a noble woman that was accoryding. *appropriate*

  Great labour was made her favour to attain
85 In the way of marriage; and, among all
  That made such labour, were specially twain
  Which more than other did busily on her call;
  On the which twain she set her mind especial,
  So that she utterly determined in her heart
90 The one of them to have, all other set apart.

  One of them was called Publius Cornelius
  Born of noble blood, it is no nay: *that's the truth*
  That other was one Gaius Flaminius
  Born of a poor stock as men do say;
95 But, for all that, many a fair day
  Thorough his great wisdom and virtuous behaviour
  He ruled the commonweal to his great honour.

---

  sharp social frontiers of the time earned them the envy of their fellows,
  the jibes of their supervisors and, in the Elizabethan era, the implacable
  hatred of the Puritans.
 81 Lit: In such a kind of way were praised and recited.

And how so be it that the vulgar opinion
Had both these men in like favour and reverence,
100 Supposing they had been of like condition,
Yet this said woman of inestimable prudence
Saw that there was some manner of difference,
For the which her answer she deferred and spared
Till both their conditions were openly declared.

105 And yet to them both this comfort she gave;
He that could be found more noble of them twain
In all godly manner, her heart should he have.
Of the which answer they were both glad and fain,
For either of them trusted thereby to attain   *both*
110 Th' effect of his desire; yet when they had do   *done*
One of them must needs his appetite forgo.

Hereupon was a-raised a great doubt and question:
Every man all, after as he was affectionate   *just as; disposed*
Unto the parties, said his opinion;
115 But, at the last, in eschewing of debate
This matter was brought before the Senate
They to give therein an utter sentence   *final*
Which of these the two men should have pre-eminence.

And finally they gave sentence and award
120 That Gaius Flaminius was to be commend
For the more noble man, having no regard
To his low birth of the which he did descend:
But only to his virtue they did therein attend,
Which was so great that of convenience   *by agreement*
125 All the city of Rome did him honour and reverence.

A.   And shall this be the process of the play?

B.   Yea, so I understand by credible information!

A.   By my faith, but if it be even as you say,
I will advise them to change that conclusion!
130 What? Will they affirm that a churl's son
Should be more noble than a gentleman born?
Nay! Beware! for men will have thereof great scorn.
It may not be spoken in no manner of case.

B.   Yes! Such considerations may be laid
135 That every reasonable man in this place
Will hold him therein right well a-paid,
The matter may be so well conveyed.

A.   Let them convey and carry clean then,
Or else he will repent that this play began!
140 How be it, the matter toucheth me never a dell;   *not at all*

For I am neither of virtue excellent
Nor yet of gentle blood; this I know well;
But I speak it only for this intent
I would not that any man should be shent;   *punished*
145   And yet there can no man blame us two:
For why? in this matter we have nought to do!

   B.   We? No, God wott! Nothing at all,
Save that we come to see this play
As far as we may by the leave of the marshall.
150   I love to behold such mirths alway;
For I have seen before this day
Of such manner things in many a good place,
Both good examples and right honest solace.
This play in like wise, I am sure,
155   Is made for the same intent and purpose,
To do every man both mirth and pleasure:
Wherefore I cannot think or suppose
That they will any word therein disclose
But such as shall stand with truth and reason
160   In godly manner according to season.

   A.   Yea! But truth may not be said alway;
For sometime it causeth grudge and despite!

   B.   Yea! Goeth the world so nowaday
That a man must say the crow is white?

165 A.   Yea, that he must, by God Almighty!
He must both lie and flatter now and then
That casteth him to dwell among worldly men.   *plans*
In some Courts such men shall most win!

   B.   Yea! But as for the parish where I abide
170   Such flattery is abhorred as deadly sin,
And specially liars be set aside
As soon as they may with the fault be spied:
For every man that favoureth and loveth virtue
Will such manner of folk utterly eschew.
175   Wherefore I can think these folk will not spare,   *hinder*
After plain truth, this matter to proceed
As the story saith. Why should they care?
I trow here is no man of the kin or seed
Of either party: for why, they were bore
180   In the city of Rome as I said before!
Therefore leave all this doubtful question
And praise at the parting even as you find!   *end*

149 The Marshall normally ruled over the Courtyard; entertainments in the
      Hall were the responsibility of the Steward.
164 See *Wit and Wisdom*, p. 169 below.

    A. Yes; be ye sure, when they have all done,
        I will not spare to shew you my mind,
185   Praise who will, or dispraise, I will not be behind:
        I will gest thereon whatsoever shall befall—   *?discourse, joke*
        If I can find any man to gest withall!

    B. Peace! No more words! for now they come;
        The players been even here at hand!

190 *A.* So they be! So help me God and halidom.   *relics*
        I pray you tell me where I shall stand.

    B. Marry, stand even here by me, I warrant!
        Give room there, Sirs! for God avow
        They would come in if they might for you!

195 *A.* Yea! but I pray thee, what calt, tell me this;
        Who is he that now cometh in?

    B. Marry! it is Fulgens, the Senator.

    A. He is? What? the father of the foresaid virgin?

    B. Yea, forsooth! He shall this matter begin.

200 *A.* And where is fair daughter Lucres?

    B. She cometh anon! I say hold thy peace!   *At once*

     Intrat Fulgens dicens. (Enter Fulgens speaking)

Fulgens. Everlasting joy with honour and praise
        Be unto our most dread Lord and Saviour
        Which doth us help and comfort many ways;
205   Not leaving us destitute of his aid and succour,
        But letteth his sun shine on the rich and poor,
        And of his grace is ever indifferent   *impartial*
        Albeit he diversely commiteth his talent.   *distributes*

        To some he lendeth the spirit of prophecy;
210   To some the plenty of tongue's eloquence;
        To some great wisdom and worldly policy;
        To some literature and speculative science;   *philosophy*
        To some he giveth the grace of pre-eminence
        In honour and degree; and to some abundance
215   Of treasure, riches and great inheritance.

        Every man oweth to take good heed
        Of this distribution: for whoso doth take
        The larger benefit, he hath the more need

---

188 This is easy to handle in performance if Fulgens's entrance is heralded
     by a drum or trumpet. Clearly, he is expected to push his way through
     the audience.
195 *what calt :* what do you call yourself.

The larger recompense and thank(s) for to make.
220 I speed these words only for mine own sake   *utter*
And for none other person, for I know well
That I am therein charged as I shall you tell.

When I consider, and call to my remembrance,
The prosperous life that I have alway
225 Hitherto endured, without any grievance
Of worldly adversity, well may I say
And think that I am bound to yield and pay
Great praise and thanks to the high King
Of whom proceedeth and groweth every good thing!

230 And, certes, if I would not praise or boast
The benefits that he hath done unto me,
Yet is it well know(n) of least and most
Throughout all Rome, the imperial city,
What place in the Senate and honourable degree   *rank*
235 I occupy, and how I demean me in the same;   *conduct*
All this can they tell that knoweth but my name.

To speak of plenty and great abundance,
Of worldly riches thereunto belonging,
Houses of pleasure and great inheritance,
240 With rich apparel and every other thing
That to a worthy man should be according,
I am, and ever have been, in metely good case;   *fittingly*
For the which I thank Almighty God of his grace.

Then have I a wife, of good condition   *standing*
245 And right conformable to mine intent   *of one mind with me*
In everything that is to be done!
And, howbeit that God hath me not sent
An heir male, which were convenient   *would be necessary*
My name to continue and it to repair,
250 Yet am I not utterly destitute of an heir!

For I have a daughter, in whom I delight
As for the chief comfort of mine old age;
And surely my said daughter Lucres doth hight.   *is called*
Men saith she is as like me in visage
255 As though she were even mine own image,
For the which cause nature doth me force and bind
The more to favour and love her in my mind.

243 This lengthy anachronistic apology, of Christian sentiments culled from
   St Matthew and *1 Corinthians* and given to a Roman Senator, is nevertheless wholly appropriate for Cardinal Morton and his guests for whom
   the play was written.

But yet to the principal and greatest occasion
That maketh me to love her as I do
260   Is this which I speak, not of affection,
But even as the truth moveth me thereto:
Nature hath wrought in my Lucres so
That to speak of beauty and clear understanding
I cannot think in her what should be lacking.

265   And, beside all that, yet a greater thing
Which is not oft seen in so young a damesell;
She is so discreet and sad in all demeaning,   *sober, serious*
And thereto full of honest and virtuous counsell
Of her own mind, that wonder is to tell
270   The gifts of nature and of especial grace.

Am not I greatly bound in this case
To God, as I rehearsed to you before?
I were void of all reason and grace
If I would not serve and praise Him therefore
275   With due love and dread: He asketh no more,
As far as he will me grace thereto send,
The rest of my life therein will I spend.

Albeit that I must partly intend   *devote myself to*
To the promotion of my daughter Lucres
280   To some metely marriage,—else God defend!   *meet, suitable*
She is my chief jewel and riches,
My comfort against all care and heaviness;
And also she is now good and ripe of age
To be a man's (*mate*) by way of marriage.   Q. *fere*

285   Wherefore, if I might see ere I die
That she were bestowed somewhat according,   *suitably*
Then were my mind discharged utterly
Of every great (*care*) to me belonging.   Q. *cure*
It was the chief cause of my hither coming
290   To have a communication in this same matter
With one Cornelius. Came there none such here?

Intrat Publius Cornelius dicens
(*Enter Publius Cornelius* [*pushing his way through the crowd
and*] *saying*)

Cornelius.   Yes! Now am I come here at the last!
I have tarried long. I cry you mercy!

Fulgens.   Nay, no offence! There is no waste
295   Nor loss of time yet hardly;   *certainly*
For this is the hour that you and I
Appointed here to meet this other day.
Now show me your mind: let me hear what you say.

[48]

Cornelius.   Then will I leave superfluity away;
For why you know already my mind in substance.

Fulgens.   I wot not whether I do; yea, or nay.

Cornelius.   Why? Is it now out of your remembrance
That my desire is to honour and advance
Your daughter Lucres, if she will agree
That I, so poor a man, her husband should be?

Fulgens.   You need not, sir, to use these words to me;
For none in this city knoweth better than I
Of what great birth (*and*) substance you be!   *Q. or*
My daughter Lucres is full unworthy
Of birth and goods to look so high,
Saving that happily her good condition
May her enable to such a promotion.   *qualify*
But if this be your mind and such intent,
Why do you not labour to her therefore?   *address yourself*
For me seemeth it were right expedient
That we know therein her mind before
Or ever we should commune thereof any more;
For, if she would to your mind apply,   *agree, consent*
No man shall be so glad thereof as I.

Cornelius.   Suppose you that I did not so begin
To get first her favour? Yes, trust me well.

Fulgens.   And what comfort would she give you therein?

Cornelius.   By my faith, no great comfort to tell
Save that she abideth to have your counsel;
For as she saith she will no thing
In such matter to do, without your counselling
Nor otherwise than you shall be content.
And thereupon it was my mind and desire
To speak with you of her, for the same intent
Your goodwill in this behalf to require:
For I am so (*burnt*) in love's fire   *Q. brent*
That nothing may my pain a-slake   *alleviate*
Without that you will my cure undertake.

Fulgens.   Sir, I shall do you the comfort that I can
As far as she will be advised by me;
Howbeit, certainly I am not the man
That will take from her the liberty
Of her own choice; that may not be:
But, when I speak with her, I shall her advise
To love you before other in all Godly wise.

Cornelius.   I thank you, sir, with all mine heart,
And I pray you do it without delay.

[49]

Fulgens.   As soon as I shall from you depart
   I will her mind therein assay.   *test her opinion*

345 *Cornelius.*   For I shall think that every hour is twain
   Till I may speak with you again.

                              Exeat Fulgens. (He goes out)

   (*To audience*) Now a wise fellow that had somewhat a brain
   And of such things had experience
   Such one would I with me retain
350 To give me council and assistance,
   For I will spare no cost or expense
   Nor yet refuse any labour or pain
   The love of fair Lucres thereby to attain.
   So many good fellows as (*be*) in this hall,   *Q. byn*
   And is there none, Sirs, among you all
   That will enterprise this geare?   *action*
   But, if you will not, then I must
   Go seek a man elsewhere.   *a servant*

       Et exeat. (He goes out.) Deinde loquitur B. (Then B speaks)

   B.   Now have I spied a meet Office for me!
360   For I will be of council, and I may,
   With yonder man—

   A.   Peace, let be!
   By God! Thou wilt destroy all the play.

   B.   Destroy the play, quotha? Nay, nay!
   The play began never till now!
365   I will be doing, I make God a vow;
   For there is not in this hundred mile
   A feater bawd than I am one!   *cleverer; handyman*

   A.   And what shall I do in the meanwhile?

   B.   Mary, thou shalt come in anon
370   With another pageant!   *tableau, show, spectacle*
               Who? I?

   B.   Yea, by St John!

   A.   What? I never used such thing before.   *tried to act*

   B.   But follow my council and do no more!
   Look that thou abide here still,
   And I shall undertake for to fulfil

   359 Medwall was clearly familiar with 'the parasite' of Roman Comedy who,
      as the slave or servant of the young gentleman in love, is the mainspring
      of the farcical incidents which follow from the mingling of his master's
      instructions with his own self-interest.

                              [50]

375 All his mind withouten delay;
    And whether I do so, yea or nay,
    At the least, well dare I undertake
    The marriage utterly to mar or make!
    If he and I make any bargain
380 So that I must give him attendance,
    When thou seest me come in again,
    Stand even still and keep thy countenance;
    For, when Gaius Flaminius cometh in,
    Then must thou thy pageant begin.

385 *A.* Shall any profit grow thereby?

B. Hold thy peace! Speak not so high!
    Lest any man of this company
    Know our purpose openly
    And break all our dance!   *wreck our chances*
390 For I assure thee faithfully,
    If thou quit thee as well as I,
    This gear shall us both advance.   *ploy, ruse*

                                    Exeat (He goes out)

A. Nay, then let me alone hardly!
    If any advantage (*hangs*) thereby,   *Q. honge*
395 I can myself thereto apply
    By help of good counsel.
    This fellow and I be masterless   *'of no fixed address'*
    And live most part in idleness:
    Therefore some manner of business
400 Would become us both well.
    At the least wise it is merry, being
    With men in time of wooing:
    For all that while they do nothing
    But dance and make revell,
405 Sing, and laugh with great shouting,
    Fill in wine with revell routing!   *tipsy jollifications*
    I trow it be a joyful thing
    Among such folk to dwell.

        Intrat Fulgens, Lucres et Ancilla et dicat
    (*Enter Fulgens, Lucres and her maid Joan, and he says*)

Fulgens. Daughter Lucres, you know well enough
410 What study and care I have for your promotion,
    And what fatherly love I bear to you;
    So that I think in mine opinion
    It were time lost and wasteful occupation
    This matter to rehearse, or tell you any more,
415 Since you it best know, as I said before.

[51]

But the special cause that I speak for
Is touching your marriage; as you know well,
Many folk there be that desireth sore
And laboureth in that behalf with you to mell.   *court*
420 You know what is for you; you need no counsel.
Howsobeit, if you list my counsel to require,   *wish*
I shall be glad to satisfy therein your desire.

Lucres.   (*Truth*) it is, father, that I am bound   **Q.** *Trought*
     As much unto you as any child may be
425 Unto the father living on the ground: *who is still alive*
     And where it pleaseth you to give unto me
     Mine own free choice and my liberty,
     It is the thing that pleaseth me well,
     Since I shall have therein your counsel

430 And now, according to this same purpose
     What think you best for me to do?
     You know right well, as I suppose,
     That many folk doth me greatly woo;
     Among the which there be specially two
435 In whom, as I trow and so do ye,
     The choice of this matter must finally be.

     In that point your mind and mine doth agree.
     But yet right now ere I came here
     For Publius Cornelius you advised me
440 As touching you would have me only rest there.
     If that be your mind, I shall gladly forbear
     All other and only to him assent
     To have me in wedlock at his commandment.

Fulgens.   Nay daughter Lucres! Not so I meant;
445 For though I did somewhat to him incline,
     Yet, for all that, it is not mine intent
     That you should so thereupon utterly define,   *determine*
     But look whom you will, on God's blessing and mine:
     For trust you me verily, it is all one to me
450 Whether Gaius Flaminius wed you or else he.

Lucres.   Then, since I have so great liberty
     And so good choice, I were unfortunable—

423–7 This was a very radical attitude to adopt in Tudor England since
       marriages among the nobility were invariably arranged by the parents
       with considerations of wealth and inheritance taking precedence over
       those of temperamental compatibility; cf. *Romeo and Juliet* and *A Mid-
       summer Night's Dream.*
448 For the actor this line is easier to speak and makes clearer sense if it is
       re-ordered to read: 'But look on whom you will, with God's blessing and
       mine.'

And also too unwise—if I would not see
That I had him which is most honourable.
455 Wherefore, may it like you to be agreeable
That I may have respite to make inquisition
Which of these two men is better of condition?

Fulgens. I hold me content! That shall be well done!
It may be respited for a day or twain:
460 But, in the meantime, use this provision—
See that you indifferently them both entertain   *impartially*
Till that your mind be set at a certain
Where you shall rest. Now, can you do so?

Lucres. At the least my goodwill shall I put thereto.

465 *Fulgens.* Then, since I have business at home for to do,
I will go thitherward as fast as I may.

Lucres. Is it your pleasure that I shall with you go?

Fulgens. Nay, I had lever that ye went your way   *rather*
About this matter.

                                Et exeat. (And he goes out)
Lucres. Well, God be with you then!

470 I shall do therein the best that I can.

                Et facta aliqua pausatione dicat Lucres.
                (And, after a short pause, Lucres continues)

I will not disclander nor blame no man;   *slander*
But, nevertheless, by that I hear say,
Poor maidens be deceived now and then,
So great dissembling nowaday
475 There is conveyed under words gay
That if—

                    (She is interrupted by her maid, Joan)

Joan. Peace, lady! You must forbear!
See you not who cometh here?

Lucres. Who is it? Wot you ere?   *Did you know beforehand?*

Joan. It is Gaius Flaminius, parde—   *by God!*
480 He that would your husband be!

Lucres. Ey! Good Lord! How wist he
For to find me here?

            Intrat Gaius Flaminius. (Enter Gaius Flaminius)

Gaius. Yes, good lady! Wheresoever you go
He that listeth to do his diligence
485 In such manner wise as I have do,   *done*

[53]

At the last he may come to your presence:
For whosoever oweth obedience
Unto love, he hath great need
To attendance if he will speed.

490 *Lucres.*   Sir, you be welcome! What is your mind?

Gaius.   Why, fair Lucres? is that your guise   *habit, custom*
   To be so strange, and so unkind,   *aloof, distant*
   To him that oweth you loving service?
   I trow I have told you twice or thrice
495 That (*my*) desire is to marry with you.   *Q. myn*
   Have you not heard this matter ere now?

Lucres.   Yes, in very truth I have heard you say
   At diverse times that you bare me affection:
   To such an intent I say not nay.   *motive*

500 *Gaius.*   What need you then to ask the question
   What I would with you at this season?
   Me seemeth you should therein doubt no more,
   Since you know well mine errand before!
   Iwis your strangeness grieveth me sore.
505 But, notwithstanding, now will I cease;
   And at this time I will chide no more,
   Lest I give you cause of heavyness.
   I came hither only for your sake, doubtless,   *believe me*
   To glad you and please you in all that I can   *cheer, gladden*
510 And not for to chide with you, as I began!
   For think it in your mind I am the man
   That would please in all that I may;
   And to that purpose I will do what I can,
   Though you forbid it and say therein nay;
515 In that point only I will you disobey.
   My heart shall you have in all goodly wise
   Whether you me take, or utterly despise!
   And to say that I will follow the guise   *fashion*
   Of wanton lovers nowaday,
520 Which doth many flattering words devise
   With gifts of rings and brooches gay
   Their lemmans' hearts for to betray,   *lovers'*
   You must have me therein excused;
   For it is the thing that I never used.
525 Therefore I will be short and plain;
   And I pray you heartily, fair Lucres,
   That you will be so to me again.   *in return*
   You know well I have made labour and business

489 He must wait constantly on his lady if he hopes to succeed.

And also desired you by words express
530 That you would vouchsafe in your heart
To be my wife till death us depart   *separate*
Lo, this is the matter that I come for;
To know therein your mind and pleasure,
Whether you set by me any store
535 To th'effect of my said desire;
And nothing else I will require   *ask for*
But that I may have a plain yea or nay
Whereto I may trust without delay.

Lucres.   Me thinketh that by that that you say
540 You force not what mine answer be!   *care*

Gaius.   Ah, will you take it that way?   Q. *A*
My lady, I meant not so, pardy!
Th' affirmative were most lief to me;   *pleasing*
For, as you yourself knoweth best
545 That was and is my principal request.
But you may say I am a homely gest   *boorish fellow*
On a gentlewoman so hastily to call.

Lucres.   Nay, nay, Sir! That guise is best;
You cannot displease me withal!
550 And, according to your desire I shall—
Even as soon as I goodly may—
Answer you therein without delay.
Howbeit, it cannot be done straight way
If I might get a realm thereby.   *even if*
555 First will I my father's mind assay
Whether he will thereunto apply;   *agree*
For, if he like you as well as I,
Your mind in this behalf shall be soon eased
If my said father can be content and pleased.

560 *Gaius.*   Gramercy, my own sweet Lucres!
Of you desire can I no more at all,
Save only that you do your business
Upon your father busily to call,   *swiftly*
So that, whatsoever shall befall,
565 Within few days I may verily know
To what effect this matter shall grow.

Lucres.   You shall know by tomorrow night
What my father will say thereto.

Gaius.   Then shall you make my heart full light
570 If it please you so to do.

560 *Gramercy:* (God have) great mercy (on you), many thanks.

[55]

Lucres. Yes, doubt you not it shall be so;
    And, for that cause, I will even now depart.

Gaius. Now farewell then, mine own sweetheart!

    Et exeat Lucres. Deinde A. accedens
    ad Gayum Flaminium dicat ei sic.
    (*And Lucres goes out. Then A approaches*
    Gaius Flaminius and says thus to him :)

A. Sir! You seem a man of great honour—
575   And that moveth me to be so bold!
    I read you, adventure not over much labour   *advise*
    Upon this woman, lest you take cold!
    I tell you the matter is bought and sold   *already fixed*
    Without you take the better heed;   *more care*
580   For all these fair words you shall not speed.   *succeed*

Gaius. Thinkest thou so in very deed?

A. Yea! so help me God! And I shall tell you why.
    Sir! Right now, this way as I yede,   *went*
    This gentlewoman came even by,
585   And a fresh gallant in her company:
    As God would, near them I stalked,
    And heard every word that they talked!

Gaius. But spake they any word of me?

A. Nay, nay! You were nothing in her thought.
590   They were as busy as they might be
    About such a matter as you have wrought,
    And, by God that me dear bought,
    Look what answer that you now have!
    Even the same words to him she gave!
595   Iwis, sir, I am but a poor knave,
    But yet I would take on me a great pain
    Your honesty in this matter to save,   *honour*
    Though it be unto me no profit nor gain:
    But therefore I speak, and have disdain
600   To see in a woman such dissemblance
    Toward a gentleman of your substance!

Gaius. Why? Hast thou of me any acquaintance?

A. Ay, sir! and some time you knew me
    Though it be now out of your remembrance!

605 *Gaius.* By my faith! It may well be!
    But nevertheless I thank thee:
    Me seemeth thou wouldest that all were well
    Betwixt me and yonder fair damesell.

A. Yea, by God! I would fight in the quarrel
610   Rather than you should lose your intent!

Gaius.   I pray thee, fellow, where dost thou dwell?

A.   By my faith I am now at mine own commandment;
  I lack a master, and that I me repent.
  To serve you and please, I would be fain,   *pleased*
615 If it might like you me to retain;
  And of one thing I will a-certain,   *for certain*
  I doubt not I shall do you better stead   *service*
  Toward this marriage than some other twain!
  And if I do not, let me be dead!

620 *Gaius.*   Well then, will I do by thy rede,   *advice*
  And in my service thou shalt be,
  If thou canst find me any surety.

A.   Yes, I can have sureties plenty
  For my truth within this place.   *reliability*
625 Here is a gentleman that would trust me   *i.e. B.*
  For as much goods as he has!

Gaius.   Yea, and that is but little percase!   *perchance, perhaps*

A.   By my faith, go where he shall,
  It is as honest a man as any in the (*realm*)   *Q. reall*
630 I have no more acquaintance within this hall:
  If I would any friends assay,
  By God, here is one best of all:
  I trow he will not say me nay,
  For he hath known me many a day.

635 (*to B*)   Sir! Will not you for my truth undertake? *reliability*
                                                         (*B joins them*)

B.   Yes, 'fore God! else would I were bake!
  Sir, my master, will you believe me,   *if you will*
  I dare trust him for all that I can make,   *earn*
  If you find me sufficient surety
640 As for his truth, doubt not ye,
  I never could by him anything espy
  But that he was as true a man as I.
  He and I dwelled many a fair day
  In one school, and yet I wot well
645 From thence he bare never away   *never stole*
  The worth of an half-penny that I can tell.
  Therefore he is able with you to dwell.
  As for his truth, that dare I well say,
  Hardily trust him therein you may.   *Assuredly*
650 *Gaius* (*to B.*).   Upon your word I shall assay.   *try him out*
  (*to A.*)   And, sir, after thy good deserving
  So shall I thy wages pay!
  But now to remember one thing;

636 *bake*: baked, roasted, i.e. in Hell.

[57]

Methought thou saidest at the beginning
655   That Lucres favoureth better than me
Another lover. What man is he?

A.   Cornelius, I ween his name should be.   *think*

Gaius.   Ay, then I know him well, by the rood!
There is not within all this city
660   A man born of a better blood.
But yet Lucres hath a wit so good
That, as I think, she will before see
Whether his conditions thereto agree;   *qualities*
And if they do not—farewell he!
665   But therein I have naught ado.   *no concern*
He shall not be dispraised for me   *by me,* or *on my account*
Without that I be compelled thereto.
I cannot let him for to woo   *prevent*
A woman being at her own liberty,
670   For why, it is as free for him as for me!
I will forbear never the more
Till I know what shall be the end.
Go thy way unto Lucres therefore,
And heartily me unto her recommend,
675   Praying her that she will me send
A ready answer of that thing
That she promised me at her departing.

A.   Marry I shall—without any tarrying;
I know mine errand well (*enough*).   Q. *Inow*
680   You shall see me appoint a meeting
Where she again shall speak with you.

Gaius.   Then shall I thy wit allow   *admit, approve*
If thou can bring that about.

A.   Yes, that I shall do, have you no doubt.

         Et exeat Gaius Flaminius et dicat B.
         (*And Gaius Flaminius goes out and B speaks*)

685 *B.*   Now, by my troth, I would not have thought
That thou haddest been half so wise;
For thou hast this matter featly wrought   *cleverly*
And conveyed it point device   *to perfection*
To bring thyself to such a service.   *To obtain such a master*
690   I see well thou hast some wit in thy head.

A.   Yea, a little! But hast thou sped?

B.   Even likewise, have thou no dread!
I have gotten a master for my prove: *gain, betterment*
I never thrived as I shall do now!

695   *A.*   No! Which way?

     B.   I shall tell thee how!
       It is no mastery to thrive at all   *skill*
       Under a man that is so liberall.
       There is now late unto him fall
       So great goods by inheritance
700   That he wot never what to do withal,
       But lashes it forth daily, escance   *lavishes; as though*
       That he had no daily remembrance
       Of time to come, nor maketh no store;
       For he careth not which end goeth before!
705   And, by Our Lady, I commend him the more!
       Why should he those goods spare
       Since he laboured never therefore?
       Nay, and every man should care   *if*
       For goods, and specially such as are
710   Of gentle blood, it were great sin;
       For all liberality in them should begin!
       Many a poor man thereby doth win
       The chief substance of his living.
       My master were worthy to be a king
715   For liberal expenses in all his dealing.
       I trow thou shalt see him come in
       Like a rutter, somewhat according,   *German Knight*
       In all apparel to him belonging.
       How much payeth he, as you suppose,
720   For the making of a pair of his hose?   *stockings*

     A.   Mary, twelve pence were a fair thing!

     B.   Yea, by the rood! Twenty times told:
       That is even twenty shillings for the making.

     A.   It cannot be so, without a man would   *unless*
725   Make them all with silk and gold!

     B.   Nay, by Jesus! None earthly thing
       But even the bare cloth and the lining—
       Save only that there is in cutting
       A new manner of fashion nowaday!
730   Because they should be somewhat strange
       They must be striped all this way
       With small slips of colours gay!
       A codpiece before, almost thus large,
       And therein restith the greatest charge!
735   To speak of gowns, and that good
          change,   *many changes of them*
       Of them he hath store and plenty,
       And that the fashions be new and strange,

For none of them passeth the mid-thigh;
And yet he putteth in a gown commonly
740   How many broad-yards, as you guess?

A.   Marry! Two or three?

B.   Nay! Seven and no less!

A.   By my troth, that is like a lie!

B.   But it is as true as you stand there!
And I shall tell you a reason why.
745   All that doth that fashion wear
They have wings behind ready to fly,
And a sleeve that would cover all the body.
Then forty pleats, as I think in my mind,
They have before—and as many behind!

750 *A.*   Well, as for gentlemen, it is full kind   *very natural*
To have their pleasures that may well pay!

B.   Yea! But then this grudgeth my mind: *annoys*
A gentleman shall not wear it a day
But every man will himself array
755   Of the same fashion even by and by   *instantly*
On the morrow after!

A.   Nay, that I defy!   *deny*
But then I marvel greatly why
You are not garnished after that guise?   *dressed*

B.   There is never a knave in that house save I
760   But his gown is made in the same wise;
And for because I am new come to service
I must, for a while, be content
To wear still mine old garment.

A.   You but abide! To what intent
765   Doth thy master take in hand
To make him so much costly raiment?

B.   Marry, that is easy to understand!
All is done for Lucres's sake:
To wed her he doth his reckoning make.

770 *A.*   I put case that she do him forsake   *I bet you*
So that she be my master's wife.

B.   By my faith! Then I say it will make
Many a man to lose his life,
For thereof will rise a great strife.

775 *A.*   Marry! I pray God send us peace.

B.   By my faith! It will be no less
If my master have not Lucres.

    A. I can no more! God speed the right!
      Lo, these folk will strive and fight
780   For this woman's sake;
      And when they have done their uttermost
      I ween verily he shall speed best
      That must her forsake!
      He is well at ease that hath a wife;
785   Yet he is better that hath none, by my life!
      But he that hath a good wife and will forsake her,
      I pray God the devil take her.

    B. Now, in good faith, thou art a mad knave!
      I see well thou hast wedded a shrew!

790   *A.* The devil I have:
      Nay, I have married two or three
      Since the time that I her lost!

    B. And keepest thou them all still with thee?

    A. Nay! That would not quit the cost
795   To say the truth; they found me most!   *kept; mostly*

    B. Then they have some manner **getting**
      By some occupation, have they?

    A. Sir, they have a pretty waye.
      The chief means of their living
800   Is lechery—leech-craft I would say—
      Wherein they labour night and day
      And ease many a man in some case!

    B. And where do they dwell?

    A. At the common place,
805   There thou mayest them all find.
      God's mercy! Where is my mind?
      By God I shall be shent!
      I should have gone to Lucres
      About my master's business;
810   Thitherward was I bent.

    B. By my faith! My master is there
      All the while that thou art here
      As I verily suppose!

    A. I shrow thy face, by St Mary!   *curse*
815   With thy chattering thou dust me **tarry**   *delay*
      Even for the same purpose!

800 The image is that of bleeding with leeches, the standard medical means
      in Tudor times for draining superfluous blood.
804 *common place:* public, i.e. tavern, brothel.

    B. I say; when thou hast with Lucres spoken,
        I pray thee, will thou deliver me a token
        In my name to her maid?

820 *A.* Nay! You must beware of that gear,   *sport, game*
        For I have been afore you there!

    B. Why? Hast thou her assayed?

    A. Yea, yea! That matter is sped full.
        I may have her and she will—
825   That comfort she me gave.

    B. And hast thou no (*other*) comfort at all?   *Q. noder*
        I trust to God then, yet I shall
        All this matter save.
        Howbeit, I will not the matter begin
830   Without I were sure she were a virgin.

    A. By my troth! This comfort shall I put thee in:
        I came never on her back in the way of sin.

                                  [Avoid the place A

    B. (*to audience*). Then all is well and fine!
        If the matter be in that case,
835   I trust that within a little space
        That wench shall be mine.   *Lucres's maid Joan*
        I tell you it is a trull of trust   *vagrant whore*
        All to quench a man's thrust
        Better than any wine.
840   It is a little pretty mouset   *diminutive mouse*
        And her voice is as doucet   *dulcet, sweet*
        And as sweet as (*roasted*) pork!   *Q. resty*
        Her face is somewhat brown and yellow;
        But for all that she hath no fellow
845   In singing hens to York.   *from here*
        But the worst that grieveth me,
        She hath no leisure nor liberty
        For an hour or twain
        To be out of her mistress's sight.
850   I watched for her this other night,
        But all was in vain.
        Howbeit, I think that at the last

                 Come in the maiden

    I shall come within two stones cast:
    Of her I ask no more.

---

838 *thrust :* so in Q (?) thirst: but cf. *Hamlet*: 'It will cost you a groaning to
take off my edge!'

855 And if I do so, then my mate
  Shall have no lust therein to prate   *desire*
  As he did before!
  Cockis body! Here she is   *by God's body*
  Now welcome, by heaven bliss,
860 The last that was in my thought!

  Joan. Tush! I pray you, let me go
  I have somewhat else to do!
  For this hour I have sought
  A man that I should speak withal
  From my mistress.

865 *B.*   What do you him call?

  Joan. Master Gaius—or his man.

  B. Am not I he that you would have?

  Joan. No! No, I would have another knave.

  B. Why? Am I a knave then?

870 *Joan.* Nay, I said not so perde!   *par dieu*
  But where trow you these folks be?

  B. I cannot verily say;
  His man went even now from me,
  And I marvel greatly that ye
875 Met him not by the way:
  For he is gone to speak with Lucres
  From his master.

  Joan. What? With my mistress? Nay!

  B. Yea, so I heard him say.

880 *Joan.* God's mercy! And I was sent
  Even hither for the same intent,
  To bring an answer
  Of the errand that he is gone for!
  Wherefore now there is no more
885 But I must go seek him there.

  B. Nay, tarry here a while, gentle Joan,
  For he will come hither anon.

  Joan. Tarry? Why should I so?

  B. Marry, to laugh and talk with me!

890 *Joan.* Nay, look where such giglottis be— *wantons, gigolos*
  For I am none of them I warn thee—
  That use so to do;

  B. I mean nothing but good, and honest,
  And for your weal, and you list   *advancement*
395 To assent thereunto.

[63]

Joan. For my weal, quotha! How may that be?
That is a thing that I cannot see.

B. Mary! This lo, is mine intent: *look you*
I mean, if you would be content
900   Or any wise agree
For to be my sacrament of penance—
By God give it a very vengeance!—
Of wedlock I would have said.

Joan. Tush! By St James you do but mock
905   To speak to me of any wedlock,
And I so young a maid.
B. Why? Are you a maid?
Joan.   Yea, else I were to blame.

B. Whereby wot ye?   *How do you know?*

Joan.   Mary, for I am!
B. (to the audience). Ay, that is a thing!
910   Hear you not, Sirs, what she sayeth?
So reasonable a cause thereto she layeth!

Joan. A straw for your mocking!
Have you noone to mock but me?

B. Mock? Nay, so mote I thee,   *as I mean to thrive*
915   I mean even good earnest.
Give me your hand, and you shall see
What I will promise you.

Joan. That way were not best for my prow.   *promotion*
Would you handfast me forth withall?   *contract marriage*
920   Nay, by the rood! First you shall
Cheap or ever you buy: *Bargain*
We must first of the price agree;
For whosoever shall have me,
I promise you faithfully,
925   He shall me first assure
Of twenty pounds of land in jointure.   *from the marriage*
                              settlement

B. Why, are you so costly?
Nay! Nay then you be not for me.
As pretty a woman as you be
930   I can some time buy—
For much less wages and hire—
As for the season that I desire
To have her in company!
Therefore, if you can find in your heart
935   To leave all such jointure apart
And take me as I am,

I shall do you as great a pleasure;
And thereto I will love you out of measure
Else I were to blame.

940 *Joan.* Yea, but our household shall be full small,
But if we have somewhat else withal   *unless*
Our charges for to bear.

B. Yea, God send us merry weather!
I may not wed and thrive all together—
945 I look not for that gear.
I shall tell you a marvellous case:
I knew twain married in a place
Dwelling together in one house,
And I am sure they were not worth a louse
950 At the beginning.
And ere ever the year were do   *done*
They were worth an hundred or two.

Joan. That was a marvellous thing!
But yet I can tell thee a greater marvel—
955 And I knew the persons right well!
Sir, I knew two certain
That when they were wedded they had in store
Scarce half a bed, and no more
That was worth an haw;   *of any value*
960 And within a year or twain
They had so great increase and gain   *children*
That at the last they were fain
To shove their heads in the straw!   *on the floor*

B. Tush! You do but mock and rail!
965 And I promise you withouten fail
If you list to have me
I (*know*) where is an hundred pound in store   *Q. woot*
And I owe never a groat there fore!

Joan. All that may be—
970 I believe it even as you say—
But you tarry me here all day.   *delay*
I pray you, let me go.
And for my marriage, that is a thing
In the which I purpose to give a sparing
975 For a year or two.

B. A year or two, quotha! Nay, God forbid!
Iwis it had be time for you to wed
Seven or eight years ago!
And you wist how merry a life
980 It is to be a wedded wife,
You would change that mind.

[65]

Joan.   Yea, so it is, as I understand
If a woman have a good husband;
But that is hard to find.
985   Many a man blameth his wife, pardy,
And she is more to blame than he.

B.   As true as the gospel now say ye!
But now tell me one thing:
Shall I have none other answer but this
990   Of my desire?

Joan.   No sir, Iwis:
Not at this meeting.

B.   Will you now need be ago? Then   *gone*
Take your leave honestly.

Joan.   See the man!
Let me alone, with sorrow!   *The devil take you!*

995   *B.*   Marry! So be it; but one word
I will kiss thee ere thou go.

> *Et conabitur eam osculari*
> (*And he tries to kiss her*)

Joan (*to audience*).   The devil's turd!
The man is mad, I trow.

B.   So mad I am that needs I must
1000   As in this point have my lust   *wish, desire*
Howsoever I do.

Joan (*relenting*).   Parde! You may do me that request
For why, it is but good and honest.

> *Et osculabitur. Intrat A.*
> (*And he kisses. Enter A*)

A.   Now a fellowship! I thee beseech,   *Hail fellows!*
1005   Set even such a patch on my breech!   *kiss my arse*

B.   A wild-fire thereon!   *plague, pestilence*

Joan.   God's mercy! This is he
That I have sought so!

A.   Have you sought me?

Joan.   Yea, that I have do!   *done*
1010   This gentlemen can witness bear
That all this hour I have stood here
Seeking even for you.

A.   Have you two be(*en*) together so long?   *Q. be*

Joan.   Yea: why not?

985–6   This couplet is difficult to construe in its present context
unless the word 'no' be inserted after 'is' and before 'more'.

A.   Marry! Then all is wrong;
1015   I fear me so now.

B.   Nay, nay! Here be too many   *have been*
            witnesses   *the audience*
        For to make any such business
        As thou weenest hardily!

Joan (*to the audience*).   Why? What is the man's thought?
1020   (*to B*).   Suppose you that I would be nought   *wanton*
            If no man were by?

B.   Nay, 'fore God! I meant not so.
        But I would no man should have to do
        With you but only I.

1025 *Joan.*   'Have to do!' quotha; What call you that?
        It soundeth (*like*) a thing I wot ne'er what!   *Q. to*

A.   Heh, God's mercy!
        I see well a man must beware
        How he speaketh, thereas you are,   *in your mood*
1030   You take it so strangely.
        Nay, I mean nothing but well;
        For by my will no man shall deal
        With you in way of marriage
        But only I—this wise I meant!

1035 *Joan.*   Yea, but though it were your intent,
        Yet, you do but rage
        To use such words unto me
        For I am yet at liberty.

A.   Yea, that I know well!
1040   But, nevertheless, (*since*) that I began   *Q. sithen*
        To love you long before this man
        I have very great marvel
        That ever you would his mind fulfil
        To stand and talk with him still
1045   So long as you have do.   *done*

B.   Before me, quotha? Nay, I make avow
        I moved this matter long before you!
        How say you thereto?

Joan.   I will nothing in the matter say
1050   Lest I cause you to make a fray;
        For thereof I would be loath.

A.   By cock's body, but whosoever it be
        That weddeth her besides me
        I shall make him wroth.   *rue it*

1055 *B.*   Yea, but he that is so hasty at every word
        For a medicine must eat his wife's turd!

[67]

Joan.   Hold your tongues there I say!
For and ye make this work for me
You shall both disappointed be
1060   As far as I may.

A.   By my troth! But mark me well,
If ever thou with this man dwell
As a woman with her mate
Thou shalt find him the most forward man
1065   That ever thou sawest since the world began:
For I dare undertake
That forty times (*in*) a day,   Q. *on*
Without any cause, he will thee affray   *assault*
And beat thee back and side!

1070 *Joan.*   He shall not need so to do
For he shall have forty causes and forty two
If I with him abide!

A.   Marry, that is a remedy according!
But I can tell thee another thing—
1075   And it is no lie—
Thou mayest well be his wedded wife
But he will never love thee in his life.

Joan.   Yet I know a remedy.

A.   How so?

Joan.   Mary, I will love him as little again:
1080   For every shrewd turn he shall have twain
And he were my brother!

B.   Iwis Joan, he speaketh but of malice.   *out of*
There is no man hence to Calais—
Whosoever be the tother—
1085   That can himself better apply
To please a woman better than I.

Joan.   Yea! So I heard you say!
But yet, be you never so wroth,   *angry*
There is never one of you both,
1090   For all your words gay,
That shall be assured of me
Till I may first hear and see
What you both can do.
And he that can do most mastery—
1095   Be it in cookery or in pastry,
In feats of war or deeds of chivalry
With him will I go!

A.   By my troth that liketh me well!
There is no mastery that a man can tell

1100 But I am meet thereto.   *equal, a match*
      Wherefore that wager I dare well undertake
      Let me see. Wilt thou go quoit for thy lady's sake?
      Or what thing shall we do?

      B. Nay, if thou wilt her with mastery win
1105 With boys' game(s) thou may'st not begin:
      That is not her intent!

      A. What is best that we do then?

      B Marry! Can'st thou sing?

      A.   Yea, that I can,
      As well as any man in Kent!

1110 *B.* What manner of song shall it be?

      A. Whatsoever thou wilt choose thee;
      I hold me well content;
      And if I meet thee not at the close   *match, equal*
      Hardily let me the wager lose   *truly*
1115 By her own judgement.
      Go to now: will you set in?   *start*

      B. Nay, by the rood, you shall begin!

      A. By St James, I assent.
      Abide Joan, you can good skill,
1120 And if you would the song fulfil   *complete*
      With a third part,
      It would do right well in my mind.

                                                 Et tunc cantabunt
                                                 (*And then they sing*)

      B. I am so hoarse, it will not be!

      A. Hoarse, quotha! Nay, so mot I thee,   *so may I thrive*
1125 That was not the thing!
      And a man should the truth say,
      You lost a crotchet or two on the way,
      To my understanding!

      B. Why, was I a minim before?

1130 *A.* Yea, by the rood, that you were—and more!

      1102 Play quoits. The quoits in question, however, were iron rings and
           they were lobbed at a stake some twenty yards away. This game was
           still played in villages in the Somerset coalfield until very recently. It
           is described by Joseph Strutt in his *Sports and Pastimes of the People
           of England* (1810), p. 69.
      1119 Thus in Q: meaning perhaps, 'you recognize skill'.
      1122 sd No song is supplied. A simple round seems called for; in per-
           formance the audience can then easily be drawn in as participants if
           the actors divide it up into three corresponding groups.

B.   Then were ye a minim behind!
Let me see. Yet sing again—
(*to Joan*) And mark which of us twain
Pleaseth best your mind.

1135 *Joan.*   Nay, nay! You shall this matter try
By some other manner of mastery
Than by your singing.

B.   Let him assay what mastery he will.

A.   Marry, and my belly were not so full
1140 I would wrestle with him a fair pull.
That were a game according
For such valiant men as we be.

B.   I shrew thine heart and thou spare me.

> *Et deinde luctabuntur*
> (*And then they wrestle*)

Joan.   Nay, by my faith! That was no fall!

1145 *B.*   Ay then, I see well you be partial
When you judge so!
Well I shall do more for your love:
Even here I cast to him my glove
Or ever I hence go,
1150 On the condition that in the plain field
I shall meet him with spear and shield
My life thereon to jeopard.   *risk, hazard*
Let me see (*if*) he dare take it!   Q. *and*

> *Tunc proiiciet cirothecam*
> (*Then he throws down a leather gauntlet*)

A.   Yes, hardily, I will not forsake it!
1155 I am not such a coward
But I dare meet thee at all assays!
When shall it be do(*ne*)?

B.   Even straightways
Without further delay!
And I shrew his heart that fears,
1160 Either with cronall or sharpe spears,   *blunted tilting lance*
This bargain to assay!

A.   And I beshrew him for me!
But, abide now; let me see.
Where shall I have a horse?

1143 sd The wrestling bout continues until B claims a victory over A
1156 This is the logical point for A to pick up the gauntlet.

[70]

1165   *B.*   Nay, we shall need no horse nor mule
        But let us joust at fart-prick-in-cule.   *buttocks*

     A.   By St James! No force!   *no matter*
        Even so be it. But where is our gear?

     B.   By my faith, all thing is ready
1170   That belongeth thereto.
        (*to Joan*) Come forth, you flower of the frying pan!
        Help you to array us as well as you can.
        And howsoever you do,
        See that you judge indifferently
1175   Which of us twain hath the mastery!

     Joan.   Yes, hardily, that I shall!
        I shall judge after my mind.
        But see you hold fast behind
        Lest you trouble us in all!

1180   *B.*   Tush! that is the least care of fifteen
        And if I do not, on my game be it seen!
        Go to! Bind me first, hardily.
        So—lo now give me my spear
        And put me a staff through here:
1185   Then am I all ready.

     A.   Abide! Who shall help to harness me?

     Joan.   That shall I do, so mot I thee,
        With a right good will.

     A.   Soft and fair! Mine arm is sore!
1190   You may not bind me straight therefore.   *tight*

     Joan.   Nay, no more I will;
        I will not hurt thee for twenty pound.
        Come off now: sit down on the ground,
        Even upon thy tail.

1195   *A.*   Heh, Good Lord, when will you have done?

     Joan.   Now all is ready, hardily. Go to!
        Bid him bail, bail!   *Charge! Charge!*

1165 In medieval and Tudor England jousting, whether on horseback or on foot, was a privileged pastime strictly reserved to the nobility. The pretensions of A and B in this matter are therefore absurd, and Medwall's purpose is to provide entertainment by offering a bawdy parody of the familiar rituals of a Tournament. Joan is thus elevated in the guise of 'the flower of the frying pan' into the lady in whose honour the jousting is taking place: but she also has to act as armourer to them both, providing them with broom and mop as spears, sauce-pans as helmets, the lids as shields and dish-cloths as slings or harnesses for the lances—or anything else immediately to hand in the hall.

1189 After the wrestling, no doubt.

A. (to audience).   Fall to prayers, Sirs. It is need
As many of you as would me good speed

1200   For this gear standyth me upon.   *this action is vital to me*

B. (to A).   Yea, and that thou shalt find ere we depart;
And if thou spare me I shrew thy heart
Let me see! Come on!

Et proiectus dicat A
(And falling down A says)

A.   Out, out, alas, for pain!
1205   Let me have a priest ere I be slain
My sin to disclose!

B.   And because he saith so, it is need;
For he is not in clean life indeed;
I feel it at my nose! For! Fo! etc.
1210   Now you are mine lady!

Joan.   Nay, never the more!

B.   No? Why so?

Joan.   For I am taken up before!

B.   Marry, I beshrew your heart therefore!
It should better content me
That you had been taken up behind!

1215   *Joan.*   Nay, nay! You understand not my mind
In that point.

B.   It may well be
But tell me how meant you (*then*)?   *Q. than*

Joan.   Marry! I am sure to another man   *assured, betrothed*
Whose wife I intend to be!

1220   *B.*   Nay, I trow by Cock's passion.   *God's*
You will not mock us of that fashion:
You may not for very shame.

Joan.   Shame or not, so shall it be!
And because that for the love of me
1225   You two have made this game,
It shall not be done all in vain;
For I will reward you both twain,
And else I were to blame.
Somewhat thereby you must needs win;
1230   And therefore to every each of you will I spin
A new pair of breeches!

1203 sd The joust concludes with B scoring a direct hit on A's backside.
1209 *For! Fo!*: exclamations appropriate to a bad smell.
1231 It is at this point that Joan starts beating B with the broomstick used
    as a spear in the jousting. She then turns to A and ties his hands
    behind his back with the sling.

[72]

Take thee that for thy dole!
And because he is black in the hole
He shall have as much!

Et utroque flagellato recedit ancilla
(*And the maid retires beating them both*)

1235   *A.*   Out, alas! What a woman was this?

       B.   It is Lucres's maid.

       A.   The devil it is!
I pray God a vengeance take her!
How sayest thou? Shall she be thy wife?

       B.   Nay! I had lever she had eaten my knife!   *rather*
1240   I utterly forsake her.

Intrat Gaius. (*Gaius enters*)

       Gaius.   How sirs? Who hath arrayed you (*thus*)?   Q. *thys*

       A.   False thieves, master, Iwis;
And all for your quarrel!

       Gaius.   What? And this other man too?

1245   *A.*   Yea: and you would our hands undo
The matter we shall tell.

       Gaius.   Yes, marry I will! Now tell on.
Who hath you these wrongs done?

       A.   Marry, that I shall. Cornelius's
1250   Servants, which is your enemy,
Espied me going towards Lucres's place
That I could bring the matter to pass
Of that (*gentlewoman*), as your desire was.   Q. *gentleman*
They laid await for me in the way,   *an ambush*
1255   And so they left me in this array.

       Gaius.   Yea; but hast thou any deadly wound?
That is the thing that feareth my mind.

       A.   I'faith, I was left for dead on the ground.
And I have a great (*gash*) here behind   Q. *garce*
1260   Out of the which there cometh such a wind
That if you hold a candle thereto
It will blow it out—that will it do!

       Gaius.   See to it betime, by mine advice,
Lest the wound (*fester*) within.   Q. *fewster*

1265   *A.*   Then have I need of a good surgeon;
For it is so deep within the skin
That you may put your nose therein,

1236 *knife*: a euphemism for genitals.
1249–50 The servants of Cornelius, who is your enemy. . . .

[73]

Even up to the hard eyes!   *?eyebrows*
Here is a man that quit him well
1270   For my defence as ever I see.
He took such part that in the quarrel
His arm was stricken off by the hard knee,
And yet he slew of them two or three.

Gaius.   Be they slain? Nay, God forbid!

1275   *A.*   Yes, so help me God! I warrant them dead.
Howbeit, I stand in great dread
That if ever he come in their way
They will cut off his arm or his head
For so I heard them—all three—say.

1280   *Gaius.*   Which? They that were slain?

A.   Yea, by this day!
What needeth me therefore to lie?
He heard it himself as well as I.

Gaius.   Well then you lie, both two!   *both of you*

Exeat B. (Exit B)

But now tell me what hast thou do
1285   As touching my commandment
That I bade thee do to Lucres?
Spakest thou with her?

A.   Yea sir, doubtless,
And this is her intent:
She commendeth her to you by the same token
1290   That with her father she hath spoken
According to your request.
And so she willeth you to be of good cheer,
Desiring you this night to appear—
Or tomorrow at the furthest—
1295   And she will meet you here in this place
To give you a final answer in this case
Whereto you shall trust.

Gaius.   That is the thing that I desire:
But said she so?

A.   Yea, by this fire,
1300   I tell you very just!
In so much that she bade me say
And warn you that you purvey   *provide, arrange*

1272 Lit. 'right through the bone'. Introduction of the word 'knee' in this
    context exposes A's story for the invention it is. Shakespeare employs
    the same device when making Falstaff say that the three knaves who
    attacked him in the dark at Gadshill were dressed in Kendal green.
1299 *by this fire:* this fire, here in the hall.

[74]

For your own business;
For then it shall determined be
1305 Whether Publius Cornelius or you
Shall have the pre-eminence.

Gaius.   All that purpose liketh me well.
But who shall be here more? Canst thou tell?

A.   Marry, here shall be Fulgens,
1310 And Publius Cornelius himself also,
With diverse other many moo   *more*
Beside(s) this honourable audience.
Wherefore, if you will your honour save
And your intent in this matter have,
1315 It is best that you go hence
For to study and call to mind
Such arguments as you can best find
And make yourself all prest.   Fr. *prêt : ready*

Gaius.   Thy council is good; be it so;
1320 And even thereafter will I do,
For I hold it best.

Et exeat Gaius. Intrat B
(*And Gaius goes out. Enter B*)

B.   God's body, sir! This was a fit!   *exciting!*
I beshrew the whore's heart yet
When I think thereon!
1325 And yet the strokes be not so sore,
But the shame grieveth me more
Since that it was done
Before so many as here be present!
But and I might take her,
1330 By my troth, I shall make her
This deed to repent!

A.   Yet thou were as good hold thy peace,
For there is no remedy doubtless.
Therefore let it go.
1335 It is to us both great folly and shame
This matter any more to rehearse or name.

B.   Well then, be it so!
And yet because she hath made me smart
I trust once to ride in her cart
1340 Be it shame or no!
I cannot suffer it patiently
To be rebuked openly
And to be mocked also!
Another thing grieveth me worst of all:

[75]

1345 I shall be shent, that I shall,   *punished*
     Of my master too,
     Because I have been so long away
     Out of his presence.

    A.   Nay, nay!
     I have heard so much since I went hence
1350 That he had little mind to thine offence.

    B. I pray you, tell me why.

    A. For as I brought my master on his way,
     I heard one of Lucres's men say
     That thy master hath been
1355 All this hour at her place,
     And that he his answer has.
     This wise as I mean:
     She hath appointed him to be here
     Soon in the evening, about supper,
1360 And then he shall have a final answer
     What she intendeth to do.
     And so then we shall know her intent;
     For, as I understand, she will be content
     To have one of them two:
1365 But first she will needs know (*for*) certain   *Q. the*
     Whether is the most noble of them twain *which of the two*
     This she sayeth alway.

    B. Why, that is easy to understand,
     If she be so wise as men bear in hand.   *maintain*

1370 *A.* Yea, so I heard you say.
     Let me see now what is your opinion
     Whether of them is most noble of condition?

    B. That can I tell hardily: *truly*
     He that hath most nobles in store
1375 Him call I the most noble evermore
     For he is most set by.
     And I am sure Cornelius is able
     With his own goods to buy a rabble *whole crowd*
     Of such as Gaius is:
1380 And, over that, if nobleness of kin
     May this woman's favour win,
     I am sure he cannot miss.

    A. Yea, but come hither soon to the end of this play

1359 The actual time that the second part of the play is to be performed.
1376 For most store is set by him.
1383 *soon* : soon after the end of the first part of the play (which is approaching now) when the debate will start.

And thou shalt see whereto all that will weigh.
1385   It shall be for thy learning.

B.   Yea, come again who will for me,
For I will not be here, so mot I thee!
It is a gentlemanly thing
That I should await and come again
1390   For other men's causes and take such pain!
I will not do it, I make God a vow!
Why might not this matter be ended now?

A.   Marry, I shall tell you why.
Lucres and her father may not attend
1395   At this season to make an end,—
So I heard them say:
And also it is a courteous guise   *good manners*
For to respite the matter this wise,   *delay; way*
That the parties may,
1400   In the meantime, advise them well;
For either of them both must tell
And show the best he can
To force the goodness of his own condition   *argue*
Both by example and good reason.
1405   I would not for a swan
That thou shouldest be hence at that season
For thou shalt hear a royal disputation
Betwixt them ere they have do—
Another thing must be considered withal:
1410   These folk that sit here in the hall
May not attend thereto.
We may not, with our long play,
Let them from their dinner all day!   *keep*
They have not fully dined!
1415   For and this play were once overpast
Some of them would fall to feeding as fast
As they had been almost pined!   *starved*
But no force hardily and they do.
Usher! Get them good wine thereto!
1420   Fill them of the best!
Let it be do(*ne*), or you will be shent!   *punished*
For it is the will and commandment
Of the master of the feast.
(*to audience*) And therefore we shall the matter forbear,
1425   And make a point even here   *stop, conclusion*
Lest we exceed a measure.   *outlive our welcome*

1418 This line, literally interpreted, means, 'But no matter, truly, if they do
resume their meal!'

And we shall do our labour and true intent
For to play the remnant
At my Lord's pleasure.

Finis prime partis
(*The end of Part I*)

Pars Secunda (*Second Part*)

Intrat A dicens. (*Enter A speaking*)

  A. Much good do it you every each one,
     You will not believe how fast I have gone
     For fear that I should come too late!
     No force! I have lost but a little sweat   *No matter*
5   That I have taken upon this heat
     My cold courage to abate.
     But now to the matter that I came for!
     You know the cause thereof before:
     Your wits be not so short.
10   Perde, my fellows and I were here   *Par dieu*
     Today when you were at dinner,
     And showed you a little disport
     Of one Fulgens and his daughter Lucres,
     And of two men that made great business
15   Her husband for to be.
     She answered to them both then,
     Look, which was the more noble man,
     To him she would agree.
     This was the substance of the play
20   That was showed here today,
     Albeit that there was
     Divers toys mingled in the same
     To stir folk to mirth and game
     And to do them solace.
25   The which trifles be impertinent   *irrelevant*
     To the matter principal;
     But nevertheless they be expedient
     For to satisfy and content
     Many a man withal.
30   For some there be that looks and gapes
     Only for such trifles and japes
     And some there be among   *also, among an audience*
     That forceth little of such madness   *careth*

1429 When the master of the feast, Cardinal Morton, bids us resume.
4–6 So in Q. The confused syntax of these three lines obscures their mean-
    ing. In performance they can be cut without significant loss.

	But delighteth them in matters of sadness	*seriousness*
35	Be it never so long!	
	And every man must have his mind,	
	Else they will many faults find	
	And say the play was nought.	
	But, no force, I care not!	
40	Let them say, and spare not!	
	For God knoweth my thought:	
	It is the mind and intent	
	Of me and my company to content	
	The least that standeth here!	
45	And so I trust you will it allow—	*accept, approve*
	By God's mercy! Where am I now?	
	It were alms to wring me by the ear	*charity*
	Because I make such digression	
	From the matter that I began	
50	When I entered the hall!	
	For, had I made a good continuance,	
	I should have put you in remembrance,	
	And to your minds call	*recall*
	How Lucres will come hither again	
55	And her said lovers, both twain,	
	To define this question:	
	Whether of them is the more noble man.	*which*
	For thereon all this matter began:	
	It is the chief foundation	
60	Of all this process, both all and some.	
	And if these players were once come	
	Of this matter will they speak.	
	I marvel greatly in my mind	
	That they tarry so long behind	
65	Their hour for to break!	
	But what, sirs, I pray you every one,	
	Have patience, for they come anon!	
	I am sure they will not fail	
	But they will meet in this place	
70	As their promise and appointment was,	
	And else I have marvel.	
	Let me see! What is now o'clock?	
	Ah! there cometh one! I hear him knock!	

35 This interesting digression on the tastes of early Tudor audiences pro-
tects Medwall, the Chaplain, and his master the Cardinal, against the
sort of criticism that the more serious Churchmen present might otherwise have levelled at provision of so secular an entertainment in the
Christmas season.

60 cf. similar use of the word 'process' in the sense of 'argument' in *The
Conversion of Saint Paul*, Introduction, p. 105 below.

He knocketh as he were wood!   *mad*
75   One of you, go look who it is!

Intrat B. (Enter B).

B. (To the member of the audience who opens the door)
Nay, nay! All the meyny of them, Iwis,   *household*
Cannot so much good!
A man may rap till his knuckles ache
Ere any of them will the labour take
80   To give him an answer!

A.   I have great marvel on thee
That ever thou wilt take upon thee
To chide any man here!
No man is so much to blame as thou
85   For long tarrying!

B.   Yea, God avow!
Will you play me that?
Marry, that shall be ammended anon!
I am late come in, and I will soon be gone
Else I shrew my cat!   *curse*
90   Cock's body, sir! It is a fair reason   *God's*
I am come hither at this season
Only at thy bidding;
And now thou makest to me a quarrel,
As though all the matter were in peril,
95   By my long tarrying!
Now God be with you, so mot I thee;
You shall play the knave alone for me.

A.   What? I am afraid
Iwis you are but lewd.   *hopeless, useless*
100   Turn again, all-be-shrewed,   *cursed by all*
Now are you fair prayed!   *courteously invited*

B.   Why, then, is your anger all do?   *done*

A.   Yea, marry; it is so.

B.   So is mine too.
105   I have done clean.
But now how goeth this matter forth
Of this marriage?

A.   By St James, right nought worth.
I wot ne'er what they mean;
110   For I can none other wise think

80 A very original and daring dramatic device comparable with the screw-
ing of money from the audience in *Mankind*. See p. 20 above.

But that some of them begin to shrink
Because of their long (*tarrying*).   Q. *tariage*

B.   Shrink now, quotha! Marry, that were marvel!
But one thing of surety I can thee tell
115   As touching this marriage.
Cornelius, my master, appointeth him   *is preparing*
   thereupon;
And doubtless he will be here anon
In pain of forty pence   *under forfeit*
In so much that he hath devised
120   Certain strangers freshly disguised   *splendidly costumed*
At his own expense
For to be here this night also.

A.   Strangers, quotha! What to do?

B.   Marry for to glad withal
125   This gentlewoman at her hither coming.

A.   Ah! then I see well we shall have a Mumming.

B.   Yea, surely that we shall;
And therefore never think it in thy mind
That my master will be behind.
130   Nor slack at his bargain.

Intrat Cornelius. (*Cornelius enters*)

Marry, here he commeth! I have him espied.
No more words! Stand thou aside,
For it is he plain.

Cornelius.   My friend, whereabout goest thou all day?

135   *B.*   Marry, sir! I came hither to assay
Whether these folk had been here;
And yet they be not come,
So help me God and halidom!
Of that I have much marvel that they tarry so.

140   *Cornelius.*   Marry, go thy way
And wit where they will or no!   *know whether*

B.   Yea, God avow, shall I so?

Cornelius.   Yea, marry! So I say!

B.   Yet in that point, as seemeth me,
145   You do not according to your degree.

126 cf. Lydgate's Mummings of 'strangers' disguised, pp. 196–7 below.
Here, of course, the 'Mumming' or 'Disguising' does not stand on its
own but is skilfully incorporated into the play. See also the Mumming of
Muscovites and Blackamoors in *Love's Labour's Lost* (V. 2) where it is as
'strangers disguised' that Navarre and his companions visit the Princess
of France and her ladies.

Cornelius.   I pray thee, tell me why?

B.   Marry, it would become them well enow
       To be here afore and to wait upon you,
       And not you to tarry
150   For their leisure and abide them here
       As it were one that were led by the ear;
       For that I defy!
       By this mean you should be their drudge!
       I tell you truth, I;
155   And yet, the worst that greeveth me
       Is that your adversary should in you see
       So notable a folly—
       Therefore withdraw you for a season.

Cornelius.   By St John, thou sayest but reason!

160 *B.* Yea, do so hardily;
       And when the time draweth upon
       That they be come, every one,
       And all thing ready,
       Then shall I come straight away
165   For to seek you without delay.

Cornelius.   Be it so hardily.
       But one thing, while I think thereon,
       Remember this when I am gone—
       If it happen so
170   That Lucres come in first, alone,
       Go in hand with her anon,   *Get on terms*
       Howsoever thou do,
       For to feel her mind toward me,
       And by all means possible to be
175   Induce her thereunto.

B.   Then some token you must give me,
       For else she will not believe me
       That I came from you.

Cornelius.   Marry, that is even wisely spoken!
180   Commend me to her by (*this*) same token: *Q. the*
       She knoweth it well, enow,
       That as she and I walked once together
       In her garden, hither and thither,   *up and down*
       There happened a strange case:
185   For, at the last, we did see
       A bird sitting on a hollow tree—
       An ash I trow it was.
       Anon she prayed me for to assay
       If I could start the bird away.

190 *B.* And did you so? Alas! Alas!

Cornelius.   Why the devil sayest thou so?

B.   By Cock's bones, for it was a cuckoo!
And men say among,   *from time to time*
He that throweth stone or stick
195 At such a bird, he is like
To sing that birdy's song!

Cornelius.   What the devil reck I therefore?   *care about that*
Hear what I say to thee evermore,
And mark thine errand well;
200 Sir, I had no stone to throw withall,
And therefore she took me her musk-ball
And thus it befell—
I kist it as straight as any pole   *cast*
So that it lighted even in the hole
205 Of the hollow ash!
Now, can'st thou remember all this?

B.   By God! I would be loath to do amiss
For, sometime(s), I am full rash.
You say that you kissed it even in the hole
210 Of the hollow ash, as straight as any pole?
Said you not so?

Cornelius.   Yes.

B.   Well then, let me alone;
As for this errand, it shall be done
As soon as you be go.   *gone*

215 *Cornelius.*   Farewell then! I leave thee here
And remember well all this gear
Howsoever thou do.

                    Et exeat Cornelius. (*And Cornelius goes out*)

B.   Yes, hardily, this errand shall be spoken.
(*To audience*) But how say you, sirs, by this token?
220 Is it not a quaint thing?
I (*thought*) he had been a (*sane*) man,   *Q. went ; Q. sad*
But I see well he is a (*mad*) man   *Q. made*
In this message doing!
But what, chose he for me!   *the decision is his*
225 I am but as a messenger, perde;
The blame shall not be mine but his;
For I will his token report.
Whether she take it in earnest or sport,

203 'Kyst' is a variant on the past tense of the verb 'to cast': B, however,
elects to take it as the past tense of the verb 'to kiss', thereby creating a
vulgar *double entendre* out of Cornelius's story that was not intended in
his telling of it.

I will not thereof miss.   *fail*
230   Be she wroth or well apaid   *angry; satisfied*
I will tell her even as he said.
God avow! Here she is!
It is time for me to be wise.

        Intrat Lucres. (*Enter Lucres*)

(*To Lucres*) Now welcome, Lady, flower of price!
235   I have sought you twice or thrice
Within this hour Iwis.

Lucres.   Me, sir? Have you sought me?

B.   Yea, that I have, by God that bought me!

Lucres.   To what intent?

240   *B.*   Marry, for I have things a few,
The which I must to you show
By my master's commandment.
Publius Cornelius is his name,
Your very lover in pain of shame,
245   And if you love him not you be to blame;
For this dare I say,
And on a book make it good,   *swear on the Bible*
He loved you better than his own heart blood.

Lucres.   His hard blood? Nay, nay;
250   Half that love would serve for me!

B.   Yet since he did you first see
In the place where he dwells,
He had loved you so in his heart
That he setteth not by himself a fart,
255   Nor by no man else!
And because you should give credence
Unto my saying in his absence,—
And trust to that I say,—
He told me tokens two or three,
260   Which I know well as he told me.   *by heart*

Lucres.   Tokens? What be they?

B.   Let me see. Now I had need to be wise
For one of his tokens is very nice   *odd, curious*
As ever I heard tell:
265   He prayed you for to believe me
By the same token that you and he
Walked together by a hollow tree.

Lucres.   All that I know well.

B.   Ah! then I am yet in the right way;
270   But I have some other thing to say

[84]

Touching my credence,
Which, as I think, were best to be spared,
For haply you would not have it declared
Before all this audience!

275 *Lucres.* Nay, nay, hardily! Spare not!
As for my deeds, I care not
If all the world it heard.

B. Marry, then I shall proceed.
He showed me also, in very deed,
280 How there sat a bird;
And then you delivered him your musk-ball
For to throw at the bird withal:
And then—as he said—you did no worse
But even fair kissed him on the nook   *cranny, crack*
of the arse.

285 *Lucres.* Nay! There thou liest falsely by my faith!

B. Truth! it was on the hole of th'arse I should say:
I wist well it was one of the two—
The nook or the hole.

Lucres.   Nay, nor yet so!

B. By my faith, you kissed him—or he kissed you—
290 On the hole of th'arse. Choose you now:
This he told me sure.
Howbeit, I speak it not in reproof,
For it was done but for good love
And for no sinful pleasure.

295 *Lucres.* Nay, nay, man, thou art far amiss.
I know what thine errand is
Though thou be negligent!
Of thy folly thou may'st well abash;
For thou should'st have said 'the hollow ash':
300 That hole thy master meant.

B. By God avow, I trow it was!
I cry you mercy: I have done you trespass!   *wrong*
But I pray you take it in patience,
For I mistook it by negligence.
305 A mischief come thereon!
He might have sent you this gear in a letter,
But I shall go learn mine errand better
And come again anon.

Et exeat. (*And he goes out*)

286 Tudor spelling permits an ambiguity here in the aural pun on 'hole',
hollow, and 'whole', and so this spelling has been retained.

[85]

Lucres.   Yea, do so hardily!

310   (*To audience*) Now, forsooth, this was a lewd message
      As ever I heard since I was bore!   *born*
      And if his master have thereof knowledge
      He will be angry with him therefore.
      Howbeit, I will speak thereof no more,

315   For it hath been my condition alway
      No man to hinder, but to help where I may.

Intrat A. (A enters)

A.   Fair (*mistress*), liketh it you to know   Q. *maysters*
      That my master (*commends*) me to you?   Q. *comaunde*

Lucres.   Commendeth you to me?

320   *A.*   Nay, commendeth you to him.

Lucres.   Well amended, by St Sim!

A.   Commendeth he to you, I would say,
      Or else you to he, now choose you may,
      Whether liketh you better!   *whichever*

325   And here he sendeth you a letter—
      God's mercy! I had it right now.
      (*To audience*) Sirs, is there none there among you
      That took up such a writing?   *picked up*
      I pray you sirs, let me have it again.

330   *Lucres.*   You are a good messenger, for certain!
      But, I pray you, sir, of one thing:
      Who is your master? Tell me that!

A.   Master? What call you him? Perde, you wot
      Whom I mean well and fine!

335   *Lucres.*   Yet I know not; so mot I go.   *survive*

A.   What, yes, perde; he that would have you so.

Lucres.   I suppose there be many of tho(*se*)
      If I would encline.
      But yet know I not who you mean!

340   I hold best that you go again
      To learn your master's name!

A.   By my faith, and I hold it best
      You may say I am a homely guest   *uncouth chap*
      In earnest and in game!

345   *Lucres.*   Abide! I shall go to you, nearhand.
      What is your own name, I would understand?

329 Q does not indicate whether the letter is found and returned or not.
344 Meaning both on and off duty and on and off the stage.

Tell me that ere I go:
I trow thou can'st not well tell!

A.   By my faith, not verily well—
350   Because you say so.

    Et scalpens caput post modicum intervallum dicat :
    (*And, scratching his head, after a short while he says :*)

By this light, I have forgotten!
Howbeit by that time I have spoken
With some of my company   *?associates, other actors*
I shall be ascertained of this gear.   *be sure of the answer*
355   But shall I find you here again?

Lucres.   Yea, that thou shalt happily!

    Et exeat A. (*And A goes out*)

[*Although there is no stage direction bidding Publius Cornelius to
enter at this point, he must do so now, or slightly earlier, since he
speaks next. B must also enter with him*]

Cornelius.   Now fair Lucres, according to th' appointment
That you made with me here this day,
Because you shall not find me there negligent,
360   Here I am come, your will to obey:
And ready am I for myself to say
That as touching the degree of noble condition
Betwixt me and Gaius, there may be no comparison:
And that shall I show you by apparent reason,
365   If it shall like you that I now begin.

Lucres.   Nay; you shall spare it for a little season
Till such time that Gaius, your adversary, come in;
For I will give you therein none audience
Till you be both together in presence.
370   And in any wise keep well your patience   *case*
Like as I have bound you both to the peace:
I forbid you utterly all manner of violence
During this matter; and also that you cease
Of all such words as may give occasion
375   Of brawling, or other ungodly condition.

Cornelius.   There shall be in me no such abusion
In word nor deed, I you promise.
But now, let me see, what occupation
Or what manner of pastime will you devise
380   While that these folk doth tarry this wise?
Will you see a base dance after the guise   *slow*
Of Spain, while you have nothing to do?
All thing have I purveyed that belongeth
    thereto.

[87]

    Lucres. Sir, I shall give you the looking on.   *watch with you*

385 *Cornelius.* Will you do so? I ask no more.
    (*To B*) Go soon and bid them come thence anon   *at once*
    And cause the minstrels to come in before!   *first, ahead*

[*The stage directions in Q are inadequate at this point. B must
have entered with Cornelius and be the person addressed by him.
B fetches the Mummers, who are preceded by the musicians, one
of whom was either indisposed (or absent), from the dressing-rooms.
He immediately apologizes for the missing piper and adopts a parody
    of a Flemish accent to get a laugh and cover up this gaff*]

    B. Marry! As for one of them, his lip is sore!
    I trow he may not pipe, he is so sick!
390   Spiel up tambourine! Ich bid owe frelike!

            Et deinde corisabunt. (And then the Mummers dance)

    Lucres. Forsooth, this was a goodly recreation.
    But, I pray you, of what nation
    Be these goodly creatures?
    Were they of England or of Wales?

395 *B.* Nay, they be wild Irish Portugales   *Portuguese*
    That did all these pleasures!
    Howbeit, it was for my master's sake.
    And he will deserve it, I undertake,
    On the largest wise.   *reward*

400 *Cornelius.* Go thyself! Why standest thou so?—
    And make them cheer! Let it be do—
    The best thou canst devise!

    B. Yes! They shall have cheer—heaven high!
    But one thing I promise you faithfully.
405   They get no drink thereto.

  Exeat. (B goes out) (taking the Mummers & musicians with him)

  Intrat Gaius. Dicat Lucres. (Enter Gaius. Lucres speaks)

    Lucres (to Cornelius). Lo, here this man is come now.
    Now may you in your matter proceed.
    You remember both what I said to you
    Touching mine answer: I trow it is no need
    Any more to rehearse it.

410 *Cornelius.*   No, in very deed;
    For much rehearsal would let the speed   *hinder*

    390 sd The strangers disguised as Spaniards who perform this Mumming
        and B's parody of a Flemish accent link this Interlude to Cardinal
        Morton's Christmas Feast for the Spanish and Flemish Ambassadors in
        1497. See Introduction, p. 37 above.

Of all this matter: it needeth no more:
Let us roundly to the matter we come for.

Lucres.   Yea, that I pray you as heartily as I can.
415   But first, me seemeth, it were expedient
That you both name some indifferent man   *impartial*
For to give betwixt you the forsaid judgement.

Cornelius.   Nay, as for that, by mine assent
No man shall have that office but ye.

420 *Gaius.*   And I hold me well content that it so be.

Lucres.   Yea, but notwithstanding that you thereto agree
That I should this question of nobless define,
It is a great matter which, as seemeth me,
Pertaineth to a philosopher or else (*to*) a divine!
425   Howbeit, since the choice of this matter is mine,
I can be content, under certain protestation,
When that I have heard you, to say mine opinion.
Lo, this wise I mean, and thus I do intend,
That whatsoever sentence I give betwixt you two
430   After mine own fantasy, it shall not extend
To any other person; I will that it be so!
For why? No man else hath therein ado.
It may not be noted for a general precedent,
Albeit that for your parts you do thereto assent.

435 *Gaius.*   As touching that point, we hold us well content.
Your sentence shall touch no man but us twain:
And, since you shall give it by our own agreement,
None other man ought to have thereat disdain.   *be indignant*
Wherefore, all this doubt you may well refrain,
440   And in the matter principal this time would be spent.

Cornelius.   Then will I begin.

Gaius.   I hold me well content.

Cornelius.   Since you have promised fair Lucres heretofore
That to the more noble man you will incline,
Vary not from that word, and I ask no more;
445   For then shall the victory of this cause be mine,
As it shall be easy to judge and define
For every creature that any reason has.
Me seemeth I durst make himself judge in this case,   *Gaius*
Save that I fear me the beauty of your face
450   Should therein blind him, so that he ne might   *could not*
Equally discern the wrong fro(*m*) the right.
And if he were half so wise a man indeed
As he reputeth himself for to be
Upon your said answer he should not need
455   To gainsay in this matter or traverse with me.   *cross*

My nobleness is known through all the city:
He knoweth himself the nobleness of my kin,
And at that one point my process I will begin.   *case*

Among all th' histories of Romans that you read
460 Where find you any blood of so great nobleness
As hath been the Cornelius's whereof I am bred?
And if so be that I would therein hold my peace
Yet all your chronicles beareth good witness
That my progenitors and ancestors have be
465 The chief aid and defence of this noble city.

How often have mine ancestors in times of necessity
Delivered this city from deadly peril
As well by their manhood as by their policy!
What jeopardy and pain they have suffered in the quarrel
470 Th' empire to increase and for the common weal!
It needeth not the specialities to rehearse or name   *details*
Since every true Roman knoweth the same.

In every man's house that histories be rife   *current*
And written in books, as in some places be
475 The gestes of Arthur, or of Alexander's life,   *romances*
In the which stories you may evidently see
And read how Carthage, that royal city,
By Scipio of Africk my great-grandsire
Subdued was, and also ascribed to his empire.

480 And many other cities that did conspire,
Against the noble senator making resistance,
As often as necessity did it require
They were reduced unto due obedience
Either by the policy or by the violence
485 Of my said ancestors: th' histories be plain
And witness that I speak not these words in vain.

My blood hath ever taken such pain
To safeguard the common weal from ruin and decay
That by one advise the Senate did ordain   *accord, decision*
490 Them to be named the fathers of the country:
And so were mine ancestors reputed alway,
For in every need they did upon them call
For help, as the child doth on the father natural.

Howbeit, to pray them it was no need at all,
495 For of their own minds they were ready alway.
In token of the same, for a memorial
Of their deserts, the city did edify   *build, erect*
Triumphal arches whereupon you may,

To my great honour, see at this day
500 Th' images of mine ancestors, even by and by   *here and now*
Because that their nobleness should never die.

In token also that they were worthy
Great honour and praise of all the country,
It is commanded, and used generally,
505 That every citizen that passeth that way
By the said Images, he must obey   *make obeisance*
And to (*those*) figures make a due reverence   *Q. that*
And else to the laws he doth great offense.

Sith it is so, then, that of convenience
510 Such honour and homage must needs be do
To these dead images, then much more reverence
To me should be given! I trow you think so;
For I am their very image and relique too,
Of their flesh and blood, and very inheritor.
515 As well of their goods as of their said honour.

To me they have left many a castle and tower
Which in their triumphs they rightfully won.
To me they have also left all their treasure
In such abundance that I trow no man
520 Within all Rome since it first began
Had half the store, as I understand,
That I have, even now at once, in my hand.

Lo, in these things my nobleness doth stand
Which, in mine opinion, sufficeth for this intent;
525 And I trow there is no man through all this land
Of Italy, but if he were here present,
He would to my saying in this matter assent,
And give unto me the honour and preeminence,
Rather than make against me resistance.

(*To Gaius Flaminius*)
530 I marvel greatly what should thy mind incense   *provoke*
To think that thy title therein should be good!
Parde, thou canst not say for thy defence
That ever there was gentleman of thy kin or blood:
And, if there were one, it would be understood
535 Without it be thyself which now of late
Among noble gentlemen playest checkmate.

Lucres.   No more thereof, I pray you! Such words I hate,

536 This phrase is said by Boas and Reed in their edition to mean 'to defeat,
bring ruin to'. This seems unnecessarily clumsy. A more simple interpretation is 'to challenge', as in chess, 'the nobility with pawns'.

And I did forbid you them at the beginning,
To eschew th' occasion of strife and debate.

540 *Gaius.*   Nay, let him alone! He speaketh after his learning:
For I shall answer him to everything
When he hath all said, if you will hear me,
As I think you will of your equity.   *in fairness*

Cornelius.   Abide! I must make an end first, perde!
545 To you, sweet Lucres, I would have said before
That if you will to my desire in this matter agree
Doubtless you shall bless the time that ever you
        were (*born*):   Q. *bore*
For riches shall you have at your will evermore,
Without care or study of laborious business,
550 And spend all your days in ease and pleasant idleness.

About your own apparel you can do none excess
In my company that should displease my mind.
With me shall you do none other manner of business
But hunt for your solace at the
        hart and hind;   *male and female deer*
555 And sometime, where we convenient game find,
Our hawks shall be ready to shew you a flight
Which shall be right pleasant and cheerful to your sight.

And if so be that in hunting you have no delight,
Then may you dance a while for your disport:
560 You shall have at your pleasure, both day and night,
All manner of minstrelsy to do you comfort.
Do what thing you will, I have to support   *enough wealth to*
Our charges and over, that I may sustain
At mine own finding an fifty or twain.

565 And, as for him, I am certain
His ancestors were of full poor degree—
Albeit that now, within a year or twain,
Because that he would a gentleman be,
He hath him gotten both office and fee,
570 Which, after the rate of his   *notwithstanding*
        wretched sparing,   *miserly behaviour*
Sufficeth scarcely for his bare living!

Wherefore, sweet Lucres, it were not according
For your great beauty with him to dwell;
For there should you have a threadbare living
575 With wretched scarceness; and I have heard tell
That maidens of your age love not right well
Such manner of husbands, without it be they
That forceth little to cast themselves away! *don't care if they*

[92]

I mean specially for such of them as may
580   Speed better if they will, as you be in (*this*) case;   Q. *the*
And therefore Lucres, whatsoever he will say
His title against you to force and embrace,
You shall do your own self too great a trespass
If you follow his part and incline thereto.
585   (*To Gaius*) Now say what you will sir, for I have all do.

Gaius (*to Cornelius*).   With right goodwill I shall go to,
So that you will hear me with as great patience
As I have heard you: reason would so.
(*To audience*) And whatsoever I shall speak in this audience—
590   Either of mine own merits or of his insolence—
Yet first unto you all, sirs, I make this request;
That it would like you to construe it to the best.

For loath would I be as any creature
To boast of mine own deeds; it was never my guise:
595   On that other side, loath I am to make any
      reporture   *mention*
Of this man's folly or him to despise;
But nevertheless this matter toucheth me in such wise
That, whatsoever you think in me, I must proceed
Unto the very truth thereof, as the matter is indeed.

600   To make a great rehearsal of that you have said,
The time will not suffer; but, nevertheless,
Two things for your self, in substance you have laid,
Which, as you suppose, maketh for your nobless;
Upon the which things dependeth all your process.
605   First, of your ancestors you allege the noble gestes;   *stories*
Secondly, the substance that you have of their bequests:

In the which things only, by your own confession,
Standeth all your nobleness; this said you before.
Whereunto, this I say, under the correction
610   Of Lucres, our judge here, that you are never the more
Worthy in mine opinion to be called noble therefore;
And without you have better causes to show than these,
Of reason you must the victory of this matter lease. *lose, yield*

To the first part, as touching your ancestors' deeds,
615   Some of them were noble—like as you declare—
Th' histories beareth witness—I must grant
      them needs;   *of necessity*
But yet, for all that some of them were
Of contrary disposition, like as you are;

606 The material possessions you have inherited.

[93]

620
For they did no profit—no more do you—
To the common weal of this noble city.

If you will the title of nobleness win,
Show me what have you done yourself therefore!
Some of your own merits, let see bring in,
If ever you did any since you were bore!
625
But surely you have no such thing in store
Of your own merits, whereby of right
You should appear noble to any man's sight!

But, nevertheless, I will you not blame,
Though you speak not of your own deeds at all:
630
And, to say the truth, you may not for shame,
Your life is so voluptuous and so bestial
In following of every lust sensual,
That I marvel nothing in my mind
If you leave your own deeds behind!

635
(*To Lucres*) He weeneth that by his proud   *supposes*
                countenance
Of word and deed, with nice array,   *fine clothes*
His great oaths, and open maintenance
Of thefts and murders every day;
Also his riotous disports and play,
640
His sloth, his cowardice and other excess,
His mind disposed to all uncleanness,
By these things only he shall have nobleness!

Nay, the title of nobleness will not ensue   *attach to*
A man that is all given to such insolence;
645
But it groweth of long continued virtue,
As I trust, lady, that your indifference   *impartiality*
Can well define by your sentence.
His ancestors were not of such condition
But all contrary to his disposition!

650
And therefore they were noble without fail
And did great honour to all the country:
But what can their said nobleness avail
To him that taketh a contrary way,
Of whom men speaketh every day
655
So great dishonour, it is marvel
The country suffereth him there to dwell!

656 The boldness of this outspoken attack on the aristocracy, so explicit in
    its details about the conduct of many of them during the Wars of the
    Roses, is perhaps surprising; but Medwall has protected himself and his
    master both by the initial appeals of Cornelius and Gaius to the audience
    not to take their speeches too personally, and by distancing both spokes-
    men into the mists of Roman antiquity.

And where he twitteth me of poor kin,
He doth me therein a wrongful offence,
For no man shall thanks or praising win
660 By the gifts that he hath of nature's influence.
Likewise, I think by a contrary sense
That if a man be born blind or lame
Not he himself, but nature therein is to blame.

Therefore he doth not me therein reprove:
665 And as for that point, this I wot well,
That both he and I came of Adam and Eve:
There is no difference that I can tell
Which maketh one man another to excel
So much as doth virtue and goodly manner,
670 And therein I may well with him compare!

Howbeit, I speak it not for mine own praise;
But certainly this hath ever be(en) my condition:
I have borne unto God, all my days,
His laud and praise with my due devotion;
675 And, next that, I bear always
To all my neighbours charitable affection:
Incontinency and uncleanness I have had in abomination,
Loving to my friend and faithful withal,
And ever I have withstood my lusts sensual.

680 One time with study my time I spend,
To eschew Idleness, the causer of sin;
Another time my country manly I defend;
And, for the victories that I have done therein,
You have seen yourself, sir, that I have come in
685 To this noble city twice or thrice
Crowned with laurel, as it is the guise.   *custom*

By these ways, lo, I do arise
Unto great honour from low degree
And if mine heirs will do likewise
690 They shall be brought to nobless by me.
But Cornelius, it seemeth by thee
That the nobless of thine ancestors every one
Shall utterly starve and die in thee alone.

And where he to twitteth me on that other side
695 Of small possession and great scarceness,   *poverty*
For all that, lady, if you will with me abide,
I shall assure you of moderate richess,

679 Here speaks Medwall, the author of the Morality Play *Nature*. cf. Idle-
    ness as the chief Vice in *The Marriage Between Wit and Wisdom*, pp.
    172–3 below.

And that sufficient for us both doubtless:
You shall have also a man according
700 To your own conditions in everything.

Now, Lucres, I have showed unto you a part
Of my title that I claim you by,
Beseeching you therefore with all my heart
To consider us both twain indifferently,   *impartially*
705 Which of us twain you will rather allow
More worthy, for nobless, to marry with you.

Lucres.   Sirs, I have heard you both at large—

Cornelius.   Nay, abide, Lucres, I pray you heartily,
Since he layeth many things to my charge,
710 Suffer that I may thereunto reply.

Lucres.   Iwis replication shall not be necessary   *reply*
Without that you have some other thing in store
To show for yourself than you did before.

Cornelius.   Why, lady, what thing will you desire more
715 Than I have showed to make for nobleness?

Lucres.   Yes: something there is that maketh therefore
Better than you have showed in your process.   *argument*
But now let me see what man of witness,
Or what other proofs will you forth bring
720 By the which either of you may justify his saying.

Gaius.   As for my part, I will stand gladly
To the common voice of all the country.

Lucres.   And you likewise, sir?

Cornelius.   Yea, certainly:
I shall in no wise your word disobey.

725 *Lucres.*   Then will I betwixt you both take this way.
I shall go enquire as fast as I may
What the common fame will therein report;
And, when I have thereof a due evidence,
Then shall I again to you resort
730 To show you th' opinion of my sentence,
Whom I will judge to have the preeminence.

Cornelius.   Nay, fair Lucres, I you require   *beg, request*
Let me not now depart in vain
Not knowing th' effect of my desire.

735 *Lucres.*   Sir, although it be to you a pain,
Yet must you do so, even both twain.
Each of you depart hence to his own place
And take no more labour or pain in this case;

For, as touching th' effect of my sentence,
740 I shall go write it by good advisement   *thought and care*
Soon after that I am departed from hence:
And then to either of you both shall be sent
A copy of the same, to this intent,
That of none other person it shall be seen,
745 Since it concerneth but only unto you twain.

Gaius. This is a good way, as in my mind.
Are not you, sir, content in like wise?

Cornelius. I wot ne'er yet; I will praise as   *I don't know yet*
    I find
And as I have cause—that is ever my guise.

750 *Gaius.* Well, Lucres, will you command me any service?

Lucres. No service at all, sir! Why say you so?
Our Lord speed you both wheresoever you go!

              Et exeant Publius Cornelius et Gaius Flaminius
              (*And Publius Cornelius and Gaius Flaminius go out*)

Lucres. Now some maid haply, and she were in my case,
Would not take that way that I do intend;
755 For I am fully determined, with God's grace,
So that to Gaius I will condescend: *consent*
For in this case I do him commend
As the more noble man, since he this wise,
By mean(*s*) of his virtue, to honour doth arise.
760 And, for all that, I will not despise
The blood of Cornelius; I pray you think not so.
God forbid that you should note me that wise;
For truly I shall honour them wheresoever I go,
And all other that be of like blood also:
765 But unto the blood I will have little respect
Where tho(*se*) conditions be sinful and abject.   *morals*
I pray you all, sirs, as many as be here,
Take not my words by a sinister way.   *to mean anything else*

              Intrat B. (*B enters*)

B. Yes, by my truth! I shall witness bear,
770 Wheresoever I be come another day,
How such a gentlewoman did openly say
That by a churl's son she would set more
Than she would do by a gentleman bore!

Lucres. Nay sir, then you report me amiss.

768 sd In performance B must enter the hall within a line or so of the
departure of Publius and Gaius if he is to overhear Lucres's decision as
he claims to have done in his first few lines.

[97]

775 *B.*   I pray you tell me how said you then?

Lucres.   For God, sir, the substance of my words was this—
I say even as I said when I began—
That for virtue excellent I will honour a man
Rather than for his blood, if it so fall
780 That gentle conditions agree not   *morals, deeds, business*
withal.

B.   Then I put case that a gentleman bore
Have goodly manners to his birth according!

Lucres.   I say of him is to be set great store:
Such one is worthy more laud and praising
785 Than many of them that hath their beginning
Of low kindred, else God forbid!
I will not affirm the contrary for my head,
For in that case there may be no comparison:
But nevertheless—I said this before—
790 That a man of excellent virtuous conditions,
Although he be of a poor stock bore,
Yet will I honour and commend him more
Than one that is descended of right noble kin,
Whose life is all dissolute and rooted in sin.
795 And therefore I have determined utterly
That Gaius Flaminius shall have his intent.
To him only I shall myself apply
To use me in wedlock at his commandment.
So that to Cornelius I will never assent;
800 Although he had as great possession
As any one man in Christian region,
I shall in no wise favour or love his condition,
Howbeit that his blood requireth due reverence.
And that shall I give him, with all submission;
805 But yet shall he never have the preeminence
To speak of very nobless, by my sentence.   *true nobility*
You be his servant, sir! Go your way
And report to your master even as I say!

(*Exit Lucres*)

B. (*to audience*).   Shall I do that errand? Nay, let be!
810 By the rood, you shall do it yourself for me!
I promise you faithfully,
I would my master had be(*en*) in Scotland
When he did put this matter in her hand
To stand to her judgement!   *to abide by*

808 sd   There is no stage-direction in Q at this point; but it is clear from the
dialogue that Lucres must leave the stage here.

815   But, for as much as it is so,
        That this wrong to him is do
        By a woman, he must let it go
        And hold him content!
        But he is of such disposition
820   That when he heareth of this conclusion
        He will be stark mad—
        Yea, by my truth, as mad as an hare!
        It shall make him so full of care
        That he will with himself fare
825   Even as it were a lad!
        And so would not I, so mot I thee!
        For this matter, and I were as he,
        It should never anger me:
        But this would I do:
830   I would let her go in the (*devil's*) name.   Q. *mare*

       Intrat A. (*Enter A*)

A (*to audience*).   What now, sirs? How goeth the game?
        What, is this woman go?

B. Yea, yea man!

A (*to B*).   And what way hath she taken?

B.   By my faith! My master is forsaken,
835   And needs she will agree
        Unto thy master. Thus she sayeth
        And many causes therefore she layeth
        Why it should so be.

A.   I marvel greatly whereof that grew.

840   *B.*   By my faith, she said—I tell thee true—
        That she would needs have him for his virtue
        And for none other thing!

A.   Virtue! What the devil is that?
        And I can tell, I shrew my cat,   *curse*
845   To mine understanding.

B.   By my faith, no more can I.
        But this she said here openly.
        All these folks can tell!

A (*to audience*).   How say you, good women? Is it your guise
850   To choose all your husbands that wise?   *way*
        By my truth, then I marvel!

B (*to A*).   Nay, this is the fear, so mot I go,
        That men choose not their wives so
        In places where I have be;

[99]

855   For wives may well complain and groan,
        Albeit that cause have they none
        That I can hear or see!
        But of wedded men there be right few
        That will not say the best is a shrew!
860   Therein they all agree!
        (*To audience*)   I warn you wedded men, every one,
        That other remedy have you none
        So much for your ease:
        And you would study till tomorrow,
865   But let them even alone, with sorrow,   *damn them*
        When they do you displease!

     A.   Tush! Here is no man that setteth a blank   *a farthing*
        By thy counsel or (*giveth*) thee thank.   Q. *konneth*
        Speak thereof no more!
870   They know that remedy better than thou!
        But what shall we twain do now?
        I care most therefore;
        Methinketh that matter would be wist.   *known*

     B.   Marry, we may go hence when we list:
875   No man sayeth us nay.

     A.   Why then, is the play all do(*ne*)?

     B.   Yea, by my faith, and we were once go(*ne*)
        It were do(*ne*) straightway!

     A.   And I would have thought in very deed
880   That this matter should have proceede(*d*)
        To some other conclusion.

     B.   Yea, thou art a master merryman;   *a king of fools*
        Thou shalt be wise I wot ne'er when!
        Is not the question
885   Of nobleness now fully defined
        As it may be so by a woman's mind?   *as it can be*
        What wouldest thou have more
        Thou toldest me (*the*) other day   Q. *that*
        That all the substance of this play
890   Was done specially therefore,
        Not only to make folk mirth and game,
        But that such as be gentlemen of name
        May be somewhat moved
        By this example, for to eschew
895   The way of vice, and favour virtue.
        For sin is to be reproved

867 *blank :* a small coin of French origin, but also current in England in the
     reign of Henry V. At first it was cast in silver, later in copper when it
     acquired its new name late in the fifteenth century.

More in them, for the degree,
Than in other persons such as be
Of poor kin and birth.
900 This was the cause principal:
And also for to do withal
This company some mirth.
And though the matter that we have played
Be not (*perchance*) so well conveyed, Q. *percase*
905 And with so great reason
As th' history itself requireth,
Yet the author thereof desireth
That, for this season
At the least, you will take it in patience.
910 And if there be any offence—
Show us wherein ere we go hence—
Done in the same,
It is only for lack of cunning
And not he, but his wit running,
915 Is thereof to blame.
And glad would he be and right fain *pleased*
That some man of stable brain
Would take on him the labour and pain
This matter to amend.
920 And so he willed me for to say,
And that done, of all this play
Shortly here we make an end.

Emprinted at London by John Rastell dwelling on the south side of
Pauls Church beside Pauls Chain.

912 I suspect that this line and the line above were set in the wrong order by
    the printer: certainly, in performance, they make much better sense if
    their order is reversed.
922 sd Here, on the printed page of the Quarto, is the MS. note 'I am Miles
    Blomefyldes booke'.

[101]

THE CONVERSION OF SAINT PAUL

Within the covers of this volume *The Conversion of Saint Paul* makes an appropriate sequel to *Mankind* and *Fulgens and Lucres* since both dialect and handwriting in the manuscript prove it to have been composed during the last quarter of the fifteenth century and then altered for subsequent revival early in the sixteenth century. The marginal annotations prescribing 'dances' between the sections of the play, and the three leaves containing the scene between the devils are the most obvious examples, while choice of Mercury as a name for Belial's Messenger is of no less obviously Renaissance, rather than Gothic, inspiration.

As a play it is spectacular, even by modern standards; for not only must the director of a revival contend with at least four live horses, but he must also arrange for Saul to be struck by lightning, for a dove and an angel to descend from heaven on separate occasions, and for devils to appear from Hell and then 'vanish away with a fiery flame and a tempest'.

Some critics might contend that the play was not an Interlude. It is constructed in three self-contained sections, which could be played with a substantial lapse of time between them; alternatively all three could be performed in sequence, and the resultant single play would still be a relatively short one. Thus its claims to be regarded as an Interlude are at least as good as the alternative possibility of describing it as a Saint Play or Miracle Play, more especially since the author avoids using any such words. The protective prologues and epilogues which frame each section, and the insertion of the word 'daunce' in the margins between the sections, only serve to reinforce the play's structural resemblance to *Mankind* and *Fulgens and Lucres* where allowance is made for performance punctuated by the principal courses of a meal or some other diversion.

The play survives in a manuscript in the Bodleian Library at Oxford (MS Digby 133), where it forms one of a group of five plays all of which were edited and printed by F. J. Furnivall for the *Early English Text Society* in 1896 under the title of *The Digby Plays*. The other plays in the group are:

1. Herod's killing of the Children

2. Mary Magdalene
3. Christ's Burial and Resurrection
4. An incomplete Morality of 'Wisdom, Who is Christ', itself a part of the Macro Plays (cf. *Mankind*, pp. 1–6 above).

At least three men took some part in compiling this manuscript either as author, or as adapter or redactor, or as simple copyist; but it is not possible to define their respective responsibilities. One of them was John Parfre, whose name appears at the end of *The Killing of the Children*: 'John Parfre ded wryte thys booke'. Another name on the manuscript is that of Myles Blomfylde (Miles Blomfield): it appears twice, once in full on the first page of *The Conversion of St Paul* and once under the initials M. B. on the first page of *Mary Magdalene*, but on both occasions in a later hand than the rest of the manuscript.

A Miles Blomfield, an alchemist of Bury St Edmunds and Cambridge, who was born in 1525 and died *c.* 1574, was an early owner of the surviving Quarto of *Fulgens and Lucres*;[1] another Miles Blomfield was a churchwarden of St Mary's, Chelmsford, in 1575 when an inventory of players' costumes was taken with his name at the head of it. What is certain is that the handwriting of this Miles Blomfield is also that in which his name and initials are inscribed on the manuscript of the Digby Plays. If it is recalled that the full text of the Morality of *Wisdom* belongs to the Macro Plays, which seem to have originated in or near Bury St Edmunds, then it would seem reasonable to suppose that the Digby Plays started life there too and later migrated to Chelmsford. Both were active centres of dramatic performances.[2]

In 1890 A. W. Pollard printed a short excerpt from *Mary Magdalene* in *English Miracles, Moralities and Interludes*, and in 1897 J. M. Manly edited and printed the whole of *The Conversion of St Paul* in *Specimens of the Pre-Shakespearean Drama*: both of these retain the original spelling and punctuation. Since then neither play has received any serious attention from students of English or Drama. It is for this reason that the extraordinary views expressed by F. J. Furnivall in the introduction to his edition of the plays for E.E.T.S. in 1896 on the staging of *The Conversion of St Paul* have gone unquestioned since: even Sir Edmund Chambers took them over without comment.[3]

Furnival thought that the three sections of this play were devised in terms of separate localities like 'the Stations of the Cross' in a Roman Catholic church, with the audience required to

---

[1] Written above the colophon is the phrase 'I am Miles Blomefyldes booke': see p. 101 above.
[2] See R. R. Wright, 'Mediaeval Theatre in East Anglia', M.Litt. Thesis University of Bristol, 1971.
[3] *The Mediaeval Stage*, ii. 428.

move from one to the next in turn (p. ix). As far as I know, this view remained unchallenged until I took up the matter myself in 'The Staging of Saint Plays in England', an essay printed in *The Mediaeval Drama*, ed. Sandro Sticca (S.U.N.Y.), 1972.

In that essay I suggested that the three 'stations' were, in reality, either mobile 'pageants' or static 'mansions', all of which were assembled within a single *platea*, or acting area, but with each in turn serving to define the locality of the action as the narrative 'progressed' or 'processed'.

The first of these pageants represents the city of Jerusalem and its famous temple with Annas and Caiaphas in residence. Saul and his knights open the play, parading and boasting like King Herod in the acting area before approaching this pageant: as Herod swore by Mahomet, so Saul swears by Belial: as Herod elected to deal with the children of Bethlehem, so Saul tells Caiaphas and Annas, when he reaches their pageant, that he will deal with Christ's disciples. Well pleased, they commission him, through the agency of a servant, with letters of authority to act as their agent in the Lebanon. Thus armed, Saul demands a horse to ride to Damascus. This request introduces a comic sequence between the servant and an ostler (not unlike the ribald exchanges between Nought, Now-a-Days and New Guise in *Mankind*, or between A and B in *Fulgens and Lucres*) which concludes with the provision of 'a palfrey . . . full goodly beseen'. The knights then parade again with Saul uttering fearsome threats before departing for Damascus and leaving the stage to Annas and Caiaphas to sum up the action. This concludes the first section which is well constructed and vigorously expressed throughout. There then follows a curious stanza allotted to the Poet-Chorus in the form of an *optional* epilogue. It is this stanza which caused Furnival to suppose that the audience had then to move to another place to view the next scene, since the Poet appears to ask the audience

> to follow and succeed,
> With all your diligence, this general procession.

In the first place, however, if the audience had to rely on this stanza for its instructions to move on, it would be an obligatory verse and not allotted to '*Poeta—si placet*', i.e. *if he wishes*. In fact the word 'procession'—the root cause of the trouble—was chosen by the author to rhyme with 'conclusion' and simply means 'process' in the sense of 'argument', as is made clear in the four concluding lines, and twice in the opening Prologue (ll. 9 and 14).

The Poet then has another stanza to open the second section or 'station'; and here he does use the word 'process'—quite clearly as a synonym for 'argument'—and rhymes it with 'redress'.[1] As the

[1] For other uses of 'process' in this context, see *Fulgens and Lucres*, Part 2, pp. 79 ff. above.

last stage direction of the first sequence requires Saul and his knights to 'ride forth . . . out of the place' and as the first stage direction of the second section requires Saul to 'ride in' it is obvious that the optional stanza has been provided to permit the play to proceed either with, or without, a formal interval at this point. It is significant that the author says nothing in either stage direction about Annas, Caiaphas or the temple in Jerusalem: the inference is that he intended them all to stay put until needed again at the start of the third section.

In the second section the focus of visual attention is shifted from Jerusalem to Damascus: this is represented by a second pageant consisting of houses for Ananias and for Saul in Damascus itself, and a well for Saul's baptism. Situated between this pageant and Jerusalem is a third representing heaven and containing God, an angel, the Holy Spirit (in the form of a dove) and the necessary machinery for the creation of wind, thunder and lightning. The action is straightforward. Saul is struck by lightning and falls, blinded and lame, from his horse. God speaks to him, and the knights, after leading him to Damascus, leave the stage to return to Jerusalem. God then tells Ananias to visit Saul and baptize him, which he does at the neighbouring well. This concludes the second section. It too is equipped with an epilogue; but as the words '*si placet*' do not recur, it would appear that the author intended this epilogue to be obligatory.

The third section starts with the return of the knights to Annas and Caiaphas in Jerusalem and their account of Saul's conversion. Then follows a short sequence, inserted into the manuscript and in another handwriting, between the devil Belial and Mercury, his messenger, which parallels both in form and content the preceding exchanges between the knights and the high priests. This sequence is thus not an irrelevant interpolation as Furnival supposed (Introduction, p. x), but links this section to Saul's own

> By the god Belial, I shall make progress
> Unto the princes both Caiaphas and Annas

in the opening stanzas of the first section and establishes all persecutors of Christians to be the devil's agents on earth. The dialogue between Belial and Mercury also provides time for Saul to change out of his knight's costume into his 'disciple's weed' to reappear as Paul to preach a sermon on the avoidance of pride and its attendant evils. He is then arrested, brought back to Jerusalem and interrogated by Caiaphas and Annas. The play ends with Paul's being warned by an angel to 'convey [himself] shortly into another place' and a statement in the final epilogue about his flight 'in the night over the wall' engineered by the disciples.

The play's subject-matter is thus carefully defined by the three sections in which it is cast. Part 1 presents Saul, the persecutor of

Christ's disciples, Part 2 Saul's conversion, and Part 3 Paul the disciple, now persecuted himself, but rescued from Hell. These three parts can be presented as separate entities with gaps of time between them, or as a single entity in sequence with the Poet's stanzas covering the changes of locality: either way the play can be presented as easily in a roofed hall as in the open air provided that allowance is made for the horses by substituting hobby-horses for live animals indoors: nor is there the least need for, or advantage to be gained from, putting an entire audience to the great inconvenience of having to move from one place to another twice during the performance as Furnivall surmised.

The author's frequent apologies for his own and his actors' 'simpleness' and lack of literary expertise strongly suggests that the play belonged—at least in its final form—to a Guild of artisans who were willing to travel and to adapt their script and presentation to the environment offered by their sponsors and hosts in exchange for hospitality and a modest fee.

EDITIONS

F. J. FURNIVALL, *The Digby Plays*, ed. for E.E.T.S., 1896.

J. M. MANLY, 'The Conversion of St Paul', *Specimens of the Pre-Shakespearean Drama*, Part II, pp. 215–38, Boston, 1897.

The Digby Play of
THE CONVERSION OF SAINT PAUL

Prologue

<table>
<tr><td>Poet.</td><td colspan="2">Rex glorie, King omnipotent!</td></tr>
<tr><td></td><td colspan="2">Redeemer of the world by thy power divine!</td></tr>
<tr><td></td><td colspan="2">And Maria, that pure virgin, queen most excellent</td></tr>
<tr><td></td><td>Which bore that blessed babe, Jesu, that for us</td><td></td></tr>
<tr><td></td><td>suffered pyne,</td><td>pain</td></tr>
<tr><td>5</td><td>Unto whose goodness I do incline,</td><td></td></tr>
<tr><td></td><td colspan="2">Beseeching that Lord, of his piteous influence,</td></tr>
<tr><td></td><td colspan="2">To preserve and govern this worshipful audience.</td></tr>
</table>

Honourable friends, beseeching you of licence
   To proceed our process, we may, under your correction,
10   (*Show*) The conversion of Saint Paul, as the Bible gives
      experience,
      Who lists to read the book, Actum Appostolorum,
      There shall he have the very noticion: *true account*
      But, as we can, we shall us redress
      Briefly, with your favour, beginning our process.

(*Exit Prologue.*) *Here entereth Saul, goodly beseen in the best wise
      like an adventurous knight, thus saying :*

15   *Saul.*   Most (*dreaded*) man I am living upon the   MS. *dowtyd*
         ground,
         Goodly beseen with many a rich
            (*garnishment*);   MS. *garment*
         My (*peer alive*) I trow is not found   MS. *pere on lyve*
         Through the world, from the orient to the occident
         My fame is best known under the firmament.
20   I am most dread of people universal;
         They dare not displease me most noble.

---

14 sd As the Prologue was spoken by the author, possibly Miles Blomfield, he
   may well have stayed on the stage (if outside the acting area) to prompt
   the actors. The word DANCE has also been added here by a later scribe.
   The knights and foot soldiers who leave with Saul for Damascus on p.
   112 must clearly enter with him at this point.

Saul is my name—I will that you notify—
  Which conspireth the disciples with threat and menace;
Before the princes of priests most noble and   *lords spiritual*
  high
25 I bring them to punishment for their trespass.
  We will them not suffer to rest in no place,
For they go about to preach and give examples
To destroy our laws, synagogues and temples.

By the god Belial, I shall make progress
30 Unto the princes, both Caiaphas and Annas,
Where I shall ask of them, in sureness,
  To pursue through all Damascus and Liba;   *Lebanon*
  And thus we shall soon after then
Bring them, that so do live, into Jerusalem,
35 Both man and child that I find of them.

Here cometh Saul to Caiaphas and Annas, priests of the
temple

Noble prelates and princes of regality,
  Desiring and asking of your benign worthiness
Your letters and epistles of most sovereignty
  To subdue rebellious that will, of frowardness,
40 Against our laws rebel or transgress,
  Nor will not incline, but make objection,
To pursue all such I will do protection.

Caiaphas.   To your desire we give perfect sentence,
  According to your petitions that you make postulation,
45 Because we know your true diligence
  To pursue all tho(*se*) that do reprobation
  Against our laws by any redarguation: *contrary advice*
Wherefore shortly we give in commandment
To put down them that be disobedient.

50 *Annas.*   And by these letters, that be most reverent,
  Take them in hand, full agree thereto!
Constrain all rebels by our whole assent!
  We give you full power so to do.
  Spare not, hardly, for friend or foe.   *truly*
55 All those you find of that life in this realm,   *Christians*
Bound look you bring them into Jerusalem.

Here Saul receiveth their letters

23 *Which conspireth :* who breathes against; cf. Acts IX. 1.
34–5 *them :* having disposed of the disciples, their converts will be the next
target.

Saul.   This precept here I take in hand
  To fulfil after your wills both,
 Where I shall spare within this land
60 Neither man nor woman—to this I make an oath—
 But to subdue I will not be loath.
 Now follow me, knights and servants true
 (*Unto*) Damascus as fast as you can sue. MS. *Into; follow*

1st Knight.   Unto your commandment I do obeissance:
65 I will not gainsay nor make delation   *delay*
 But with good mind and hearty pleasaunce *delight*
  I shall you succeed and make perambulation
  Throughout Damascus with all delectation,
 And all that rebel and make resistance,
70 For to oppress I will do my diligence.

2nd Knight.   And in me shall be no negligence,
  But to this precept myself I shall apply,
 To do your behest with all convenience,
  Without any frowardness or any obstinancy—
75 None shall appear in me, but verily,
 With all my mind I you insure,   *assure*
 To resist tho(*se*) rebels I will do my cure.

Saul.   Truly, to me it is great consolation
  To hear this report that you do advance.
80 For your (*beneficial counsel*) I give MS. *sapyencyall wyttes*
  commendation.
  Ever at my need I have found you constant:
 But, knights and servants, that be so pleasant,
 I pray you anon my palfrey you bring,
 To speed my journey without letting.   *delay*

  Here goeth Saul forth a little aside for to make him ready
   to ride, the servant thus saying:

85 *Servant.*   Ho! Ostler, ho! A peck of oats and a bottle of hay!
 Come off apace, or I will to another inn!
 What, ostler! Why comest not thy way?
 Hie thee faster, I beshrew thy skin!   *curse*

 Ostler.   I am no ostler, nor none ostler's kin,
90 But a gentleman's servant, if thou dost know!
 Such crabbish words do ask a blow.

 Servant.   I cry you mercy, sir! I wist well somewhat *knew*
  you were
 Either a gentleman—or a knave, methinketh by your
  physiognomy!
 If one look you in the face that never see you ere,

[110]

95   Would think you were at the next door by.
    In good faith, I (*guessed*) you had been an   MS. *wenyd*
     ostler, verily;
   I saw such another gentleman with you a barrow-full bear
   Of horsedung and dogs' turds and such other gear.

   And how it happened a marvellous chance betide: *occurred*
100   Your fellow was not sure of foot, and yet he went very
     broad,
   But in a cow-turd both did you slide
    And, as I wene, your nose therein rode
    Your face was be-painted with
     sowter's code   *cobbler's shoe polish*
   I (*saw*) never such a sight, I make God a vow MS. *sey*
105   Ye were so be-grimed and it had been a sow!

Ostler. In faith, thou never sawest me till this day!
   I have dwelled with my master this seven year and more:
   Full well I have pleased him, he will not say nay,
   And mickle he maketh of me therefore.   *much*

110 *Servant.* By my troth, then you be changed
    to a new lore: *have been translated*
   A servant you are, and that a good:
   There is no better looketh out of a hood.

Ostler. Forsooth! and a hood I use for to wear,
   Full well it is lined with silk and chamlet; *satin*
115 It keepeth me from the cold, that the wind doth me not
    dere   *harm*
   Neither frost nor snow that I thereby do set.

Servant. Yea, it is a double hood and that a fet! *well tailored*
   He was a good man that made it, I warrant you.
   He was neither horse nor mare, nor yet yoked sow!

Here cometh the first knight to the stable-groom, saying:

120 *1st Knight.* Now, stable-groom, shortly bring forth away
    The best horse, for our lord will ride!

Ostler. I am full ready. Here is a palfrey,
   There can no man a better bestride!
   He will conduct our lord, and guide
125 Through the world: he is sure and able:
   To bear a gentleman he (*is*) easy and profitable.

Here the knight cometh to Saul with a horse.

1st Knight. Behold, Sir Saul, your palfrey is come,
   Full goodly beseen, as it is your desire,
   To take your voyage through every region.

[111]

130   Be not in doubt, he will speed your matter;
        And we, as your servants, with glad cheer,
      Shall give attendance—we will not gainsay,
      But follow you where you go by night or day.

Saul.   Unto Damascus I make my progression
135   To pursue all rebellious, being froward and obstinate
      Against our laws by any transgression.
        With all my diligence myself I will preparate   *prepare*
        Concerning my purpose to oppress and separate:
      None shall rejoice that doth offend,
140   But utterly to reprove with mind and intend.   *intention*

     Here Saul rideth forth with his servants about the place
        (and) out of the pl(ace)

Caiaphas.   Now Saul hath taken his worthy voyage
        To pursue rebellious, of what degree they be: *whatever*
      He will none suffer to reign nor have passage
      Within all this region, we be in certainty.
145   Wherefore I commend his goodly dignity,
      That he thus always taketh in hand
      By his power to govern thus all this land.

Annas.   We may live in rest by his consolation.
      He defendeth us: wherefore we be bound
150   To love him entirely with our hearts' affection,
        And honour him as champion in every stownde. *movement*
      There is none such living upon the ground
      That may be like him nor be his peer,
      By east nor west, far nor near.

      Poeta (si placet) (*The Poet—if he wishes*).

Conclusion

155 *Poet.*   Finally, of this station thus we make a conclusion,
      Beseeching this audience to follow and succeed,
      With all your diligence, this general procession.
      To understand this matter, who list to read
      The Holy Bible for the better speed,
160   There shall he have the perfect intelligence.
      And thus we commit you to Christ's magnificence.

      Finis istius stacionis et altera sequitur
      (*The end of that section and the second follows*)

154 sd (si placet) appears thus in MS. Following the word 'Conclusion'
    the word 'Daunce' has been added in the MS. by a later hand.
155–61 On the meaning and significance of these words, see Introduction,
    p. 105.

Poet.   Honourable friends, we beseech you of audience
        To hear our intention and also our process
        Upon our matter: by your favourable licence
165   Another part of the story we will redress.   *rehearse*
        Here shall be briefly showed with all our business
        At this pageant, Saint Paul's conversion.
        Take you good heed, and thereto give affection.   *attention*

        Here cometh Saul riding in, with his servants.

Saul.   My purpose to Damascus fully I intend;
170   To pursue the disciples my life I apply.
        For to break down the churches thus I condescend;
            None I will suffer that shall edify.   *build*
            Perchance our laws then might thereby—
        And the people also—turn and convert,
175   Which should be great heaviness unto mine heart.

        Nay, that shall not be, but laid apart!
            The princes have given me full potestation.   *powers*
        All that I find, they shall not start,
            But, bound, to Jerusalem, with furious violation,
180   Before Caesar, Caiaphas and Annas (*have*) presentation.
        Thus shall be subdued those wretches of that life
        That none shall enjoy, neither man, child nor wife.

        Here cometh a fervent with great tempest,
        and Saul falleth down off his horse: that done, Godhead
            speaketh in heaven.

God.   Saul! Saul! Why dost thou me pursue?
        It is hard to prick against the spore!   *resist the spur*
185   I am thy Saviour that is so true,
            Which made heaven and earth and each creature;
        Offend not my goodness! I will thee recure!   *redeem*

Saul.   O Lord! I am afeared! I tremble for fear!
        What wouldest I did? Tell me here!

190   *God.*   Arise, and go thou with glad cheer
            Into the City a little beside,
        And I shall thee succour in every dere   *danger*
            That no manner of ill shall betide:

---

162 f. This stanza exists as a precautionary measure to supply continuity
        covering whatever stage action was needed to take Caiaphas and Annas
        out of sight of the audience.
177 *The princes:* a reference back to Caiaphas and Annas in the first station
        or scene.
182 sd The equivalent stage direction, in modern parlance, would be 'wind,
        thunder and lightning': 'fervent' means 'flames', here lightning.

[113]

And I will there for thee provide
195   By my great goodness what thou shalt do.
Hye thee as fast thither as thou mayest go!

Saul. O merciful God! What aileth me?
I am lame, my legs be take(n) me fro: *from*
My sight likewise—I may not see!
200   I cannot tell whither to go!
My men hath forsake me also!
Whither shall I wend, or whither shall I pass?   *go*
Lord, I beseech thee, help me of thy Grace.

1st Knight. Sir, we be here to help thee in thy need
205   With all our affiance; we will not cease.   *trust, faithfulness*

Saul. Then in Damascus I pray you me lead,
I' God's name, according to my promise.

2nd Knight.   To put forth your hand, look
    you dress.   *address yourself*
Come on your way: we shall you bring
210   Into the city without tarrying.

*Here the knights lead forth Saul into a place and
Christ appeareth to Ananias, saying:*

God. Ananias! Ananias! Where art thou Ananias?

Ananias. Here, Lord, I am here, truly!

God. Go thy way and make thy course,
As I shall assign thee by mine advice,
215   Into the street *qui dicitur rectus*,   *which is called straight*
And in a certain house, of warrantise,   *assuredly*
There shall you find Saul in humble wise,
As a meek lamb, that a wolf before was named.
Do my behest: be nothing ashamed!

220   He wanteth his sight, by my punishment constrained!
Praying unto me, I assure, thou shalt him find.
With my stroke of pity sore is he pained
Wanting his sight, for he is truly blind.

Ananias. Lord, I am afeared; for always in my mind
225   I hear so much of his furious cruelty
That, for speaking of thy name, to death he will put me.

God. Nay, Ananias; nay, I assure thee!
He will be glad of thy coming.

Ananias. Ah, Lord! But I know of a certainty
230   That thy saints in Jerusalem to death he doth bring.
Many ills of him I have be(en) kenning,

For he hath the power of the princes all
To save or spill—do which he shall.

God. Be nothing adread! He is a chosen vessel
235   To me assigned by my godly election.
He shall bear my name before the kings and children of Israel,
By many sharp showers suffering correction,
A great doctor, of benign complexion,   *dignified bearing*
The true preacher of the high divinity,
240   A very pinnacle of the faith, I assure thee.

Ananias. Lord! Thy commandment I shall fulfil.
Unto Saul I will make my way.

God. Be nothing in doubt for good nor ill!
Farewell, Ananias. Tell Saul what I do say.

Et exiat Deus. (*And God goes out*)

245 *Ananias.* Blessed Lord, defend me, as thou best may!
Greatly I fear his cruel tyranny:
But, to do thy precept, myself I shall apply.

Here Ananias goeth towards Saul

1st Knight. I marvel greatly what it doth mean
To see our master in this hard stounde.   *time, moment*
250   The wonder-great-lights that were so sheen   *bright*
(*Smote*) him down of his horse to the ground: MS. *Smett*
And me thought that I heard a sound
Of one speaking with voice delectable,
Which was to wonder full   *very wonderfully*
mirable.   *marvellous*

255 *2nd Knight.* Certainly this light was fearful to see!
The sparks of fire that were very fervent: *flaming*
It inflamed so grievously about the country
That, by my troth, I went we should have   *thought*
been brent.   *burnt*
But now, Sirs, let us relent   *return*
260   Again to Caiaphas and Annas, to tell this chance
How it befell to us this grievance.

Here Saul is in contemplation

Saul. Lord, of thy comfort much I desire,
Thou mighty Prince of Israel, King of pity,
Which me has punished as thy prisoner
265   That neither ate nor drank this days three:
But, gracious Lord, of thy visitation I thank thee.
Thy servant shall I be as long as I have breath,
Though I therefore should suffer death.

Here cometh Ananias to Saul, saying

[115]

Ananias.   Peace be in this place and goodly mansion!
270   Who is within? Speak, in Christ's holy name!

Saul.   I am here,—Saul. Come in, on God's benison!
      What is your will? Tell, withouten blame.   *fearlessly*

Ananias.   From Almighty God, certainly, to thee sent I am,
      And Ananias men call me where as I dwell.

275 *Saul.*   What would you have? I pray you me tell.

Ananias.   Give me your hand for your
           avail!   *profit, advantage*
      For, as I was commanded, by his gracious sentence
      I bid thee be steadfast, for thou shalt be hale
      For this same cause he sent me to thy presence:
280   Also he bade thee remember his high excellence
      By the same token that he did thee meet
      Toward the city, when he appeared in the street.

      There mayest thou know his power celestial,
      How he disposeth everything as him list;
285   Nothing may withstand his might essential.
      To stand upright, or else down to thrust;
      This is his power; it may not be missed;
      For who that it wanteth, lacketh a friend.
      This is the message that he doth thee send.

290 *Saul.*   His mercy to me is right welcome:
      I am right glad that it is thus.

           Hic aparebit Spiritus Sanctus super eum
      (*Here, the Holy Spirit [in the form of a dove] appears above him*)

Ananias.   Be of good cheer and perfect jubilation
      Discendet super te Spiritus Sanctus
      (*The Holy Spirit descends upon you*)
      Which hath with his grace illumined us;
295   Put forth thy hand and go with me.
      Again to thy sight, here I restore thee.

Saul.   Blessed Lord, thanks to You ever be!
      The swame is fallen from my eyes twain: (?) *sward = skin*
      Where I was blind and could not see,
300   Lord, thou has sent me my sight again.
      From sobbing and weeping I cannot refrain
      My pensive heart, full of contrition:
      For my offences, my body shall have punition;   *punishment*

      And, where I have used so great persecution
305   Of thy disciples through all Jerusalem,
      I will (*aid*) and defend their predication   *preaching*
      That they did teach (*in*) all this realm: MS. *on*

Wherefore, Ananias, at the watery stream
Baptise me, heartily I thee pray,
310 Among your number that I elect and chosen
(*may be*).   MS. *be may*

Ananias. Unto this well of much virtue
We will us hye with all our diligence.

Saul. Go you before, and after I shall sue,   *follow*
Lauding and praising our Lord's benevolence.
315 I shall never offend his mighty magnificence,
But always observe his precepts and keep.
For my great unkindness my heart doth weep.

Ananias. Kneel you down upon this ground,
Receiving this christening with good intent,
320 Which shall make you whole of your deadly wound,
That was infect with venom nocent.   *noxious, poisonous*
It purgeth sin; and fiend's powers so fraudulent *the Devil*
It putteth aside—where this doth attain,
In every stead, he may not obtain.

325 I christen you with mind full perfect,
Receiving you into our religion,
Ever to be steadfast and never to flit,   *defect*
But ever constant without variation.
Now is fulfilled all our observation;
330 Concluding, thou mayest it ken,   *know*
In nomine Patris et Filii et Spiritus Sancti, Amen!
(*In the name of the Father and of the Son and of the Holy Spirit,
Amen!*)

Saul. I am right glad as (*bird on wing*)   MS. *foule on flyte*
That I have received this blessed sacrament!

Ananias. Come on your way, Saul; for nothing let!   *delay*
335 Take you some comfort for your body's nourishment.
You shall abide with the disciples, verament,   *truly*
This many days in Damascus city,
Until the time more perfect you may be.

Saul. As you command, holy father Ananias;
340 I fully assent at your request
To be guided and ruled as you will have me,
Even at your pleasure, as you think best.
I shall not offend for most nor least.
Go forth your way: I will succeed
345 Into what place you will me lead.

345 sd See footnote to p. 112 above.

[117]

Conclusion

Poet.　Thus Saul is converted, as you see express,
　　The very true servant of our Lord Jesu.
　None may be like to his perfect holiness,
　　So noble a doctor, constant and true.

350　　After his conversion, never mutable, but still issue　*seek*
　The Laws of God to teach ever more and more,
　As Holy Scripture telleth, who-so list to look there-for.

　Thus we commit you all to the Trinity,
　　Concluding this station as we can or may,
355　Under the correction of them that lettered be:
　　Howbeit unable, as I dare speak or say,
　　The compiler hereof should translate veray　*accurately*
　So holy a story, but with favourable correction
　Of my favourable masters of their benign
　　supplection.　*supplication*

　　　　Finis istius secunde stacionis et sequitur tercia
　　　　(*The end of that second section, and the third follows*)

360　*Poet.*　The might of the Father's (*powerful*) deity MS. *potential*
　Preserve this honourable and worshipful
　　congregation　*audience*
　That here be present of high and low degree,
　　To understand this pageant at this little station,
　　Which we shall proceed with all our delectation,
365　If it will please you to give audience favourable.
　Hark wisely thereto; it is good and profitable.

　　(*Caiaphas and Annas, to whom enter the knights*)

1st Knight.　Noble prelates, take heed to our sentence!
　　A wonderful chance fell and did betide
　Unto our master, Saul, when he departed hence,
370　　Into Damascus purposed to ride.
　　A marvellous light from the elements did glide,
　Which smote down him to ground, both horse and man,
　With the fearfullest weather that ever I in came.

2nd Knight.　It ravished him, and his spirits did benumb;
375　　A sweet, dulcet voice spake him unto
　And asked wherefore he made such persecution
　　Against His disciples, and why he did so.
　　He bade him into Damascus to Ananaias go,
　And there he should receive baptism, truly.
380　And now clean against our laws he is truly.

Caiaphas.　I am sure this tale is not true!
　　What! Saul converted from our law?
　　He went to Damascus for to pursue

[118]

All the disciples that did with-draw
385   From our faith—this was his saw.   *claim, saying*
How say you, Annas, to this matter? This is a marvellous chance.
I cannot believe that this is of assurance.

Annas.   No, Caiaphas; my mind truly do (*I*) tell,
    That he will not turn in no manner wise,
390   But rather to death put, and expel,
      All miscreants and wretches that doth arise
      Against our laws by any enterprise.
    (*To the knights*) Say the truth with(*out*) any cause fraudulent
    Or else for your tales you be like to be shent!   *punished*

395 *1st Knight.*   Else our bodies may (*you*) put to pain!
    All that we declare, I saw it with mine eye;
    Nothing offending, but truly do justify!

Caiaphas.   By the great God, I do marvel greatly!
    And this be true that you do rehearse,
400   He shall repent his rebellious (*treachery*)   MS. *traitory*
    That all shall beware of his falseness.
    We will not suffer him to
      obtain doubtless,   *maintain this story*
    For many perils that might betide
    By his subtle means on every side.

405 *Annas*   The law is committed to our
      advisement   *we are its interpreters*
    Wherefore we will not see it decay!
    But rather uphold it,—help and augment—
    That (*no*) reproof to us fall may   MS. *ony*
    Of Caesar, the emperor, by night or day.
410   We shall to such matters hark and attend,
    According to the laws, our wits to spend.

[*At this point in the MS three separate leaves have been bound in,
written in a later hand: these contain the whole of the following
scene of Belial and the diablerie including the stage directions which
begin and end it.*]

*Here to enter a devil with thunder and fire, and to avaunt himself
[stride about] saying as followeth; and his speech spoken, to sit down
in a chair*

Belial.   Ho! ho! Behold me, the mighty prince of the parts
      infernal
    Next unto Lucifer I am in majesty;
    By name I am nominate the god Belial;

397 i.e. 'Far from giving offence, I tell the truth'. It seems that four lines
    may be missing from the start of this stanza.

415   None of more might nor of more excellency!
      My power is principal and now of most sovereignty.
    In the temples and synagogues who denyeth me to honour?
    My bishops, through my motion, they will him   *Saul*
      soon devour.

    I have moved my prelates Caiaphas and Annas,
420   To pursue and put down by power royal,
    Through the cities of Damascus and Liba,
      All such as do worship the high God supernal.
      Their death is conspired without any favour at all.
    My bishops have chosen one most rigorous
425   Them to pursue, whose name is Saul.

    Ho! thus as a god, most high in majesty,
      I reign and I rule over creatures human.
    With sovereign suit sought to is my deity:
      Man's mind is (*as pliable*) as I list to   *MS. applicant*
      ordain.
430   My law still increaseth; whereof I am fain.   *pleased*
    Yet of late I have heard of no news truly,
    Wherefore I long till I speak with my messenger, Mercury.

Here shall enter another devil, called Mercury, with a firing, coming
    in haste, crying and roaring, and shall say as followeth :

Mercury.   Ho! out! out! alas, this sudden chance!
    Well may we bewail this cursed adventure!

435 *Belial.*   Mercury, what ailest thou? Tell me thy grievance!
    Is there any that hath wrought us displeasure?

Mercury.   Displeasure enough! Thereof you may be sure!
    Our law at length it will be clean down laid,
    For it decayeth sore—and more will, I am afraid!

440 *Belial.*   Ho! How can that be? It is not possible!
    Consider, thou fool, the long continuance.
    Decay, quotha? It is not credible!
    Of false tidings thou makest here utterance.
    Behold how the people have no pleasaunce   *pleasure*
445   But in sin, and to follow our desire,
    Pride and voluptuosity their hearts doth so fire!

    Though one do swerve away from our law,
      Yet is our power of such nobility
    To have him again and two (*more?*) therefore   *not in MS.*
450   That shall prefer the praise of our majesty.

433f It should be noticed that this passage exactly parallels the earlier
      exchange between the knights and Caiaphas and Annas, whom Belial
      claims to be his mortal agents.

What is the tidings? Tell out! Let us see!
Why art thou amazed so? Declare (*before*) us   MS. *afore*
What fury is fallen that troubleth thee thus!

Mercury. Ho! out! out He that I most trusted to,
455   And he that I thought would have been to us most special,
Is now of late turnéd, and our cruel foe.
    Our special friend, our chosen Saul,
      Is become servant to the high God eternal.
As he did ride on our enemies' persecution
460   He was suddenly stricken by the high provision,

And now is baptized, and promise hath made
    Never to vary; and such grace he hath obtained,
That, undoubted, his faith from him cannot fade.
    Wherefore to complain I am constrained,
465   For much by him should we have prevailed.

Belial. Ho! out! out! What! have we lost
    Our darling most dear whom we loved most?
But is it of truth that thou dost here specify?

Mercury. It is so, undoubted. Why should I feign?
470   For thought I can do none other but cry!   *At the*

Here they shall roar and cry, and then Belial shall say:

Belial. Out! This grieveth us worse than hell-pain!
    The conversion of (*a*) sinner, certain,
Is more pain to us and persecution
Than all the furies of the infernal dungeon.

475 *Mercury.* It doth not avail us thus to lament,
    But let us provide for remedy shortly.
Wherefore, let us both by one assent
    Go to the bishops and move them privily
    That by some subtle means they may cause him to die.
480   Then shall he in our law make no disturbance,
Nor hereafter cause us to have more grievance.

Belial. Well said, Mercury! Thy counsel is profitable.
    Ho, Saul! Thou shalt repent thy unstableness!
Thou hadst been better to have been confirmable
485   To our law: for thy death, doubtless,
    It is conspired to reward thy falseness.
Though one hath deceived us, yet now-a-days
Twenty doth gladly follow our lays: *laws*

Some by pride, some through envy,
490   There reigneth through my might so much disobedience:
There was never among Christians less charity

[121]

Than is at this hour; and as for concupiscence,
(*He*) reigneth as a lord through my violence;
Gluttony and wrath every man doth devise
495   And most now is praiséd my cousin Covetise.   *covetousness*

Come Mercury! Let us go and do as we have said;
To delay it any longer, it is not best.

Mercury.   To bring it about I would be well a-paid;
Till it be done, let us not rest.

500 *Belial.*   Go we then shortly! Let us depart
His death to devise, since he will not revart.   *revert*

Here they shall vanish away with a fiery flame and a tempest.

[*This concludes the three leaves in a later hand inserted into the MS.*]

Here appeareth Saul in a disciple's weed, saying :

Saul (*Paul*).   That Lord that is shaper of sea and of sand
And hath wrought with his word all thing(*s*) at his will,
Save this (*assembly*) that here sitteth or   MS. *semely*
    stand
505   For His mercy's sake, that we do not spill!   *fail*
Grant me, good Lord, thy pleasure to fulfill,
And send me such speech that I the truth say,
My intentions profitable to move if I may.

(*To audience*) Well-beloved friends! There be seven mortal sins,
510   Which be proved principal and princes of poisons;
Pride, that of bitterness all bale   *envy; trouble, sorrow*
    begins—
    With-holding all faith—it feedeth and foisons,   *fattens*
As Holy Scripture beareth plain witness:
Inicium omnium peccatorum superbia est,
(*Pride is the origin of all sins,*)
515   That often destroyeth both most and least.

Of all vices and folly, pride is the root.
    Humility may not reign, nor yet endure;
Pity, alack, that is flower and boot,   *virtuous and healing*
    Is exiled where pride hath succour.
520 *Omnis qui se exaltat humiliabitur :*
(*Whoever exalts himself, he shall be brought low :*)
Good Lord, give us grace to understand and persevere,
This word, as thou biddest, to fulfil ever.

Whoso in pride beareth him too high,
    With mischief shall be meeked, as I make   *made meek*
    mention;
525   And I therefore assent and fully certify
    In text, as I tell, the true intention

Of perfect goodness and very locution   *true speech*
Noli, tibi dico, in altum sapere, sed time—
(*Do not, I tell you, trust in exalted social status, but be
    modest—*)
This is my counsel—bear thee not too high,

530   But dread always sin and folly,
          Wrath, envy, covetise and sluggishness;
      Exeunt out of thy sight gluttony and lechery,   *Let go*
          Vanity and vainglory and false idleness.
          These be the branches of all wickedness:
535   Who that in him these vices do root
      He lacketh all grace and bale is the boote.   *sorrow; cure*

      'Learn at myself, for I am meek in heart',   *by my example*
          Our Lord to his servants thus he sayeth;
      'For meekness I have suffered a spear at my heart;
540   Meekness all vices annulleth and delayeth,
          Rest to souls it shall find, in faith.'   *supply*
      Discite a me, quia mitis sum, et corde humilis;
      Et invenietis requiem animabus vestris.
      (*Learn from me, because I am gentle and humble in heart;
      And you will acquire rest for your souls.*)

      So our Saviour sheweth us examples of meekness,
545   Through grace of His goodness
              (*meekness is grounded*);   MS. *mekly ys groundys*
          Truly it will us save from the sin's sickness;
              For pride and his progeny meekness
                  confounds:
              Quanto maior es, tanto humilia te in omnibus.
      (*The greater you are, by the same measure humble yourself in
          all things.*)
      The greater thou art, the lower look thou be;
550   Bear thee never the higher for thy degree.

      From sensuality of flesh thyself look thou lead,   *avoid*
          Unlawfully therein use not thy life.
      Whoso therein delighteth, to death he must need: *of necessity*
          It consumeth nature, the body slayeth without knife.
555   Also it stinteth not but manslaughter and strife.
      Omnis fornicator aud immundus non habet hereditem Christi.
      (*No fornicator or lecherous minded person shall inherit Christ's
          kingdom.*)
      None shall in heaven possess that be so unthrifty.

550 i.e. 'Don't flaunt your social position'.
555 In the context of this stanza, cf. *Nice Wanton*, pp. 153–8 below.
557 This line makes better sense (and scans as well) if the word 'in' is
    dropped.

Flee fornication, nor be no lecher,
But spare your speech and speak not thereon:
560 *Ex habundancia cordis os loquitur.*
(*The mouth speaks from the fullness of the heart.*)
Who moveth it oft, chastity loveth none.
Of the heart's abundance the tongue maketh locution:
'What man's mind is laboured, thereof it   *obsessed with*
speaketh':
That is of sureness, as Holy Scripture treateth.

565 Wherefore I rehearse this with mine own mouth:
Caste viventes templum Dei sunt.
(*Those that live virtuously are the Temple of God.*)
Keep clean your body from sin uncouth.
Stable your sights and look you not stunt,
For of a certainty I know, at a brunt   *ardently, burningly*
570 *Oculus est nuncius peccati*
(*The eye is the messenger of sin*)
That the eye is ever the messenger of folly.

(*Enter the servant of the high-priests*)

Servant. What! Is not this Saul that took his voyage
Into Jerusalem, the disciples to oppress?
Bound he would bring them, if any did rage
575 Upon Christ; this was his process
To the princes of priests; he said doubtless
Through all Damascus and also Jerusalem
Subdue all temples that he found of them!

Saul. Yes, certainly, Saul is my proper name,
580 That had in power the full dominion!—
To hide it from you, it were great shame
And mortal sin, as in my opinion—
Under Caesar and priests of the religion
And temples of Jews, that be very hideous,
585 Against almighty Christ, that king so precious!

Servant. To Annas and Caiaphas you must make your recourse!
Come on your way, and make no delation!   *excuses, delay*

Saul. I will you succeed, for better or worse,   *follow*
To the princes of priests with all delectation!   *pleasure*

(*They go to Annas and Caiaphas*)

590 *Servant.* Holy priests of high potestation,   *puissance, power*
Here is Saul! Look on him wisely:
He is another man than he was, verily!

568 Lit. do not stare like a man stunned.
578 Compressed to omit 'that he would'.

[124]

Saul.   I am the servant of Jesu Almighty,
    Creator and maker of sea and sand,
595   Which is king cunctipotent of heaven('s)   *omnipotent*
      glory
    Chief comfort and solace both to free and bound,
    Against whose power nothing may stand:
    Emperor he is both of heaven and hell,
    Whose goodness and grace all thing(s) doth excel.

                             Recedit paulisper
                       *(**He** retires for a short while)*

600 *Caiaphas.*   Unto my heart this is great admiration,
    That Saul is thus marvellously changed;
    I trow he is bewitched by some conjuration,
    Or else the devil on him is avenged!
    Alas! to my heart it is descended   *sunk*
605   That he is thus taken from our religion!
    How say you, Annas, to this conversion?

Annas.   Full marvellously, as in my conception,
    This wonderful case how it be-fell
    To see this chance so suddenly done,
610   Unto my heart it doth great ill.
    But for his falseness we shall him spill;   *destroy*
    By mine assent to death we will him bring,
    Lest that more mischief of him may spring.

Caiaphas.   You say very true; we might it all rue!
615   But shortly in this we must have advisement,
    For, thus against us, he may not continue—
    Peradventure then of Caesar we may be shent.   *punished*

Annas.   Nay, I had liever in fire he were brent,   *rather*
    Than of Caesar we should have displeasure
620   For such a rebel and subtle false traitor.

Caiphas.   We will command the gates to be kept about,
    And the walls surely on every stead,   *place*
    That he may not escape no-where out;
    For die he shall, I ensure you indeed.   *assure*

625 *Annas.*   This traitor rebellious, evil may he speed,
    That doth this unhappiness against all!
    Now every custodian keep well   *sentry*
      his wall!   *his section of the wall*

Servant.   The gates be shut; he cannot escape:
    Every place is kept well and sure,
630   That in no wise he may, till he be take,
    Get out of the city, by any conjecture.

Upon that caitif, and false traitor
Look you be avenged with death mortal,
And judge him as you list to what end he shall.

(*They go out : an angel appears to Saul*)

635 *Angel.*   Holy Saul, I give you monition: *warning*
 The princes of Jews intend, certain,
 To put you to death; but by God's provision
  He wills you shall live longer, and obtain;   *survive*
  And, after thy death, thou shalt reign
640 Above in heaven, with our Lord's grace.
 Convey yourself shortly into another place.

Saul.   That Lord's pleasure ever may be done
 Both in heaven and hell, as His will is!
 In a bearing basket, or (*by*) a leap, anon,   *not in MS.*
645 I shall me convey with help of the disciples;
  For every gate is shut and kept with multitude of peoples.
 But I trust in our Lord, that is my succour,
 To resist their malice and cruel furor.   *fury*

Conclusion

Poet.   Thus leave we Saul within the city
650 The gates kept by commandment of Caiaphas and Annas;
 But the disciples in the night over the wall, truly,
  As the Bible sayeth: *dimiserunt eum summitentes in sporta.*
  (*They contrived his escape by lowering him in a wicker basket.*)
  And Saul after that, in Jerusalem, *vera,*   *truly*
 Joined himself and there accompanied
655 With the disciples, where they were
  unfeigned.   *not dissembling*
 This little pageant thus conclude we
  As we can, lacking littural science;   *knowledge of literature*
 Beseeching you all, of high and low degree,
  Our simpleness to hold excused and license(*d*),
660 That of Rhetoric have none intelligence;
 Committing you all to our Lord Jesus,
 To whose laud you sing: *Exultet celum laudibus!*   *praise*

Finis convercionis Sancti Pauli

634 *to what end he shall :* how he shall be executed.

JOHN BALE:
THE TEMPTATION OF OUR LORD

This play was intended by its author to form a self-contained part of a sequence of four interrelated religious plays. Thus, unlike the other Interludes in this volume, it loses some of the controversial significance it possessed for the audiences to whom it was originally addressed when printed on its own. Against this disadvantage, however, must be set the fact that John Bale's plays are documents of such historical importance for anyone seeking to understand why English drama developed so differently during the sixteenth century from that in other countries, that to neglect them entirely would be a more serious fault. In this context his career speaks for itself.

John Bale was one of those friars who, early in the fifteen-thirties, were 'induced to leave the monstrous *Corruption of Popery* and to embrace the Purity of the Gospel'. Born in 1495—the year to which *Everyman* is usually assigned and two years before Henry Medwall wrote *Fulgens and Lucres*—he was educated at the Carmelite Convent in Norwich and at Jesus College, Cambridge, taking the degree of Bachelor of Divinity in 1529 and his Doctorate *c.* 1533. Converted there to Protestantism, Bale, like St Paul on arrival in Damascus, wasted no time in earning himself a formidable reputation as a militant propagandist for the new faith. Having cast aside his religious vows, he married, became a parish priest and devoted his energies to writing. Between 1533 and his death in 1563 he wrote twenty-one plays, revising many of them several times. Through the outspokenness of his plays and other writings he made many enemies and became, again like St Paul, a victim of continuous persecution. He was imprisoned in 1536, dismissed from his parish of Thorndon (Suffolk) in the following year, and forced into exile, following the downfall of Thomas Cromwell, in 1540. On the accession of Edward VI in 1548 he was recalled from Germany to livings, first in Hampshire, then in Norfolk, and finally promoted to the Bishopric of Ossory in Ireland. No sooner had he been consecrated in Dublin than Edward died and was succeeded by the Roman Catholic Queen Mary I. After a long and hazardous journey, Bale and his family finally found refuge in Basle. On the accession of Elizabeth I he again returned to England,

and was made a prebendary of the Cathedral at Canterbury, where he died in 1563.

All his plays were written in the decade after leaving Cambridge, where he had attracted the attention of Archbishop Cranmer and Thomas Cromwell, the Lord Chancellor to whom Henry VIII owed his divorce from Katherine of Aragon and the transfer to himself of supremacy over the English Church from the Pope in Rome. With Cromwell's support he set about transforming the traditional moral interlude into a weapon of religious (and thus social and political) propaganda. The principal objects of his virulent satire were the Pope, whom he equated with Antichrist, and the superstition and corruption of the Roman Catholic clergy, whom he stigmatized as Satan's agents.

Characters drawn from modern history had appeared on the stages of City Pageants a century earlier in Lydgate's day; but it was Bale who took the great leap forward of giving the abstract personifications familiar in moral interludes a specific name and identity drawn from English history; if others forestalled him, their plays have not survived. Bale's *Kyng Johan* (*c.* 1536) looks backwards through such characters in its cast list as Nobility, Verity and Sedition to *Mankind*, but forwards through such characters as Stephen Langton, Simon of Swinstead and King John himself to Elizabethan Chronicle Plays. His aim in *Kyng Johan* is to equate John, whom he portrays as an aspiring Protestant hero trying to free 'Widow England' from her oppressors, with John the Baptist, and Christ with Imperial Majesty (Henry VIII).

In *The Temptation of Our Lord* and the other three plays with which it is associated his purpose is simpler, but no less self-evidently Protestant in intention. The starting point is *Three Lawes*, a long play in five acts for five actors four of whom take three parts each; the fifth actor is given two roles. In it Bale argues that God ordered the world for men by providing them first with the Law of Nature, then with the Law of Moses and finally with the Law of Christ: he then claims that these laws have all been corrupted and overthrown—natural law by Idolatry and Sodomy, that of Moses by Avarice and Ambition, and that of Christ by Hypocrisy and Pseudodoctrine. The prime begetter of all these corrupting Vices, he insists, has been Infidelity, alias Roman Catholicism. Men, having been thus brought to ignore their natural understanding of God, to reject the commandments revealed through Moses, and to desert Christ, will become the slaves of Antichrist if they do not rebel and free themselves from the ministrations of the Pope, Cardinals and other Roman Catholic clergy.

The three plays which follow—*God's Promises*, *John the Baptist*, and *The Temptation of Our Lord*—each offer a signpost to redemption from a strictly Protestant standpoint. In one sense this sequence of plays may be considered as a corrective to the traditional Mystery

Cycles. The Cycles, starting with the Creation and Fall of Lucifer and ending with Doomsday, urged audiences to acknowledge their sins and repent while time permitted. Bale also urges repentance, but of a different kind: his plea to them is to cast away the spiritual blindness in which Roman Catholicism has trapped them, and to return to the Bible as the source of all truth and inspiration. Their condition is no worse than that of earlier generations, but they have the chance to change things. As Thora Blatt observes in *The Plays of John Bale*, 'the idea of a repeated pattern of events and a perpetual spiritual legacy seen in *Three Lawes* recurs in the rest of the plays' (p. 86).

In *The Temptation of Our Lord* Bale discusses two subjects, fasting and persecution. The frequent references to the latter suggest that the play was written after Parliament had passed the Act of the Six Articles in 1539 and before Bale's departure to Germany following the execution of his patron and protector, Thomas Cromwell. His purpose is to dismiss Roman Catholic insistence on fasting in the conventional, literal sense as not only a hypocritical irrelevance, but also as a deliberate impediment to any true understanding of how to combat persecution and still serve Christ. This is made explicit in the Prologue.

> To persecution let us prepare us then
> For that will follow in them that seek the truth.

The fable or story chosen by Bale to figure this idea outwardly on the stage is that of Satan's assaults on Christ in the wilderness recounted by Luke and Matthew in their Gospels. The defence, then as now, is to be recognized in Christ's answers to Satan.

> For assaults of Satan (*the Roman Catholic establishment*) learn
>   here the remedy;
> Take the word of God; let that be your defence;
> So will Christ teach you, in our next comedy.

Satan presents himself to Christ as a hermit. His costume, however, puts an entirely different complexion on the whole of the subsequent dialogue.

> Subtlety must help; else all will be amiss;
> A godly pretence, outwardly, must I bear,
> Seeming religious, devout and sad in my gear.

Reference back to *Three Lawes* leaves no doubt as to the nature of the disguise that Satan then assumes when he steps forward 'simulating religion'; for in that play Bale obligingly provides a costume rubric on 'the apparelling of the six vices, or fruits of infidelity'. This reads,

Let Idolatry be decked like an old witch, Sodomy like a monk of all sects, Ambition like a bishop, Covetousness like a pharisee or spiritual lawyer, False Doctrine like a Popish Doctor, and Hypocrisy like a grey friar.

Satan is thus presented in the dialogue as himself attempting to destroy Christ, in strict accord with the Gospel story; but, as his costume reveals, he is just as recognizably a Roman Catholic priest trying to provoke all adherents to Protestant beliefs into actions that will bring destruction upon them.

As dramatic poetry, *The Temptation of Our Lord* may not have much to recommend it to students of literature; but as dramatic propaganda it is well wrought and effective. As an example, therefore, not only of Bale's work, but of all those interludes both of Protestant polemic and of subsequent Catholic imitations which forced successive governments between 1534 and 1589 to impose an ever more rigorous censorship on English drama, it justifies its place in this volume.

The play survives in a unique printed copy, now in the Bodleian Library in Oxford.

EDITIONS

A brefe Comedy or enterlude concernynge the temptacyon of our lorde and saver Jesus Christ by John Bale. Anno. M. D. XXXVIII. Printed by ? D. van den Straten, ? Wesel, n.d. (1547–8?);

J. S. FARMER, *The Dramatic Writings of John Bale*, for the Early English Drama Society, London, 1907; reprinted by Charles W. Traylen, Guildford, 1966.

CRITICAL WORKS

W. T. DAVIES, 'A Bibliography of John Bale', *Oxford Bibliographical Society*, Proceedings and Papers, V, Pt IV, 1939, O.U.P. 1940;

H. MCCUSTER, *John Bale: Dramatist and Antiquary*, Bryn Mawr, 1942;

THORA B. BLATT, *The Plays of John Bale*, Copenhagen, 1968.

A BRIEF COMEDY OR INTERLUDE CONCERNING THE TEMPTATION OF OUR LORD AND SAVIOUR, JESUS CHRIST, BY SATAN IN THE DESERT

Compiled by John Bale Anno MDXXXVIII

'Jesus was led from thence of the spirit into the wilderness, to be tempted of the devil.
And when he had fasted forty days and nights, he was at last an hungered.' *Matthew* IV.

Interlocutores

Jesus Christus   Satan Tentator
Angelus Primus   Angelus Alter

Baleus Prolocutor

PRAEFATIO (*PREFACE*)

Baleus Prolocutor (Bale as Prologue)

After his baptism, Christ was God's son declared
By the Father's voice, as ye before have heard;
Which signifieth to us that we, once baptised,
Are the sons of God by His gift and reward.
5 And, because that we should have Christ in regard,
He gave unto him the mighty authority
Of his heavenly word, our only teacher to be.
Now is he gone forth into the desert place
With the Holy Ghost, his office to begin;
10 Where Satan, the devil, with his assaults apace,
With colours of craft, and many a subtle gin,   *trap*
Will undermine him; yet nothing shall he win
But shame and rebuke in the conclusion final:
This tokeneth our raise, and his unrecurable fall.   *irrecoverable*
15 Learn first, in this act, that we, whom Christ doth call,
Ought not to follow the fantasies of man,
But the Holy Ghost, as our guide special;
Which to defend us is he that will and can.
To persecution let us prepare us than;
20 For that will follow in them that seek the truth:
Mark in this process what troubles to Christ ensueth.
Satan assulteth him with many a subtle drift;
So will he do us if we take Christ's part.
And when that helpeth not, he seeketh another shift,

25   The rulers among, to put Christ unto smart;
      With so many else as bear him their good heart.
      Be ye sure of this, as ye are of daily meat—
      If ye follow Christ, with him ye must be beat.
      For assaults of Satan learn here the remedy:
30   Take the word of God; let that be your defence;
      So will Christ teach you, in our next comedy;
      Earnestly print it in your quick intelligence;
      Resist not the world, but with meek patience
      If ye be of Christ. Of this, hereafter, ye shall
35   Perceive more at large by the story as it fall.

(Exit Prologue)

INCIPIT COMOEDIA (*HERE THE COMEDY BEGINS*)

(Enter Christ and Satan)

Jesus Christus.   Into this desert the Holy Ghost hath brought
    me,
      After my baptism, of Satan to be tempted:
      Thereby to instruct of man the imbecility
      That, after he hath God's holy spirit received,
40   Diversely he must of Satan be impugned;
      Lest he, for God's gift, should fall into a pride,
      And that, in peril, he take me for his guide.
      Think not me to fast because I would you to fast;   *want*
      For then ye think wrong, and have vain judgment.
45   But, of my fasting, think rather this my cast—   *objective*
      Satan to provoke to work his cursed intent;
      And to teach you ways his mischiefs to prevent
      By the word of God, which must be your defence
      Rather than fastings, to withstand his violence.
50   I have fasted here the space of forty days,
      Performing that fast which Moses had in figure
      To stop their mouths with, which babble and prate always,
      'Thus did our fathers', my name and fame to disfigure.
      Therefore, now I taste of fasting here the rigour;
55   And am right hungry after long abstinence:
      This mortal body complaineth of indigence.

(Here Christ retires and Satan advances)

Satan Tentator.   Nowhere I further, but everywhere   *help*
    I noy;   *obstruct*
      For I am Satan, the common adversary,
      An enemy to man, him seeking to destroy
60   And to bring to nought, by my assaults most crafty.
      I watch everywhere; wanting no policy

To trap him in snare, and make him the child of hell.
What number I win, it were very long to tell.
I heard a great noise in Jordan, now of late,
65 Upon one Jesus sounding from heaven above;
'This is mine own son which hath withdrawn all hate,
And he that doth stand most highly in my love.'
My wits the same sound doth not a little move—
He cometh to redeem the kind of man, I fear;
70 High time is it, then, for me the coals to stear.   *stir*
I will not leave him till I know what he is,
And what he intendeth in this same border here:
Subtlety must help; else all will be amiss;
A godly pretence, outwardly, must I bear,
75 Seeming religious, devout and sad in my gear.
If he be come now for the redemption of man,
As I fear he is, I will stop him if I can.

Hic simulata religione Christum aggreditur
(Here, simulating religion, he approaches Christ)

It is a great joy, by my halidom! to see
So virtuous a life in a young man, as you be;
80 As here thus to wander, in godly contemplation,
And to live alone in the desert solitary.

Jesus Christus.   Your pleasure is it to utter your fantasy.

Satan.   A brother am I, of this desert wilderness,
And full glad would be to talk with you of goodness,
85 If ye would accept my simple company.

Jesus Christus.   I disdain nothing which is of God truly.

Satan.   Then will I be bold a little with you to walk.

Jesus Christus.   Do so, if ye list, and your mind freely talk.

Satan.   Now, forsooth and God! it is joy of your life
90 That ye take such pains; and are in virtue so rife
Where so small joys are to recreate the heart.

Jesus Christus.   Here are, for pastime, the wild beasts of the
desert;
With whom much better it is to be conversant
Than with such people as are to God repugnant.

95 *Satan.*   Ye speak it full well; it is even as ye say;
But tell me how long ye have been here, I you pray.

Jesus Christus.   Forty days and nights, without any sustenance.

Satan.   So much I judged by your pale countenance;
Then is it no marvel, I trow, though ye be hungry.   *that*

100 *Jesus Christus.*   My stomach declareth the weakness of my body.

    Satan.   Well, to be plain with you, abroad the rumour doth run,
       Among the people, that ye should be God's son.
       If ye be God's son, as it hath great likelihood,
       Make of these stones bread, and give your body his food! *its*

105 *Jesus Christus.* No offence is it to eat when men be hungry;
       But, to make stones bread, it is unnecessary.
       He which, in this fast, hath been my special guide,
       Food for my body is able to provide.
       I thank my Lord God I am at no such need
110   As to make stones bread, my body so to feed.
       When I come in place where God hath appointed meat,
       Giving him high thanks I shall not spare to eat.

    Satan.   Not only for that this similitude I bring;
       But my purpose is to conclude another thing.
115   At the Father's voice ye took this life in hand,
       Minding now to preach, as I do understand.
       In case ye do so, ye shall find the office hard;
       My mind is, in this, ye should your body regard:
       And not, indiscreetly, to cast yourself away:
120   Rather take some ease than ye should so decay.
       I put case: ye be God's son—what can that further?
       Preach ye once the truth, the bishops will ye murther!
       Therefore, believe not the voice that ye did hear,
       Though it came from God; for, it is
         unsavoury gear,   *a devilish trap*
125   Beyond your compass: rather than ye so run,   *run into it*
       Forsake the office, and deny yourself God's son!

    Jesus Christus. Ye speak, in that point, very unadvisedly.
       For, it is written, in the Eighth of Deuteronomy:
       Man liveth not by bread, or corporal feeding, only,
130   But by God's promise, and by His scriptures heavenly.
       Here ye persuade me to recreate my body,
       And neglect God's word, which is great blasphemy.
       This caused Adam from innocency to fall;
       And all his offspring made miserable and mortal.
135   Whereas in God's word, there is both spirit and life;
       And, where that is not, death and damnation is rife.
       The strength of God's word mightily sustained Moses
       For forty days' space; thereof such is the goodness.
       It fortified Helias; it preserved Daniel;
140   And helped, in the desert, the children of Israel;
       Sore plagues do follow, where God's word is reject;
       For no persuasion will I, therefore, neglect
       That office to do which God hath me commanded;
       But, in all meekness, it shall be accomplished.

   113 *this similitude I bring:* do I make this comparison.

145 *Satan.*   I had rather nay, considering your feebleness;
     For ye are but tuly; ye are no strong person doubtless.   *weak*

    Jesus Christus.   Well, it is not the bread that doth a man uphold;
     But the Lord of Heaven, with his graces manifold.
     He that man create(*d*) is able him to nourish;
150 And, after weakness, cause him again to flourish.
     God's word is a rule for all that man should do;
     And, out of that rule, no creature ought to go.
     He that it followeth cannot out of the way,
     In meat nor in drink, in sadness nor in play.

155 *Satan.*   Ye are stiff-necked; ye will follow no good counsel.

    Jesus Christus.   Yes, when it is such, as the Holy Scripture tell.

    Satan.   Scriptures? I know none; for I am but an hermit, I.
     I may say to you, it is no part of our study;
     We religious men live all in contemplation:
160 Scriptures to study is not our occupation;
     It longeth to doctors. Howbeit, I may say to you:
     As blind are they as we in the understanding now.
     Well, shall it please ye any farther with me to walk?
     Though I little profit, yet doth it me good to talk.

165 *Jesus Christus.*   To tarry, or go—it is all one to me.

    Satan.   Let us then wander into the holy city
     Of Jerusalem, to see what is there ado.

    Jesus Christus.   I shall not say nay, but am agreeable thereto.

    Satan.   My purpose is this: a voice in your ear did ring
170 That ye were God's son, and well-beloved darling;
     And you believe it; but, it was some subtle practice.
     Well, upon that voice, ye are given to perfectness;
     Not else regarding; but to live in ghostliness.
     Ye watch, fast, and pray, ye shine in contemplation,
175 Leading here a life beyond all estimation;
     No meat will ye eat, but live by God's word only;
     So good are ye wext, so perfect, and so holy,   *waxed, grown*
     I will bring ye (I trow) to the well of ghostliness,
     Where I shall fill ye and glut ye with holiness.
180 What, holy, quoth he? Nay, ye were never so holy
     As I will make ye, if ye follow handsomely.
     Here is all holy; here is the holy city;
     The holy temple, and the holy priests here be.

145 For you are certainly very frail, having let your strength waste away.
162 These references to 'the Scriptures' embody Protestant sentiment
    about the need to replace the Latin Vulgate with versions of the Old and
    New Testaments in the vernacular: they also contain a satiric attack on
    the pedantic quality of monastic learning.

Ye will be holy: well, ye shall be above them all
185 Because ye are God's son; it doth ye so befall.
Come here! on the pinnacle we will be, by and by.

Jesus Christus.   What mean ye by that? show forth your
fantasy!

Satan.   When ye were hungry, I did ye first persuade
Of stones to make bread; but, ye would none of that trade.
190 Ye laid for yourself that scripture would not serve it—
That was your buckler; but now, I am for ye fit,
For the suggestion that I now shall to ye lay,
I have scripture at hand; ye shall it not deny.

Jesus Christus.   Keep it not secret, but let it then be
hod.   *heard*

195 *Satan.*   If ye do believe that ye are the son of God,
Believe this also: if ye leap down here, in scoff,
From this high pinnacle, ye can take no harm thereof;
And, therefore, be bold, this enterprise to jeopard—
If ye be God's son cast down yourself here backward.

200 *Jesus Christus.*   Truly, that need not; here is other remedy,
To the ground to go, than to fall down foolishly!
Here are gresings made, to go up and down thereby—   *steps*
What need I then leap to the earth, presumptuously?

Satan.   Say that ye did it upon a good intent.

205 *Jesus Christus.*   That were neither good nor yet convenient:
Dangers are doubtful where such presumption is.

Satan.   Tush! scripture is with it; ye cannot fare amiss.
For, it is written how God hath given a charge
Unto his angels; that, if ye leap at large,
210 They shall receive ye in their hands tenderly,
Lest ye dash your foot against a stone thereby.
If ye do take scathe, believe God is not true;   *hurt*
Nor just of his word. And then, bid him adieu!

Jesus Christus.   In no wise ye ought the scriptures to deprave;
215 But, as they lie whole, so ought ye them to have;
No more take ye here than serve for your vain purpose,
Leaving out the best, as ye should trifle or gloss.
Ye mind not, by this, towards God to edify;
But of sincere faith to corrupt the innocency.

220 *Satan.*   Why, is it not true that such a text there is?

Jesus Christus.   Yes, there is such a text, but ye wrast   *twist*
it all amiss—
As the Psalm doth say: God hath commanded angels
To preserve the just from dangerous plagues and perils.

Satan.   Well then, I said true, and as it lieth in the text.

225 *Jesus Christus.*   Yes, but ye omitted four words which
        followeth next,
    As: in all thy ways—which, if ye put out of sight,
    Ye shall never take that place of scripture a-right.
    Their ways are such rules as God hath them commanded
    By his living word, justly to be observed.
230   If they pass those rules the angels are not bound
    To be their safeguard; but, rather, them to confound.
    To fall down backward, of a wanton peevishness,
    Is none of those ways that God ever taught, doubtless.
    Then, if I did it, I should tempt God very sore,
235   And deserve to have his anger evermore.
    I will not so do: for, their fathers in the desert
    Did so tempt him once, and had the hate of his heart.
    The clause that ye had maketh for none outward working
    If ye mark the Psalm throughly from his beginning.
240   But what is the cause ye went not forth with the next verse?

Satan.   It made not for me; if ye will, ye may it rehearse.

Jesus Christus.   Thou shalt (saith the Psalm) subdue the cruel
        serpent,
    And tread under foot the lion and dragon pestilent.

Satan (aside).   No nigher (I say), for there ye touch   *nearer*
    freehold.

245 *Jesus Christus (hearing, nonetheless).*   Some love in no wise to
        have their rudeness told;
    To walk in God's ways it becometh a mortal man;
    And, therefore, I will obey them if I can.
    For it is written in the Sixth of Deuteronomy:
    Thou shalt in no wise tempt God presumptuously.

250 *Satan.*   What is it to tempt God, after your judgement?

Jesus Christus.   To take of His word an outward
      experiment   *a casuistical argument*
    Of an idle brain; which God neither thought nor meant.

Satan.   What persons do so? Make that more evident!

Jesus Christus.   All such as forsake any grace or remedy
255   Appointed of God, for their own policy:
    As they that do think that God should fill their belly
    Without their labours, when His laws are contrary;
    And they that will say the Scripture of God doth slee, *slay*
    They never searching thereof the verity.

244 *ye touch freehold:* you become personal.

[137]

260   Those also tempt God that vow presumptuously,
       Nor having His gift to keep their continency.
       With so many else, as follow their good intents
       Not grounded on God nor yet on his commandments.
       These throw themselves down, into most deep damnation.

265   *Satan.*   Little good get I by this communication!
       Will ye walk farther, and let this prattling be?
       A mountain here is, which I would you to see;
       Trust me and ye will, it is commodious thing   *splendid sight*

    Jesus Christus.   If it be so good, let us be thither going.

270   *Satan.*   Lo, how say ye now; is not here a pleasant sight?
       If ye will, ye may have here all the world's delight.
       Here is to be seen the kingdom of Arabia;
       With all the regions of Afric, Europe, and Asia;
       And their whole delights, their pomp, their magnificence,
275   Their riches, their honour, their wealth, their concupiscence.
       Here is gold and silver, in wonderful habundance;
       Silks, velvets, tissues, with wines and spices of pleasance.
       Here are fair women of countenance amiable,
       With all kinds of meats to the body delectable.
280   Here are camels, stout horses, and mules that never will tire;
       With so many pleasures as your heart can desire.

    Jesus Christus.   Well, He be praised which is of them the giver.

    Satan.   Alas! it grieveth me that ye are such a believer.
       Nothing can I lay but ever ye avoid me
285   By the word of God; leave that point once, I pray ye!
       If I bid ye make of stones bread for your body,
       Ye say man liveth not in temporal feeding only.
       As I bid ye leap down from the pinnacle above,
       Ye will not tempt God, otherwise than you behove.
290   Thus are ye still poor: thus are ye still weak and needy.

    Jesus Christus.   And what, suppose ye, will that need remedy?

    Satan.   Forsake the belief that ye have in God's word,
       That ye are His son, for it is not worth a turd!
       Is he a father, that see his son thus famish?
295   If ye believe it, I say ye are too foolish.
       Ye see these pleasures—if you be ruled by me,
       I shall make ye a man; to my words, therefore, agree.
       Look on these kingdoms, and incomparable treasure;
       I, the lord of them, may give them at my pleasure.
300   Forsake that father which leaveth thee, without comfort
       In this desolation; and, henceforth, to me resort.
       Knowledge me for head of this world   *acknowledge*
         universal,
       And I will make thee possessor of them all.

Thou shalt no longer be desolate and hungry;
305 But have all the world to do thee obsequy.
Therefore, kneel down here, and worship me this hour;
And thou shalt have all with their whole strength and power.

Jesus Christus. Avoid thou, Satan! thou devil! thou adversary!
For now thou persuadest most damnable blasphemy.
310 As thou art wicked, so is thy promise wicked;
Not thine the world, but His that it created;
Thou canst not give it, for it is not thine to give.
Thus didst thou corrupt the faith of Adam and Eve;
Thus didst thou deceive both Moses and Aaron,
315 Causing them to doubt, at the lack of contradiction.
Get thee hence, thou fiend and cruel adversary!
For it is written in the Tenth of Deuteronomy:
God thou shalt worship and magnify alone;
Hold him for thy lord, and make to him thy moan.
320 He is the true God; he is the lord of all—
Not only of this, but the world celestial.
Thy persuasion is, I should not His word regard—
O venomous serpent! damnation is thy reward!
Provide will I so that thy kingdom shall decay;
325 God's word shall be heard of the world though thou say nay.

Satan. Well then, it helpeth not to tarry here any longer;
Advantage to have I see I must go farther:
So long as thou livest I am like to have no profit.
If all come to pass, I may sit as much in your light
330 If ye preach God's word, as methink ye do intend.
Ere four years be past I shall you to your father send
If Pharisees and scribes can do anything thereto—
False priests and bishops, with my other servants mo.   *more*
Though I have hindrance, it will be but for a season;
335 I doubt not thine own, hereafter, will work some treason;
Thy vicar at Rome I think will be my friend:
I defy thee, therefore, and take thy words but as wind.
He shall me worship, and have the world to reward;
That thou here forsakest he will most highly regard.
340 God's word will he tread underneath his foot for ever;
And the hearts of men from the truth thereof dissever;
Thy faith will he hate, and slay thy flock: in conclusion,
All this will I work to do thee utter confusion.

Jesus Christus. Thy cruel assaults shall hurt neither me nor
mine,
345 Though we suffer both, by the providence divine.

336 In this glaring anachronism the Pope, in line with Protestant thought, is directly equated with Antichrist.

[139]

Such strength is ours that we will have victory
Of sin, death, and hell, and of thee in thy most fury.
For God hath promised that His shall tread the dragon
Under their feet, with the fierce roaring lion.

Hic angeli accedunt, solacium administraturi
(*Here two angels enter to administer comfort*)

350 *Angelus primus.*   The father of comfort and heavenly con-
solation
Hath sent us hither to do our administration.
We come not to help, but to do our obsequy,
As servants becometh, to their lord and master meekly.
If our office be to wait on creatures mortal,
355 Why should we not serve the Master and Lord of all?

Angelus alter.   It is our comfort, it is our whole felicity,
To do our service and in your presence to be.
We have brought ye food to comfort your weak body
After your great fast and notable victory.
360 Unto all the world your birth we first declared;
And now these victuals, we have for you prepared.

Jesus Christus.   Come nigher to me! Sweet Father! thanks to
thee
For these gracious gifts of thy liberality.

Hic coram angelis ex appositis comedet
(*Here he eats, standing between the angels gathered round him*)

Angelus primus.   How meek art thou, Lord! to take that nature
on thee,
365 Which is so tender, and full of infirmity
As man's nature is; both feeble, faint, and weary;
Weak after labour, and after fasting hungry.
Forsooth! heaven and earth, yea, hell may be astonished
The Godhead to see to so frail nature joined.

370 *Angelus alter.*   In His own He is, for He the world first create:
Yet seemeth the world to have Him in great hate.
About thirty years hath he been here among them:
Sometime in Jewry, and sometime in Jerusalem.
But few, to this day, have done him reverence;
375 Or, as to their lord, showed their obedience.

Jesus Christus.   My coming hither is for to seek no glory,
But the high pleasure and will of my father heavenly.
He will require it at a certain day, no doubt,
And shall revenge it, look they not well about.   *if they do not*

Angelus primus plebem alloquitur
(*The first angel addresses the audience*)

[140]

380   *Angelus primus.*   The Lord here, for you, was born and
        circumcised;
        For you, here also he was lately baptised;
        In the wilderness this lord, for you, hath fasted;
        And hath overcomen, for you, the devil that tempted.
        For you, friends! for you, this heavenly lord doth all;
385   Only for your sake he is become man mortal.

     Angelus alter.   Take the shield of faith and learn to resist the
        devil,
        After his teachings that he do you none evil.
        Full sure shall ye be to have us on your side
        If ye be faithful, and hold Him for your guide.

390   *Jesus Christus.*   If they follow me they shall not walk in
        darkness,
        But in the clear light, and have felicity endless;
        For, I am the way, the life, and the verity:
        No man may attain to the Father but by me.

     Angelus primus.   In man's frail nature ye have conquered the
        enemy;
395   That man, over him, should always have victory.

     Angelus alter.   Our manner is it most highly to rejoice
        When man hath comfort, which we now declare in voice.

         Hic dulce canticum coram Christo depromunt
       (Here the angels sweetly sing a sweet song before Christ)

           Baleus Prolocutor (Bale, as Epilogue)

     Let it not grieve you in this world to be tempted,
     Considering your Lord, and your high bishop, Jesus,
400   Was here, without sin, in every purpose proved;
     In all our weakness to help and succour us;
     Furthermore, to bear with our frailty thus.
     He is unworthy of him to be a member,
     That will not, with him, some persecution suffer.
405   The life of man is a proof or hard temptation,
     As Job doth report, and Paul confirmeth the same.
     Busy is the devil, and laboureth his damnation.
     Yet, have no despair, for Christ hath
        got the game;   *won the fight*
     Now is it easy his cruelness to tame.
410   For Christ's victory is theirs that do believe;
     Where faith take rooting the devil can never grieve.
     Resist (saith Peter), resist that roaring lion,
     Not with your fastings—Christ never taught ye so—
     But with a strong faith withstand his false suggestion;

415 And with the Scriptures upon him ever go:
Then shall he no harm be able you to do.
Now may ye be bold; ye have Christ on your side
So long as ye have his verity for your guide.
What enemies are they that, from the people, will have
420 The Scriptures of God, which are the mighty weapon
That Christ left them here, their souls from hell to save,
And throw them headlondes into the devil's   *headlong*
   dominion!
If they be no devils I say there are devils none.
They bring in fasting, but they leave out *Scriptum est*;
425 Chalk they give for gold, such friends are they to the beast.
Let none report us, that here we condemn fasting,
For it is not true; we are of no such mind.
But this we covet: that ye do take the thing
For a fruit of faith, as it is done in kind,
430 And only God's word, to subdue the cruel fiend.
Follow Christ alone! for, he is the true shepherd;
The voice of strangers do never more regard.

*Thus endeth this brief comedy concerning the temptation of Jesus
Christ in the wilderness.*

NICE WANTON

The full title of this play in the edition printed by John King at
'the Sign of the Swan' in Paul's Churchyard, London, in 1560—
two years, that is, after Elizabeth I's accession—is given as *A Pretty
Interlude called Nice Wanton*. No author's name is attached and no
manuscript survives: only two copies of the printed text exist, one
at Chatsworth and the other in the British Museum.

From the second stanza of the Prologue it appears that the play
was written during the reign of the boy King, Edward VI (1549–
1553): it must therefore have been revived for performance before
Queen Elizabeth before it was printed, as may be judged from
Barnabas's last eight lines and the date of printing. That this closing
prayer has been hastily revised is clear from the rhyme scheme of
the second, fourth and fifth lines where the word 'things' was
originally intended to rhyme with 'Kings'. Curiously, the change to
'Queens', which does not rhyme, has been overlooked in the Prologue where there is no requirement for it to rhyme, and again in
the line of Judge Daniel's second speech and in Ismael's reply.
Granted a date of original composition and performance *c*. 1550,
the attribution of authorship to Thomas Ingland (known author of
The Disobedient Child) seems reasonable as the two plays share
several features in common including an unhappy ending and
remarkable dramatic vitality throughout.

Nice Wanton is a highly melodramatic cautionary tale directed at
parents and guardians of children rather than at children themselves, and as such the play has by no means lost its topicality
despite the lapse of more than four hundred years. Granted this
bias and the certainty of Court performance, this Interlude can be
categorized as one of those written for the young choristers known as
the Children of the Chapel, who were to attain such prestige under
the direction of Richard Farrant and John Lyly between 1576 and
1584 as to warrant the conversion of rooms in the dissolved
monastery of the Blackfriars, near St Paul's Cathedral, into a
Private Playhouse; and so these boy actors were the precursors of
'the eyrie of children, little eyases' pilloried by Shakespeare in
Hamlet as serious rivals of the adult companies.

Two further pointers to this as being a boys' play lie within the text. The first is the group of twelve 'extras', described in the cast list as Jurors, who make a single appearance in the Court scene with only one of them having a couple of lines to speak: such extras were easy enough to muster in a school, and their use frequently characterizes a boys' play since wages were not in question. The second is the use of songs, including, in this case, a duet and a trio. A Clerk to the Court and at least two warders seem also to be needed in this scene. 'Worldly Shame', however, can (and probably should) be doubled with 'Iniquity'.

The play is divided into two distinct sections of equal length. An interval is prescribed which allows for a passage of time: this permits the substantial changes called for in the text in Dalilah's costume and make-up; from representing a buxom young girl at line 253 (her last in Part I) she has to transform herself into a pox-scarred prostitute by line 261 (her first in Part II). This may indicate that the author intended the play to be performed, like *Fulgens and Lucres* (see pp. 37–8 above) in between the principal courses of a banquet.

The plot is a simple one built around the proverb 'spare the rod: spoil the child'. The two young miscreants who are central to it might, a century earlier, have been called Sensuality and Prodigality, but in this case are given the names of Dalilah and Ismael respectively. Both are well born, well educated and extravagantly dressed in the trendiest of fashions: they thus pre-figure, in embryo, the wilful self-indulgence of Vittoria and Flamineo in Webster's *The White Devil*, the most flamboyant of all stage courtesans and gallants in the Jacobean drama. Dalilah and Ismael, however, need not be regarded as remote figures from the historical past, since the desire to play truant from school is as familiar to spirited teenagers today as it was to the choirboys of the sixteenth century: nor, unfortunately, despite our own estimation of ourselves as progressives, are love-ins, drug addiction, mugging, and their effects on the career prospects of the individuals concerned, together with the results of hysteria and violence attaching to pop concerts and football matches, unknown to parents and teachers in our own schools. The director, therefore, who can visualize *Nice Wanton* imaginatively in these terms of reference should have no difficulty in making this play relevant to audiences today. It is this sense of mischief, topicality and fun that explains the use of the word 'Pretty' in the play's full title: *A Pretty Interlude called Nice Wanton*. This should be exploited in production to provide the proper counter-weight to the more serious moral purpose of this Interlude.

Given such an approach, even the abstract personifications of Iniquity and Shame, together with the purveyors of conventionally sound advice, Eulalia, Barnabas and Judge Daniel, are less daunting than they may appear to be on a first reading of the text.

When revived in 1964 as part of the Shakespeare Quatercentenary festivities under the aegis of the Bristol Old Vic Trust, the play performed well. On this occasion the director took pains to avoid any suspicion of a naturalistic approach to dialogue and situation, preferring to insist that the actors should approach their roles from within the 'game' conventions of the medieval stage. This ensured that the double image of actor and character was the dominant reality, and that the moral was clearly pointed in a manner that avoided priggishness and boredom by being consistently amusing.

EDITIONS

JOHN KING, London, 1560;

W. C. HAZLITT, in Vol. 2 of Robert Dodsley's *A Select Collection of Old Plays*, 15 vols., 4th ed., 1874–6;

J. M. MANLY, in *Specimens of the Pre-Shakespearean Drama*, Boston, 1897;

J. S. FARMER, in 'The Writings of Richard Wever and Thomas Ingelend', *Early English Dramatists*, for the Early English Drama Society, London, 1905: Reprinted by Charles W. Traylen, Guildford, 1966;

J. S. FARMER, *Tudor Facsimile Texts*, 1908.

A Pretty Interlude
called
NICE WANTON

Wherein ye may see
Three branches of an ill tree:
The mother and her children three,
Two naught, and one godly.

Early sharp, that will be thorn,
Soon ill, that will be naught:
To be naught, better unborn;
Better unfed than naughtily taught.

Ut magnum magnos, pueros puerilia doctus.

Personages:

The Messenger (The Prologue)

Barnabas (Son of comfort) *Iniquity* (A vice: later, as
Ismael (His hand against   Baily Errand, appears as a
 every man)   corrupt official)
Dalilah (A nice wanton) *Xantippe* (A foolish mother)
Eulalia (With goodly speech) *Worldly Shame* (A tempter)
Daniel (The Judge)   *Jury* (Twelve good men and
          true)

Anno Domini MDLX

THE PROLOGUE

The Messenger. The prudent Prince Solomon doth say,
'He that spareth the rod, the child doth hate';
He would youth should be kept in awe alway
By correction in time, at reasonable rate:
5 To be taught to fear God, and their parents obey,
To get learning and qualities, thereby to maintain
An honest quiet life, correspondent alway
To God's law and the king's; for it is certain,
If children be noseled in idleness and ill,   *cosseted*
10 And brought up therein, it is hard to restrain,
And draw them from natural wont evil,   *habit*
As here in this interlude ye shall see plain:
  By two children brought up wantonly in play,
Whom the mother doth excuse, when she should chastise;
15 They delight in dalliance and mischief alway,
At last they end their lives in miserable wise.
  The mother, persuaded by Worldly Shame
That she was the cause of their wretched life,

[146]

So pensive, so sorrowful, for their death she became,
20 That in despair she would slay herself with a knife.
  Then her son Barnabas (by interpretation
The son of comfort) her ill-purpose doth stay,
By the scriptures he giveth her godly consolation,
And so concludeth. All these parts will we play.

(*Exit*)

Barnabas cometh

25 *Barnabas.*   My master, in my lesson yesterday,
  Did recite this text of Ecclesiasticus:
  'Man is prone to evil from his youth' did he say,
  Which sentence may well be verified in us—
  Myself, my brother, and sister Dalilah,—
30 Whom our parents to their cost to school do find;
  I tarry for them here; time passeth away,
  I lose my learning, they ever loiter behind.
    If I go before, they do me threat
  To complain to my mother: she, for their sake,
35 Being her tender tidlings, will me beat: *darlings*
  Lord, in this perplexity, what way shall I take?
  What will become of them? Grace God them send
  To apply their learning, and their manners amend. *behaviour*

  Ismael and Dalilah come in singing :

      Here we comen, and here we lonen!   *belong*
40   And here will abide, abide-ay!

Barnabas.   Fie, brother, fie! And specially you, sister Dalilah!
  Soberness becometh maids alway.

Dalilah.   What, ye dolt! Ye be ever in one song!

Ismael.   Yea, sir. It shall cost you blows ere it be long.

45 *Barnabas.*   Be ye not ashamed the truants to play,
  Losing your time and learning, and that every day?
  Learning bringeth knowledge of God and honest living to get.

Dalilah.   Yes, marry, I warrant you, master hoddypeak.

Barnabas.   Learn apace, sister, and after to spin and sew,
50 And other honest housewifely points to know.

Ismael.   Spin, quotha? Yea, by the mass, and with
      your heels up-wind,   *roll over*
  For a good mouse-hunt is cat after Saint Kind.

Barnabas.   'Lewd speaking corrupteth good manners,' Saint
      Paul doth say!
  Come, let us go, if ye will to school this day;
55 I shall be shent for tarrying so long.   *reprimanded*

Barnabas goeth out

[147]

Ismael.   Go, get thee hence, thy mouth full of horse-dung!
   Now, pretty sister, what sport shall we devise?
   Thus palting to school, I think us unwise: *trudging*
   In summer die for thirst, in winter for cold,
60   And still to live in fear of a churl—who would?

Dalilah.   Not I, by the mass! I had rather he hanged were,
   Than I would sit quaking like a mome for fear.   *an idiot*
   I am sun-burned in summer; in winter the cold
   Maketh my limbs gross, and my beauty decay;
65   If I should use it, as they would I should,
   I should never be fair woman, I dare say.

Ismael.   No, sister, no! But I can tell,
   Where we shall have good cheer,
   Lusty companions two or three,
70   At good wine, ale, and beer.

Dalilah.   O good brother, let us go;
   I will never go more to school.
   Shall I never know,
   What 'pastime' meaneth?
75   Yes, I will not be such a fool.

Ismael.   Have with thee, Dalilah! (*They sing*)

   Farewell our school!
   Away with books and all,

                    [*They cast away their books*

   I will set my heart
80   *On a merry pin,*
   Whatever shall befall!   (*Exeunt, singing*)

          (*Enter Eulalia*)

Eulalia.   Lord, what folly is in youth!
   How unhappy be children now-a-days!   *discontented*
   And the more pity, to say the truth,
85   Their parents maintain them in evil ways:
   Which is a great cause that the world decays,
   For children, brought up in idleness and play,
   Unthrifty and disobedient continue alway.
      A neighbour of mine hath children hereby,
90   Idle, disobedient, proud, wanton, and nice.
   As they come by, they do shrewd turns daily;
   Their parents so to suffer them surely be not wise.
   They laugh me to scorn, when I tell them mine advice;
   I will speak with their elders and warn them neighbourly—
95   Never in better time! their mother is hereby.

          (*Enter Xantippe*)

90 *nice:* effeminate, a slave of fashion.

[148]

God save you, gossip, I am very fain   *pleased*
That you chance now to come this way;
I long to talk with you a word or twain;
I pray you take it friendly that I shall say:
100   Ismael your son and your daughter Dalilah,
Do me shrewd turns, daily more and more,
Chide and beat my children—it grieveth me sore.
    They swear, curse, and scold, as they go by the way,
Giving other(s) ill example to do the same,
105   To God's displeasure, and their hurt another day.
Chastise them for it, or else ye be to blame!

Xantippe.   Tush! tush! if ye have no more than that to say,
Ye may hold your tongue and get ye away.
Alas! Poor souls, they sit a-school all day
110   In fear of a churl; and if a little they play,
He beateth them like a devil. When they come home,
Your mistress-ship would have me lay on.
If I should beat them, so oft as men complain,
By the mass, within this month I should make them lame.

115 *Eulalia.*   Be not offended, I pray you; I must say more;
Your son is suspect light-fingered to be:
Your daughter hath nice tricks three or four;
See to it in time, lest worse ye do see.
He that spareth the rod, hateth the child, truly.
120   Yet Salomon sober correction doth mean,
Not to beat and bounce them to make them lame!

Xantippe.   God thank you, mistress, I am well at ease!
(*Aside*) Such a fool to teach me, preaching as she please!
(*To Eulalia*) Dame, ye belie them deadly, I know plain;
125   Because they go handsomely, ye disdain.   *are well-dressed*

Eulalia.   Then on the other as well would I complain,
But your other son is good, and no thanks to you!
These will ye make nought, by sweet Jesu!

Xantippe.   Gup, liar! My children nought? Ye lie!
130   By your malice they shall not set a fly;
(*Aside*) I have but one mome, in comparison of his brother:
Him the fool praiseth, and despiseth the other!

Eulalia.   Well, Xantippe, better in time than too late!
Seeing ye take it so, here my leave I take.   [*Exit*

135 *Xantippe.*   Marry, good leave have ye, the great God be with
you!
My children or I be cursed, I think;

130 They don't care a damn for your spite.

[149]

They be complained on wherever they go,
That for their pleasure they might drink.
Nay, by this the poor souls be come from school weary;
140   I will go get them meat to make them merry.   (*Exit*)

Iniquity, Ismael and Dalilah come in together, singing

Iniquity.   Lo, lo, here I bring her.

Ismael.   What is she, now ye have her?

Dalilah.   A lusty minion lover.

Iniquity.   For no gold will I give her—

145   *All together.*   Welcome, my honey-a!

Iniquity (here he speaketh).   O my heart! This wench can sing,
    And play her part.

Dalilah.   I am yours, and you mine, with all my heart.

Iniquity.   By the mass, it is well sung!
    Were ye not sorry ye were a maid so long?

150   *Dalilah.*   Fie, master Iniquity, fie, I am a maid yet.

Ismael.   No, sister, no, your maidenhead is sick.

Iniquity.   That knave your brother will be a blabber still,
    Iwis, Dalilah, ye can say as much by him, if ye will.

Dalilah.   By him, quotha? He hath whores two or three;
155   (*To Ismael*) But ich tell your minion doll, by Gog's   *I shall*
    body
    It skilleth not she doth hold you as much.

Ismael.   Ye lie falsely, she will play me no such touch.   *trick*

Dalilah.   Not she? Yea, to do your heart good,
    I could tell you who putteth a bone in your hood!

160   *Ismael.*   Peace! whore! or ye bear me a box on the ear.

Dalilah.   Here is mine ear, knave; strike, and thou
    dare!   (*He does*)
    (*To Iniquity*) To suffer him thus ye be no man,
    If ye will not revenge me, I will find one;   *one who will*
    To set so little by me ye were not wont—
165   Well, it is no matter; though ye do, *ceteri nolunt.*

Iniquity.   Peace, Dalilah; speak ye Latin, poor fool?

Dalilah.   No, no, but a proverb I learned at school—

Ismael.   Yea! Sister, you went to school, till ye were past
    grace:—

156 No matter: she does the same by you.
159 Who shares her with you.

Dalilah.   Yea, so didst thou, by thy knave's face!

170 *Iniquity.*   Well, no more a-do, let all this go.
We kinsfolk must be friends; it must be so,
Come on! come on! come on!—

> [*He casteth dice on the board*

Here they be that will do us all good.

Ismael.   If ye use it long, your hair will grow through your
hood.

175 *Iniquity.*   Come on, knave, with Christ's curse,
I must have some of the money
Thou hast picked out of thy father's purse!

Dalilah.   He, by the mass, if he can get his purse,
Now and then he maketh it by half the worse!   *Ismael*

180 *Ismael.*   I defy you both, whore and knave—

Iniquity.   What, ye princocks, begin ye to rave?   *cheeky fellow*
Come on—

Dalilah.   Master Iniquity, by your leave,
I will play a crown or two here by your sleeve.

Ismael.   Then be ye servant to a worshipful man;
185 Master Iniquity—a right name, by Saint John!

Dalilah.   What can ye say by Master Iniquity?   *about*
I love him and his name most heartily.

Iniquity.   God-a-mercy, Dalilah, good luck, I warrant thee,
(*Aside*) I will shrive you both by and by.

> [*He kisseth her*

190 *Ismael.*   Come on; but first let us have a song.

Dalilah.   I am content, so that it be not long.   *provided*

Iniquity and Dalilah sing :

Iniquity.   *Gold locks*
She must have knocks,
Or else I do her wrong.

195 *Dalilah.*   *When ye have your will*
Ye were best lie still,
The winter nights be long.

Iniquity.   *When I ne may*   *When I can't manage*
Another assay ;
200 *I will take it for no wrong :*

174 *If ye use it long :* if you don't throw the dice soon.

[151]

Dalilah.   *Then, by the rood,*
  A bone in your hood
  I shall put, ere it be long.

Ismael.   She matcheth you, sirrah!

205   *Iniquity.*   By God's blood, she is the best whore in England!

Dalilah.   It is knavishly praised; give me your hand.

Iniquity.   I would thou had'st such another.

Ismael.   By the mass, rather than forty pound, brother.

Iniquity.   Here, sirs, come on; seven—

                                                          [They set him

210   Eleven at all—

Ismael.   Do ye nick us? beknave your   *cheat*
  noly!—   *curse your head*

Iniquity.   Ten mine!

Ismael (casteth dice).   Six mine,
  Have at it, and it were for all my father's kine.
  It is lost by His wounds,—and ten to one!

215   *Iniquity.*   Take the dice, Dalilah, cast on—

                                            [She casteth, and they set

Dalilah.   Come on; five!
  Thrive at fairest—

Ismael.   Gup, whore, and I at rest.   *[He loseth*
  By God's blood, I ween God and the devil be against me—

220   *Iniquity.*   If th' one forsake thee, th' other will take thee!

Ismael.   Then is he a good fellow; I would not pass,   *care*
  So that I might bear a rule in hell, by the mass!
  To toss firebrands at these pennyfathers' pates; ·   *misers*
  I would be porter, and receive them at the gates.

225   In boiling lead and brimstone I would seeth them each one!
  The knaves have all the money, good fellows have none!

Dalilah.   Play, brother,—have ye lost all your money now?

Ismael.   Yea, I thank that knave and such a whore as thou.
  'Tis no matter, I will have money, or I will sweat;

230   By God's blood, I will rob the next I meet—
  Yea, and it be my father!   *[He goeth out*

Iniquity.   Thou boy! By the mass, ye will climb the
  ladder.   *be hanged*
  Ah, sirrah, I love a wench that can be wily,—
  She perceived my mind with a twink of   *in the twinkle*
  mine eye,

235   If we two play boody on any man,   *dishonestly*
          We will make him as bare as Job anon!
          Well, Dalilah, let see what ye have won.
                      They tell it   *count*

Dalilah.   Sir, I had ten shillings when I begon,
          And here is all—every farthing.

240   *Iniquity.*   Ye lie like a whore; ye have won a pound!

      Dalilah.   Then the devil strike me to the ground!

      Iniquity.   I will feel your pocket, by your leave, mistress—

      Dalilah.   Away, knave, not mine, by the mass!

      Iniquity.   Yes, by God, and give you this to boot—   *as well*

                              [*He giveth her a box*

245   *Dalilah.*   Out, whoreson knave, I beshrew thy heart-root!
          Wilt thou rob me and beat me too?

      Iniquity.   In the way of correction, but a blow or two!

      Dalilah.   Correct thy dogs, thou shalt not beat me!
          I will make your knave's flesh cut, I   *have you whipped*
          warrant thee.
250   Ye think I have no friends? Yes, I have in store
          A good fellow or two, perchance more.
          Yea, by the mass, they shall box you for this gear,   *mischief*
          A knave I found thee, a knave I leave thee here.

                              [*She goeth out*

      Iniquity.   Gup, whore! (*To audience*) Do ye hear this jade?
255   Loving, when she is pleased:
          When she is angry, thus shrewd!
          Thief, brother: sister, whore;
          Two grafts of an ill tree!
          I will tarry no longer here,
260   Farewell! God be with ye!

                              [*He goeth out*

(AN INTERVAL)

Dalilah cometh in ragged, her face hid, or disfigured, halting on a
staff

Dalilah.   Alas, wretched wretch that I am!
          Most miserable caitiff that ever was born!
          Full of pain and sorrow, crooked and lorn: *lost*
          Stuff'd with diseases, in this world forlorn!

260 sd In production a song or a piece of instrumental music can be used to
      cover the change of costume and make-up if no break in continuity is
      desired at this point.

265   My sinews be shrunken, my flesh eaten with pox;
      My bones full of ache and great pain;
      My head is bald, that bare yellow locks;   *carried*
      Crooked I creep to the earth again.
        Mine eyesight is dim; my hands tremble and shake;
270   My stomach abhorreth all kind of meat;
      For lack of clothes great cold I take,
      When appetite serveth, I can get no meat.   *food*
        Where I was fair and amiable of face,
      Now am I foul and horrible to see;
275   All this I have deserved for lack of grace;
      Justly for my sins God doth plague me.
        My parents did tiddle me; they were to blame;   *spoil*
      Instead of correction, in ill did me maintain.
      I fell to naught, and shall die with shame.
280   Yet all this is not half of my grief and pain.
        The worm of my conscience, that shall never die,
      Accuseth me daily more and more:
      So oft have I sinned wilfully,
      That I fear to be damned evermore.

(Enter Barnabas)

285 *Barnabas.* What woeful wight art thou, tell me,
      That here most grievously dost lament?
      Confess the truth, and I will comfort thee
      By the word of God omnipotent:
      Although your time ye have misspent,
290   Repent and amend, while ye have space,
      And God will restore you to health and grace.

 Dalilah. To tell you who I am, I dare not for shame;
      But my filthy living hath brought me in this case,
      Full oft for my wantonness you did me blame;
295   Yet to take your counsel I had not the grace.
      To be restored to health, alas, it is past;
      Disease hath brought me into such decay.
      Help me with your alms, while my life doth last,
      That, like a wretch as I am, I may go my way.

300 *Barnabas.* Show me your name, sister, I you pray,
      And I will help you now at your need;
      Both body and soul will I feed.

 Dalilah. You have named me already, if I durst be so bold:
      Your sister Dalilah, that wretch I am;
305   My wanton, nice toys ye knew of old.
      Alas, brother, they have brought me to this shame!
        When you went to school, my brother and I would play,
      Swear, chide, and scold with man and woman;

To do shrewd turns our delight was alway;
310 Yet were we tiddled, and you beaten now and then.
    Thus our parents let us do what we would,
And you, by correction, they kept thee under awe:
When we grew big, we were sturdy and bold;
By father and mother we set not a straw.
315   Small matter for me; I am past!
But your brother and mine is in great jeopardy:
In danger to come to shame at the last,
He frameth his living so wickedly.

Barnabas.   Well, sister, I ever feared ye would be nought,
320 Your lewd behaviours sore grieved my heart:
To train you to goodness all means have I sought,
But in vain; yet will I play a brotherly part;
    For thy soul is more precious, most dearly bought
With the blood of Christ dying therefore.
325 To save it, first a mean must be sought
At God's hand, by Christ, man's only Saviour.
    Consider, Dalilah, God's fatherly goodness,
Which for your good hath brought you in this case,
Scourged you with his rod of pure love doubtless,
330 That, once knowing yourself, ye might call for grace.
    Ye seem to repent; but I doubt whether
For your sins or for the misery ye be in!
Earnestly repent for your sin rather,
For these plagues be but the reward of sin.
335   But so repent that ye sin no more,
And then believe with steadfast faith
That God will forgive you evermore
For Christ's sake, as the Scripture saith.
    As for your body, if it be curable,
340 I will cause it to be healed, and during your life
I will clothe and feed you as I am able.
Come, sister, go with me; ye have need of relief.

                        [They go out

         Enter the Judge (and a Clerk)

Daniel (the judge).   As a judge of the country, here am I come,
    Sent by the King's Majesty, justice to do:
345 Chiefly to proceed in judgment of a felon:
I tarry for the verdict of the quest, ere I go.   *inquest, jury*

Iniquity, dressed as Baily Errand, comes in; the judge sitteth down

309 *To do shrewd turns:* to play cruel practical jokes.
315 Never mind about me; I'm done for!
342 sd In production another musical intermission is useful here to give
    time to set furniture and properties for the ensuing trial scene.

Go, Baily, know whether they be all agreed, or no;
If they be so, bid them come away,
And bring their prisoner: I would hear what they say.

350 (*Baily*). I go, my Lord, I go! Too soon for one:
He is like to play a cast will break his neck-bone.
I beseech your lor'ship be good to him:
The man is come of good kin.

He telleth him in his ear [so loud] that all may hear

If your lordship would be so good to me
355 As for my sake to set him free,
I could have twenty pound in a purse,
Yea, and your lordship a right fair horse,
Well worth ten pound—

Daniel (*the judge*).   —Get thee away, thou hell-hound!
If ye were well examined and tried,
360 Perchance a false knave ye would be spied.

Iniquity goeth out; the judge speaketh still

Bribes (saith Salomon) blind the wise man's sight,
[*So*] that he cannot see to give judgment right.
Should I be a briber? Nay! He shall have the law,
As I owe to God and the king obedience and awe.

They bring Ismael in, bound like a prisoner. (Jury enter)

365 *Iniquity* (*aside to Ismael*). Ye be tied fair enough for running
    away!
If ye do not after me, ye will be hanged, I dare say;
If thou tell no tales, but hold thy tongue,
I will set thee at liberty, ere it be long,
Though thou be judged to die anon.

(The jurors sit down)

370 *Judge* (*to the jury*). Come on, sirs, I pray you, come on!
Be you all agreed in one?

[*One of them speaketh for the quest*

Quest (*i.e. jury*). Yea, my lord, every one.

Judge. Where Ismael was indicted by twelve men
Of felony, burglary, and murder,

351 An ambiguous line: it is easiest for the actor to take it as an aside making
    'He' refer to the judge, and 'his' to Ismael.
353 sd *all*: Judge and audience but not the Jury.
364 sd This stage direction suggests the presence of two Warders or Con-
    stables although this is not stipulated in the cast-list. A Justice's Clerk to
    record the proceedings is also needed. '*They*' must include Iniquity.

375   As the indictment declareth how, where, and when—
       You heard it read to you lately, in order—
       You, with the rest,—I trust all true men—
       Be charged upon your oaths to give verdi(*c*)t directly,
       Whether Ismael thereof be guilty or not guilty.

                                             [One for the rest

380 *Quest.*   Guilty, my lord, and most guilty.

     Iniquity.   Wilt thou hang, my lord, (*this*) whoreson noddy?

     Judge (*to Iniquity*).   Tush, hold thy tongue, and I warrant
         thee—
       (*To Ismael*). The Lord have mercy upon thee!
385   Thou shalt go to the place thou cam'st fro,
       Till tomorrow, nine of the clock, there to remain;
       To the place of execution then shalt thou go,
       There to be hanged to death, and after, again,
       Being dead, for ensample to be hanged in a chain.
       Take him away, and see it done,
390   At your peril that may fall thereupon!

     Ismael.   Though I be judged to die, I require respite;
       For the king's advantage some things I can recite.

     Iniquity.   Away with him, he will speak but of
       spite—   *only spitefully*

     Judge.   Well, we will hear you say what you can;
395   But see that ye wrongfully accuse no man.

     Ismael.   I will belie no man, but this I may say—
       Here standeth he that brought me to this way.

     Iniquity.   My lord, he lieth like a damned knave,
       The fear of death doth make him rave—

400 *Ismael.*   His naughty company and play at dice
       Did me first to stealing entice:
       He was with me at robberies, I say it to his face;
       Yet I can say more in time and space.   *given the chance*

     Iniquity (*aside*).   Thou hast said too much, I beshrew thy
       whoreson's face!
405   Hang him, my lord, out of the way,
       The thief careth not what he doth say.
       (*Aside*) Let me be hangman, I will teach him a sleight;
       For fear of talking, I will strangle him straight;
       Tarry here that list, for I will go—

                                       [He would go

410 *Judge.*   No, no, my friend, not so!
       I thought always ye should not be good
       And now it will prove, I see, by the rood!

             They take him in a halter : he fighteth with them

[157]

Take him, and lay him in irons strong;
We will talk with you more, ere it be long.

415 *Iniquity.*   He that layeth hands on me in this place,
Ich lay my brawling iron on his face!   *my sword*
By Gog's blood, I defy thy worst!
If thou shouldest hang me, I were accurst.
I have been at as low an ebb as this,
420 And quickly aloft again, by Gis!   *by Jesus*
I have more friends than ye think I have;
I am entertained of all men like no slave:
Yea, within this moneth, I may say to you,
I will be your servant and your master too.
425 Yea, creep into your breast! will ye have it so?

Judge.   Away with them both: lead them away:
At his death tell me what he doth say,
For then, belike, he will not lie.

Iniquity.   I care not for you both, no, not a fly!

[They lead them out

430 *Judge.*   If no man have here more matter to say,
I must go hence some other way.

He goeth out. (Exeunt Jurors and others)

(Enter Worldly Shame)

Worldly Shame.   Ha, ha! though I come in rudely, be not
aghast!
I must work a feat in all the haste;
I have caught two birds; I will set for the dame,
435 If I catch her in my clutch, I will her tame!
Of all this while know ye not my name?
I am right worshipful Master Worldly Shame;
The matter that I come now about,
Is even this, I put you out of doubt.
440   There is one Xantippe, a cursed shrew—
I think all the world doth her know—
Such a jade she is, and so curst a quean,   *whore*
She would out-scold the devil's dame, I ween.   *guess*
Sirs, this fine woman had babes three,
445 Twain the dearest darlings that might be,
Ismael and fair Dalilah these two;
With the lout Barnabas I have nothing to do.

418 I'm damned if you'll hang me.
431 sd There is a strong case, deriving from the first three lines of Worldly
   Shame's speech, for this role to be played by Iniquity in disguise. In
   production the shock of his sudden return is very striking and justifies
   use of the word 'aghast'.

[158]

All was good, that these tiddlings do might:
Swear, lie, steal, scold, or fight:
450   Cards, dice, kiss, clip, and so forth: *cuddle*
All this our Mammy would take in good worth.   *part*
    Now, sir, Dalilah my daughter is dead of the pox,
And my son hang'th in chains, and waveth his locks.
These news will I tell her, and the matter so frame,
455   That she shall be thine own, master Worldly Shame!
Ha, ha, ha!—   *[Enter Xantippe*
Peace, peace, she cometh hereby,
I spoke no word of her, no, not I,—
    O Mistress Xantippe, I can tell you news:
460   The fair wench, your dear daughter Dalilah,
Is dead of the pox taken at the stews;   *brothel*
And thy son Ismael, that pretty boy,
Whom, I dare say, you loved very well,
Is hanged in chains, every man can tell.
465   Every man said thy daughter was a strong whore,
And thy son a strong thief and a murderer too.
It must needs grieve you wond'rous sore
That they died so shamefully both two.
Men will taunt you and mock you, for they say now
470   The cause of their death was even very you.   *you yourself*

Xantippe.   I the cause of their death?

        [She would swoon

Worldly Shame (aside).   Will ye swoon? The devil stop thy
    breath?
Thou shalt die (I trow) with more shame;
I will get me hence out of the way,
475   If the whore should die, men would me blame;
That I killed her, knaves should say.

        (Exit, leaving her a knife)

Xantippe.   Alas, alas, and well-away!
I may curse the time that I was born!
Never woman had such fortune, I dare say;
480   Alas, two of my children be forlorn:
    My fair daughter Dalilah is dead of the pox:
My dear son Ismael hanged up in chains—
Alas, the wind waveth his yellow locks—
It slayeth my heart, and breaketh my brains!
485   Why should God punish and plague me so sore?
To see my children die so shamefully!

---

455 Despair, and commit suicide: cf. Iago's treatment of Othello.

I will never eat bread in this world more!
With this knife will I slay myself by and by.   *here and now*

        [*She would stick herself with a knife*

    (*Enter Barnabas*)

Barnabas.   Beware what ye do! Fie, mother, fie!
490   Will ye spill yourself for your own offence,   *destroy*
      And seem for ever to exclude God's mercy?
      God doth punish you for your negligence:
      Wherefore take His correction with patience,
      And thank him heartily, that of His goodness
495   He bringeth you in knowledge of your trespass.
         For when my brother and sister were of young age,
      You saw they were given to idleness and play,
      Would apply no learning, but live in outrage.
      And men complained on them every day.
500   Ye winked at their faults, and tiddled them alway;
      By maintenance they grew to mischief and ill,
      So, at last, God's justice did them both spill.
         In that God preserved me, small thank(s) to you!
      If God had not given me special grace,
505   To avoid evil and do good, this is true,
      I had lived and died in as wretched case
      As they did, for I had both suffrance and space;
      But it is an old proverb, you have heard it, I think:
      'That God will have see, shall not wink.'
510   Yet in this we may all take comfort:
      They took great repentance, I heard say,
      And as for my sister, I am able to report,
      She lamented for her sins to her dying day:
      To repent and believe I exhorted her alway;
515   Before her death she believed, that God of his mercy
      For Christ's sake would save her eternally.
         If you do even so, ye need not despair,
      For God will freely remit your sins all,
      Christ hath paid the ransom—why should ye fear
520   To believe this and do well? To God for grace call!
      All worldly cares let pass and fall.
      And thus comfort my father I pray you heartily.

                     [*Xantippe goeth out*

I have a little to say; I will come by and by.

523 In performance it is better at this point for Barnabas to exit, but in
     another direction (without cutting this line), and for the Messenger:
     speak the Epilogue and closing prayer.

EPILOGUE

Right gentle audience, by this interlude ye may see
525 How dangerous it is for the frailty of youth,
Without good governaunce, to live at liberty;
Such chances as these oft happen of truth: *in real life*
Many miscarry, it is the more ruth,   *pity*
By negligence of their elders and not taking pain,
530 In time, good learning and qualities to attain.
        Therefore exhort I all parents to be diligent
In bringing up their children aye to be circumspect,
Lest they fall to evil. Be not negligent,
But chastise them, before they be sore infect:
535 Accept their well-doing, in ill them reject.
A young plant ye may plant and bow as ye will: *bend, train*
Where it groweth strong, there will it abide still.
        Even so by children: in their tender age
Ye may work them, like wax, to your own intent;
540 But, if ye suffer them long to live in outrage,
They will be sturdy and stiff, and will not relent.
O ye children, let your time be well-spent,
Apply your learning, and your elders obey;
It will be your profit another day.
545   Now, for the Queen's Royal Majesty let us pray,

[*He kneeleth down*

That God (in whose hands is the heart of all queens),
May endow her highness with godly puissance alway:
That Her Grace may long reign and prosper in all things,
In God's word and justice may give light to all queens,
550 Let us pray for the Honourable Council and Nobility,
That they may always counsel us wisdom with tranquillity
God save the Queen, the Realm, and Commonalty!

[*He maketh courtesy and goeth out*

FINIS

A SONG

It is good to be merry
But who can be merry?
He who hath a pure conscience,
    He may well be merry.

552 sd This song almost certainly belongs to Iniquity, Dalilah and Ismael
    having by now changed back into their original costumes. As such it
    serves as 'the Curtain Call'.

[161]

Who hath a pure conscience, tell me?
No man of himself, I assure thee.
Then must it follow of necessity,
    That no man can be merry.

Purity itself may pureness give;
You must ask it of God in true belief:
Then will He give it, and none reprove:
    And so we may be merry.

What is the practice of a conscience pure?
To love and fear God, and other allure,   *persuade others*
And for his sake to help his neighbour:
    Then may he well be merry.

What shall we have, that can and will do this?
After this life everlasting bliss.
Yet not by desert, but by gift, iwis,
    There God make us all merry!

FINIS

Imprinted at London, in Paules Churche yearde at the Sygne of
of the Swane by John Kyng.

THE MARRIAGE BETWEEN
WIT AND WISDOM

This play survives as a single manuscript in the British Museum (Additional MS. 26782). The full, original title is surmised to have been 'The Interlude of a Contract of Marriage between Wit and Wisdom'; but the top edge of the first page of the manuscript is so severely damaged that only the lower part of the letters of the text prior to the word 'marriage' remain visible.[1]

The play was written by Francis Merbury (who later became a preacher of some repute) in student days at Christ's College, Cambridge, between 1571 and 1578. The manuscript in the British Museum, however, is neither Merbury's original (since it is in two hands, neither being his own), nor a prompt-copy made from it: rather is it a transcript of a printed edition published in 1579, no copy of which is known to exist. If the printed edition was not the source, there would be no reason for the words 'never before in-printed' to appear on the title-page, since inclusion of the word 'before' is only necessary if the copy in question is a first edition.

We can say with confidence therefore that this Interlude was in print by 1579. Who printed it, and why it is not recorded in the Stationers' Register, are difficult questions to answer; Trevor Lennam, in his introduction to the Malone Society Reprint (1971), discusses both these topics, and adduces good reasons for supposing that the printer was John Allde, who was responsible for printing Thomas Preston's *Cambises* and William Wager's *Enough is as Good as a Feast* some ten years earlier.

Firm assignment of this play to the 1570s assumes a particular importance from the fact that this decade saw not only the final suppression of overtly religious plays in the Midlands and the North of England, but also the granting of a licence (or Patent) to the Earl of Leicester's players led by James Burbage (1574) to perform plays regularly on weekdays in London, and the opening of both the first Private Playhouse in the Blackfriars and the building of the Theatre in Shoreditch (1576). *The Marriage Between Wit and Wisdom*, like *Cambises*, can thus be regarded as typical of the sort of play that a company of six professional actors saw fit to

---

[1] See the facsimile of this page reproduced in the Malone Society edition (1971) and placed between the introduction and the text.

place in the repertory for public performance in the years when Marlowe and Shakespeare were at school. Its popularity is to some extent authenticated by the reference to it in *Sir Thomas More* (c. 1590), where, from a list of seven plays in the repertoire of a travelling company of actors, this is the one chosen for performance.[1]

A further point of special interest arises from Merbury's unashamed borrowings from John Redford's *Wit and Science* (1539), *Gammer Gurton's Needle* (1553), *Cambises* (c. 1569) and *Misogonus* (1570), all of which we might describe as plagiary, but which any Elizabethan dramatists would have taken for granted as 'redaction', or adaptation of old material to new ends, a practice which Shakespeare himself employed in the composition of such plays as *King John*, *Hamlet* and *King Lear*.

As the starting point for his plot Merbury took Redford's *Wit and Science*, and then set about modifying it in two interrelated directions. First, he greatly reduced the academic and moralizing elements of the original: then he amplified the structural skeleton he had left himself with humorous characters and farcical incidents extracted from other plays. Thus the gist of scenes 6 and 7, set before and within Mother Bee's cottage, is lifted from *Gammer Gurton's Needle*; the characters of Snatch and Catch who dominate scene 3 are developed from Huff, Ruff and Snuff in Preston's *Cambises*; and those parts of scenes 5 and 6 where Idleness confronts the audience in the role of a beggar can be described as improvisations on Cacurgus's antics and complaints in *Misogonus*: all of these borrowings, however, have been skilfully reworked to fit the needs of their new narrative environment.

The resulting variety enables Merbury to lighten the serious, if witty, tone of Redford's *Wit and Science* (appropriate enough for the choristers of St Paul's) and thus to provide public audiences (who demanded amusement rather than instruction in return for their money) with a much more light-hearted entertainment. How much of this professionalism, so evident within the script as a whole, is Merbury's own, and how much is the result of alterations and adjustments made subsequently by the actors in whom the copyright was vested once the script had been paid for, must remain an open question.[2] No actor, however, even today, can view the prospect of playing the Vice, Idleness, with its many changes of costume, and make-up and its many shifts of dialect, vocal pitch

---

[1] *More. The Marriage of Wit and Wisdom!* That, my lads!
   I'll none but that. The theme is very good,
   And may maintain a liberal argument. (Scene ix)

In fact, the play when acted turns out to be *Lusty Juventus* rearranged to dovetail with this title.

[2] It was unusual for actors to release a play to a printer while it continued to attract audiences, since only by keeping it in manuscript could they retain their copyright in it.

and personality, with anything but delight. It is a role that demands technical virtuosity that is at once assured and relaxed. This role provides the play with its centre of gravity and engages audiences as much by the bravura quality of its insolence as by its variety.

This lively comedy was originally scripted in a straightforward sequence of ten scenes. The printer, however, appears to have inserted the words 'The Second Act' between the end of scene 3 and the start of scene 4, and this was copied by the scribe of the manuscript; but, as the words 'The First Act' do not appear before the start of scene 1, it is reasonable to infer that the author never conceived of his play as formally structured in acts, but only as ten scenes grouped into two parts, which would provide the actors with an interval, if required, between scenes 3 and 4. This break, coming as it does after the defeat and death of Irksomeness, allows his den or cave to be transformed into Fancy's prison for use in scene 5, and Wantonness's house to be adapted to represent Mother Bee's cottage in readiness for scene 6. No further changes are needed. Granted this to have been Francis Merbury's intention, the localizing of the stage settings (which then becomes simple, and easy to handle in production) is as follows:

Prologue—Open Stage

Scene 1—Unlocalized: open stage
Scene 2—Before and within Wantonness's house
Scene 3—Before and within Irksomeness's den

Interval: modest scenic alterations

Scene 4—Unlocalized: open stage
Scene 5—Before and within Fancy's prison
Scene 6—Before and within Mother Bee's cottage
Scene 7—The same as scene 6
Scene 8—Before and within Fancy's prison
Scene 9—Unlocalized: open stage
Scene 10—Unlocalized: open stage

Epilogue—Open Stage

This Interlude can thus be presented on the simplest of booth stages with the booth modelled on the woodcuts illustrating Renaissance editions of Terence's plays and divided into two curtained cubicles. These two cubicles will then serve to represent respectively Wantonness's House and Mother Bee's Cottage in Part I, and Irksomeness's Den and Fancy's Prison in Part II. All the other scenes, being unlocalized, can be presented on the open stage with the curtains of both cubicles closed. Given these staging arrangements, each of the two Parts (scenes 1–3 and 4–10) can proceed with unbroken continuity: in performance, the resultant sense of pace goes far, of itself, to dispel the awkward questions that can otherwise arise about the play's time scheme and matters of naturalistic detail.

When this Interlude was revived by students of the Drama Department of Bristol University in 1972 and taken to Southwark under the sponsorship of the Bankside Globe Theatre Trust for performance in the George Inn and elsewhere in the borough, the script proved to be remarkably resilient. The wealth of humanity dormant in the dialogue beneath the abstract names of the characters blazed into new life, provoking forms of audience participation that were as unexpected as they were demanding on the wits of the actors. Replies to questions which, in rehearsal, had been regarded as strictly rhetorical, had in performance to be answered not only with lines invented on the spur of the moment, but in lines framed in an attempt to preserve the metre and the rhyme. Some young spectators, who were sufficiently moved to involve themselves in the stage action, had firmly, if politely, to be disengaged.

Since the manuscript has been admirably printed in a verbatim transcription (including all its deficiencies in annotated footnotes) by Trevor N. S. Lennam for the Malone Society as recently as 1971, I have felt free to gloss the text which follows as an acting edition, opting in all cases of doubtful legibility and ambiguity to prefer the reading which is easiest for the actor who has to speak the line. Such stage directions as I have added (again, for clarity) are clearly recognizable by the brackets in which they are placed.

EDITIONS

J. O. HALLIWELL, *Shakespeare Society*, 1846;

J. S. FARMER, *Five Anonymous Plays*, 4th series, 1908; reprinted, 1966;

J. S. FARMER, *Tudor Facsimile Texts*, 1909;

T. N. S. LENNAM, *Malone Society Reprints*, 1971.

[The Interlude
of a
CONTRACT OF MARRIAGE
between
WIT AND WISDOM]

[The Contract
of a]
Marriage between Wit and Wisdom
very fruitful and mixed full
of
pleasant mirth as well for
the beholders as
the readers or hearers:
never before inprinted.

The division of the parts for six to play this interlude:

The Prologue⎫   *Wantonness*⎫
Idleness ⎬ For one   *Fancy* ⎬ For one
Epilogue ⎭   *Doll* ⎭

Severity ⎫   *Wit* ⎫
Irksomeness ⎬   *Search* ⎬ For one
Snatch ⎬ For one *Inquisition* ⎭
Honest Recreation ⎭

Indulgence ⎫   *Good Nurture* ⎫
Wisdom ⎬ For one *Catch* ⎬ For one
Mother Bee ⎭   *Lob* ⎭

1579

THE PROLOGUE

Who marks the common course of youthful wandering wits,
Shall see the most of them frequent where Idleness still sits;
And how (*that*) Irksomeness doth murder many a one, MS. *the*
Before that they, to wisdom's-ward, the half way yet have gone.
5 Except good Nurture do, with some severity,
Conduct them to Parnassus mount well nurt with levity.   *graced*
But if it hap, in fine, that Wit the mate be made
Of Wisdom, such a worthy wife, to follow godly trade,
Then shall you see whereon Dame Virtue doth depend;
10 Not all the world besides, forsooth, so meet a match can mend!
But else, if Wit should wag, and hap to wave awry,

[167]

Without, then, any rightful rule, and reasons good supply,
Then Fancy frames effects to bring his brain aboard,
And shelves his ship in haven's mouth, ere it the seas have
    scoured.
15 Whereby you may perceive that Wisdom
(*is the wight*)   *missing in MS.* (*see l. 37*)
That must conform a youthful Wit and bring it in good plight.
The proof, the sequel shows, for I have done my charge,
And to the actors must give place to set it forth at large.

                                                 Exit

THE FIRST SCENE

Enter Severity and his wife, Indulgence, and their son, Wit

Severity.   My son, draw near, give ear to me, and mark the
    cause aright
20 For which I call thee to this place. Let all thy whole delight
Be still in serving God aright and treading virtue's trace;
And labour learning for to get whilst thou hast time and space.
I now have brought thee on the way the thing for to attain,
Which, son, if thou might'st hap to hit, will turn unto thy gain.
25 Thou knowest how changeable a thing thy learning is to me;
Thou knowest also the care I take for to provide for thee;
And now, since that thine age draw(*s*) on to nature's riper
    state,
My purpose is, and full intent, to find for thee a mate
With whom thou mayest dispend the rest of this thy life to
    come;
30 And joy as I, thy father, have with this, thy mother, done.

Indulgence.   Indeed, good husband, that were good—we have no
    more but he;
My heart, methinks, would be at rest—him matched for to see.
But yet, my dear Severity, be heedful, for your life,   *own sake*
That she be able for to live that he shall take to wife.

35 *Severity.*   Well, as for that I shall foresee; for why, I know right
    well
That she whom I do mean is rich, and highly doth excel.
Wherefore, son Wit, mark well my tale! Dame Wisdom is the
    wight
Whom you shall labour to espouse with all your main and
    might.
And if that she will be your wife, look what I leave behind:
40 You shall possess it full and whole, according unto kind;
But if you find some worser haunt, and hap to run by rote,
I promise thee, before these folk, thoust never cost me groat.

    42 You will never get a penny of it.

[168]

Wit. Dear father, for your grave advice right humble thanks I
    give,
    Intending to obey your charge so long as I shall live;
45   Now if that Wit with Wisdom may be linked fast in love,
    Then Wit shall think himself right blest of God that sits above!

Indulgence. Well said, good Wit! and hold thee there, I tell thee
    this before:
    Indulgence, when thou married art, hath butter pence in store.

Severity. Such pamp'ring mothers do more harm than e'er
    they can do good.

50 *Indulgence.* If you had felt the pain we feel, you then would
    change your mood.

Severity. You show that you the mother are of this the
    outward man,   *body*
    And not of mind; for, if you were, you would be careful then
    To give him counsel, how to use himself for to aspire
    To Wisdom's friendships and her love, the which we do desire.

55 *Indulgence.* Alas! good sir! Why, harken, Wit, what counsel I
    can give;
    Whenas thou com'st to Wisdom's house, then may'st thou it
    approve:
    Take heed that thou art neat and fine, and go straight bolt
    upright,
    And cast a cheerful look on her, smiling at the first sight.
    And when thou com'st to talk with her, forget not for to praise
60   Her house, herself, and all her things, and still be glad to
    please;
    Be diligent to do for her, be pleasant in her sight,
    Say as she saith, although that she do say the crow is white;
    And if she have a mind to ought, although it cost red gold,
    Provide it for her, and thou may'st be more welcome and more
    bold!

65 *Severity.* See! see! what counsel you can give; you show your
    nature plain!
    This counsel liketh Wit right well, and mak'th him
    all-too fain.   *glad*
    But, sirrah! if thou list to thrive, mark well what I shall say,
    That Wisdom may become your wife this is the ready way:
    Apply your book and still beware of Idleness, I say,
70   For he a(n) enemy hath been to Virtue many a day.
    Beware of Irksomeness, I say, which is a monster fell,
    And near to lady Wisdom's house doth always use to dwell;
    For he will have a fling at you, and so will Idleness;
    Therefore, beware of these two foes, and God will sure you
    bless.

75 *Wit.*   As duty doth require in me, I thank you humbly
For these your fatherly precepts, and purpose ernestly
For to observe that you command, and these my foes to
watch,
Lest they, perhaps—ere I beware—me in their snares should
catch!

Indulgence.   Well, yet before thee goest, hold! hear my blessing
in a clout,
80 Well fare the mother at a need, stand to thy tackling stout!

Wit.   Mother, I thank you heartily, and you, father, likewise;
And both your blessings here I crave in this my enterprise.

Both.   God bless thee, Wit, our son, and send thee good
success.

Wit.   I thank you both, and pray to God to send to you no less!

Exeunt Severity and Indulgence

85 *Wit.*   God grant this my purpose may come unto good effect;
Well, now I must about this gear! I must it not forget.   *task*

Exit

THE SECOND SCENE

Enter, Idleness, the vice

(Idleness).   Ah! sirrah! my masters! how fare you at this blessed
day?
What, I ween all this company are come to see a play!
What lookest thee, good fellow? didst see ne'er a man before?
90 Here is a gazing! I am the best man in the company, when
there is no more!
As for my properties, I am sure you know them of old!
I can eat till I sweat, and work till I am a-cold.
I am always troubled with the litherlurden, I love   *lethargy*
so to linger;
I am so lazy the moss groweth an inch thick on the top of my
finger!
95 But if you list to know my name,—Iwis I am too   *indeed*
well known to some men—
My name is Idleness, the flower of the frying-pan!
My mother had two whelps at one litter, both born in Lent;
So we were both put into a mussel-boat,
And came sailing in a sow's ear over sea into Kent.

79–80   In production the obscurity of this couplet can be clarified by letting
Indulgence give Wit a hamper or cloth-bundle of provisions at this
point.

[170]

100 My brother, Irksomeness, and I, (catch the dog)
Being disposed to make merry,
We got us both down to Harlowe-bery.
But what is that to the purpose—perhaps you would know?
Give me leave but a little, and I will you show!
105 My name is Idleness, as I told you before.
And my mother, Ignorance, sent me hither.
I pray thee, sirrah! what more?
Marry, my masters! she sent me the counterfeit
crank for to play;   *hypocrite, deceiver*
And to lead Wit, Severity's son, out of the way!
110 He should make a marriage with Wisdom, in all haste, as
they talk;
But stay there awhile!—soft fire makes sweet malt—
I must be firm to bring him out of his brown study; on this
fashion
I will turn my name from Idleness to Honest Recreation;
And then I will bring him to be Mistress Wantonness's man;
115 And afaith! then he is in for a bird, get out how he can!
But soft yet, my masters! who is within?
Open the door and pull out the pin!

Wantonness entereth, and sayeth:

Wantonness.   What, Doll, I say, open the door! Who is in the
street?
What, Mr Idleness! lay a straw under your feet,
120 I pray you, and one may ask you what wind brought you
hither?

Idleness.   A little wind. I warrant you I am as light as any feather!
But, hark thee! (*Whispers*)

Wantonness.   What? it is not so? will he come indeed?

Idleness.   Nay, if I say the word thou mayest believe, as thy
creed;
But when he comes, you must be courteous, I tell you,
125 And you shall find him as gentle as a falcon,
Every fool's fellow.
What, methinks you are with child!

Wantonness.   Nay! My belly doth swell with eating of eggs.

Idleness.   Nay, by St Anne, I am afraid it is a timpany   *drum*
with two legs!
130 Away, get thee in!   [*Exit*

115 *in for a bird*: like a bird in a net.
117 sd Her head is seen by the audience as if at a window. Her actual entry
follows at the end of the next line.

Enter Wit

(*Wit*).   My father, he hath charged me the thing to take in hand,
    Which seems to me to be so hard, it cannot well be scanned;
    For I have toiled in my book where Wisdom much is praised,
    But she is so hard to find that I am nothing eased;
135 I would I had been set to blow, or to some other trade,
    And then I might some leisure find, and better shift have made.
    But now I swink and sweat in vain; my labour hath no end;
    And, moping in my study still, my youthful years I spend.
    Would God that I might hap to hit upon some good resort,
140 Some pleasant pastime for to find, and use some better sport!

Idleness.   Marry! no better. I am even as fit for that purpose as
    a rope for a thief!
    And you will be lusty, cry Hay! amongst knaves I am the
    chief!

Wit.   What, good fellow, art thou? what is thy name?

Idleness.   In faith I am *Ipse*. He! Even the very same!
145 A man of great estimation in mine own country:
    I was never stained but once, falling out of my mother's
    plum tree.

Wit.   Thou art a merry fellow and wise and if thou keep
    thyself warm.

Idleness.   In faith, I have a mother-wit, but I think no harm.

Wit.   I pray thee, what is thy name? To me it declare!

150 *Idleness.*   Nay! I am no niggard of my name! For that I will
    not spare!
    Ha! by the mass! I could have told you, even now,
    What a short-brained villain am I! I am as wise as my mother's
    sow!
    I pray you, sir, what is my name? Cannot you tell?
    (*To audience*) Is there any here that knows where my god-
    father doth dwell?
155 Gentlemen, if you will tarry while I go look,
    I am sure my name is in the church book.

Wit.   I prithee, come off! and tell me thy name with readiness.

Idleness.   Faith, if you will needs know, my name is Idleness.

Wit.   Marry! fie on thee, knave! I need not thy company!

160 *Idleness.*   What! because I spoke in jest, will you take it so
    angrily?
    For my name is Honest Recreation, I let you well to wit,
    There is not in all the world a companion for you more fit.

Wit.   And if thy name be Honest Recreation thou art as
    welcome as any in this land.

Idleness.   Yea, marry is it!

[172]

Wit.   Why, then, give me thy hand.

165 *Idleness.*   In faith, I thank you. You are come of a gentle birth;
And, therefore, I will bring you acquainted with a gentlewoman called Modest Mirth.

Wit.   Yea, marry! with all my heart, and God have mercy too!

Idleness.   Why then, come away, come! let us go.

(*He returns to the house of Wantonness, leaving Wit behind*)

(*Knocking*) How, God be here!

170 *Wantonness.*   What, Master Honest Recreation, I pray you draw
near.

Idleness.   Nay, I pray you come hither; come, I pray ye.

Wantonness.   I come.

Idleness.   Nay, but in any wise hide your belly.

Wantonness.   It is a child of your getting.

175 *Idleness.*   I? It hath fathers at large;
But here comes in Wit that is like to bear all the charge.

(*Wantonness enters : Wit approaches the house*)

Gentleman, here is the gentlewoman!
Kiss her, I say! (*Aside*) I am a whoreson else!
If I had know(n) you would not have kissed her,

180 I would have kissed her myself!   [*Wantonness kisses Wit*

Wit.   Gentlewoman, this shall be to desire you of more
acquaintance.

Wantonness.   Sir, a ought I may pleasure you I will give
attendance;
To have many suitors my lot doth befall,
But yet methink I like you best of all.

185 *Idleness* (*aside*).   Yea, she might have had many men of
knavery and of stealth!

Wantonness.   What sayest thou?

Idleness.   Marry! You might have had many men of
bravery and wealth;
But yet methinks there cannot be a match more fit
Than between Mistress Modest Mirth and you, Master Wit.

190 *Wantonness.*   That is well said.

Idleness (*aside*).   Yea, and that will be a ready carriage to the
rope.

Wantonness.   What sayest thou?

170 She should again appear at the window and take her first three lines
from there.
181 He gives her his portrait, or some other jewelled token like a ring.

Idleness. That will be a speedy marriage, I hope.

Wantonness. By my troth! I am so weary, I must needs sit
down!

195 My legs will not hold me.

Wit. Then I will sit down by you, if I may be so bold.

Idleness (assisting them). Here is love, sir reverence! (*Aside*)
This gear is even fit;
Oh! here is a head hath a counting-house full of wit!

Wit. I am sure you are cunning in music,

200 And therefore, if you please, sing us a song.

Wantonness. That will I, if it were for your ease.

*Here shall Wantonness sing this song to the tune of 'Attend thee, go
play thee'; and having sung him asleep upon her lap, let him snort;
then let her set a fool's bauble on his head, and colling (blacking) his
face; and Idleness shall steal away his purse from him, and go his
ways*

THE SONG

Lie still, and here nest thee;
Good Wit, lie and rest thee,
And in my lap take thou thy sleep;

205 Since Idleness brought thee
And now I have caught thee,
I charge thee let care away creep.
So now that he sleeps full soundly,
Now purpose I roundly,

210 Trick this pretty doddy   *parasite*
And make him a noddy,   *fool*
And make him a noddy!
Since he was unstable,
He now wears a bauble, *fool's, dunce's cap*

215 Since Idleness led him away;
And now of a scholar   *from being*
I will make him a collier, *paint his face black*
Since Wantonness beareth the sway:
Well, now I have him changed,

220 I needs must be ranging;
I now must go pack me,
For my gossips will lack me.
For my, *etc.*   [*Exit*

Enter Good Nurture, speaking this:

Good Nurture. I wonder where my schollard, Wit, is now of
late become?

225 I fear lest with ill company he happen for to run;
For I Good Nurture commonly among all men am counted,

But Wit, by this his straying so, I fear hath me renounced.
Severity, his father, sure is grave and wise withal,
But yet his mother's pampering will bring his son to thrall.

Here he stayeth, stumbling at Wit as he lieth asleep

230   Why, how now! ho! what wight is this on whom we now have hit?
Soft! Let me see. This same is he: yea, truly, this is Wit!

[*Here he awaketh him*

What, Wit, I say, arise for shame! O God! where hast thou been?
The company made thee a fool that thou of late wast in.

Here he riseth, rubbing his eyes, and saying:

Wit.   O, arrant strumpet! that she was, that raid   *arrayed*
me in this case!

235 *Good Nurture.*   Nay, rather thou art much to blame to be with such in place.

Here he washeth his face and taketh off the bauble

Come on, I say, amend this gear, beware of all temptation;
Your weariness for to refresh, take Honest Recreation.

He delivereth him Honest Recreation

Wit.   I thank you, Mr Nurture, much for this your gentleness,
And will do your commandments henceforth with willingness.

240 *Good Nurture.*   God grant you may! (*To Honest Recreation*)
And, sirrah! you await upon him still.

Exit

Wit.   I thank you, sir, with all my heart, for this your great good will;
One journey more I mean to make, I think I was accurst!
God grant the second time may be more happy than the first!

[*They both go out*

THE THIRD SCENE

Enter Idleness

245 (*Idleness*).   Ah! sirrah! it is an old proverb and a true, I swear by the rood!
It is an ill wind that blows no man to good.

237 sd No direction is supplied in the manuscript for his entrance; in production he can enter with Good Nurture and stand at a respectful
distance, looking demure, but allowing the audience to recognize
Idleness through his disguise.

[175]

When I had brought Wit into Wantonness'
    hampering,   *entanglements*
Then thought I it was time for me to be tempering.   *to be off*
The cook is not so soon gone as the dog's head is in the
    porridge-pot;
250   Wit was not so soon asleep but my hand was in his hose.
Wantonness is a drab! for the nonce she is an old rig;
But as for me, my fingers are as good as a lime twig.
Now I am new arrayed like a physician! Now do I not pass,
I am as ready to cog with Mr Wit as ever I was;
255   I am a very turncoat as the weathercock of St Paul's;
For now I will call my name Due Disport, fit for all souls—
Yea, so, so findly I can turn the cat in the pan.   *strongly*
Now shall you hear how findly Master Doctor can play the
    outlandish man.   *foreigner*
Ah! by Got! Me be the Doctor! Me am the fine knave, I tell ye,
260   Me have the good medicine for the maiden's belly!
Me have the excellent medicine for the blains and blister!
Ah! me am the knave to give the fair maid the glister! *enema*
How like you this, my masters?
The bee have no so many herbs whereout to suck honey,
265   As I can find shifts whereby to get money.

Enter Snatch and Catch (Sailors, home from the Netherlands)

But, soft, awhile, my masters! who have we here?
These be crafty knaves; and, therefore, lie thou there!

[*Lays down the purse in a corner*

The song that Snatch and Catch singeth together

I hath been told, been told, in proverbs old
That soldiers suffer both hunger and cold,
270   That soldiers suffer both hunger and cold;
And this sing we, and this sing we,
We live by spoil, by spoil, we moil and toil;
Thus Snatch and Catch doth keep a coil!   *make a noise*
And thus live we, and thus live we,
275   By snatching a(*nd*) catching, thus live we.
We come from sea, from sea, from many a fray,
To pilling and polling every day,   *pillaging; plundering*
To pilling and polling every day:
And thus skip we, and thus skip we,
280   And over the hatches thus skip we!

Catch.   Hey, lively! by the guts of a crab-louse, Snatch,
This is an excellent sport!
Now we are come from Flushing to the English port,

[176]

There shall not a fat pouch
285 Come nodding by the way
But Snatch and Catch will desire him to stay.

Snatch. Yea, by the hogshead, Catch! now we will lick
the spickets;   *spicy dishes*
But, by the mass! my hose be full of Spanish crickets!
Sirrah, dost thou not know Idleness, that counterfeit knave?

290 *Catch.* Yea! by St Anne! I know him well for a knave.
He hath his purse full of money if we could him get.

Snatch. Where had he it?

Catch. I tell thee, Snatch, he stole it from Wit.

Snatch. Who told thee so? declare it with readiness.

295 *Catch.* By the brains of a black pudding!
'Tis such a knave thou hast not heard:
It was told me of Wantonness.

[Here they espy him

Idleness. Ah, that drab! she can cackle like a caddow; *jackdaw*
I pray you behold, my masters!
300 A man may shape none by their shadow.

Snatch. O, wonderful! I would he were burst.

Catch. Nay, I pray thee let me speak first.
Master Idleness, I am glad to see you merry, heartily.

Idleness. In faith, I thank you.
305 But I had rather have your room than your company.

Snatch. Master Idleness, how have you done in a long time?
         (Tries to shake hands)

Idleness. Come, come! An hand of yours to pick a purse of mine?

Catch. Nay, sir! I hope you trust us better!
I must needs borrow your ring to seal a letter.

310 *Idleness.* By my leave? In spite of my teeth, God a mercy on us!
This is that must needs be, quoth the good man,
When he made his wife pin the basket. Patience, perforce!
Well, my masters, if you will go with me,
I will carry you to an old wife that
315 Makes puddings with her arse: hold your nose there!
And, if you will, you may have legs of mutton stuffed with
hair.

Catch. This is a crafty fox, but, by
a herring toke!   *a sailor taken*
I have a good nose to be a poor man's sow:
I can smell an apple seven mile in a hay mow.

289 *Spanish crickets:* my legs itch.

320   *Ubi animus, ibi ovulus*; where he loves there he looks.
Hey, lively! these will help to bring me out of John Tapster's
books.

> *Now he shall find the purse. Here after they have
> sc(r)ambled for the money, they shall spit in the purse
> and give it him again*

Snatch.   Hold, here! thou shalt not lose all;
Thy purse shall not come home weeping for loss;
And as for thee, thou shalt be commist to   *dumped at*
Dawe's cross.

325   *Idleness.*   Evil gotten worse spent, by theft this money came;
I got it with the devil, and now it is gone with his name!

Catch (to Snatch).   But, sirrah! if we let him escape, perhaps
we may have a check;
If we should chance to look through an hemp window, and
our arse break our neck.

Snatch.   Why, we will pull him up by a rope to the top of the
house,
330   And then let him fall.

Catch.   Nay, then, I know a better way;
We will run his arse against the wall!

Snatch.   Nay, by the mass! I have a devise much more meet.
Where I lay last night, I stole away a sheet:
335   We will take this, and tie it to his head,
And so we will blind him!
And, sirrah! I charge you, when you hear anybody coming,
If they ask you any question, say you go a-mumming!

> *Here they turn him about, and bind his hands behind
> him, and tie the sheet about his face.*

Idleness.   A-mumming, quoth you? why, there can be nothing
worse
340   Than for a man to go a-mumming when he hath no money in
his purse.

Catch.   Well, yet we charge you to do on this fashion.

Snatch.   Farewell, Mr Idleness, and remember your lesson.

> *Here they run one to one corner of the stage, and the other
> to the other, and speak like countrymen, to beguile him.*

Idleness.   Ah, sirrah! in faith this gear cottons! I go   *tickles*
still a-mumming;
Even poor I, all alone, without either pipe or drumming.

321 to pay my liquor bills.
328 Obscure, but meaning, 'if we let him go, he may turn the tables on us'.

345   *Snatch.*   Good day, neighbour, good day!
         'Tis a fair grey morning, God be blessed!

      Catch.   I, by Gis! 'twould be trim weather and if it were not for
         this mist.
         What! those fellows be all day at breakfast! I ween they make
         feasts.
         What! Jack, I say! I must zwinge you before you will   *whip*
         serve the beasts!
350   How now? God's daggers! death! who have we here?

      Idleness.   Oh, for the passion of God, loose me!
         False knaves have robbed me of all the money I got this year!

                                  [Here they beat him

      Snatch.   Yea, ye rascal, is the matter so plain?
         Come, come! We must teach him his lesson again.

355   *Catch.*   Sirrah! now you have learnt a trick for your coming:
         When anybody cometh, say you go a-mumming.

                          Exit Snatch (and) Cat(ch)

      Idleness.   A-mumming, quoth you? why, this gear will not
         settle;
         Either I rose on my left side to-day, or I pissed on a nettle.
         Here is news, (quoth) the fox, when he let a fart in the
         morning;
360   If Wantonness knew this, she will never lin scorning;   *stop*
     This same is kind cuckold's luck;
     These fellows have given me a dry pluck;
     Now I have never a cross to bless me.
     Now I go a-mumming,
365   Like a poor penniless spirit,
     Without pipe or drumming!

        Enter Wit, and Honest Recreation awaiting on him

      Wit.   Fie, fie! what kind of life is this to labour all in vain?
         To toil to get the thing the which my wit cannot attain?
         The journey seemeth wondrous long the which I have to
         make,
370   To tear myself and beat my brains, and all for Wisdom's sake!
     And yet, God knows what may befall, and what luck God
     will send,
     If she will love me when I come at this my journey's end.
     This Honest Recreation delights me not at all;
     For, when I spend the time with him I bring myself in thrall!

        Here he steppeth back, having espied Idleness

362-3 stripped me naked: they have even stolen my crucifix.

[179]

375   But soft! what have we here? some ghost or deadly sprite,
         That comes our journey for to stay, and us for to affright!

Idleness.   Yea, by the mass! what, are ye coming?
         In faith, I am a penniless spirit: I go still a-mumming.

Wit.   I conjure thee to tell me what art thou?
380   A man, a monster, a spirit, or what would'st thou have?

Idleness.   I am neither man, monster, nor spirit, but a poor,
         penniless knave!

Wit.   Wherefore is thy coming?

Idleness.   Marry, to go a-mumming!

Wit.   Yea, but what art thou? May not that be known?

385 *Idleness.*   Why, what am I but a knave when all my money is
         gone?

Wit.   Come, tell me thy name: I pray thee have done.

Idleness.   A good honest knave's: have ye forgot so soon?

Wit.   Why, but will ye not tell me how thou camest thus
         dressed?

Idleness.   In faith, gentle thieves! you yourselves know best.

390 *Wit.*   Do I? why, thou dost not know me, thou whoreson patch!

Idleness.   Yes, I know it is either Snatch or Catch.
         But in faith, gentle thieves! I go still a-mumming,
         Although it be without either pipe or drumming.

                        Here shall Wit pull off the sheet, saying,

Wit.   How sayest thou now? canst thou not see?
395   I pray thee tell me, dost thou know me?

Idleness.   Oh, the body of a gorge, I would I had them here;
         In faith! I would chop them—they were not so hack(*ed*) this
         seven year!
         Why, I am so cold that my teeth chatter in my head!
         I have stood here three days and three nights without either
         meat or bread.

400 *Wit.*   I pray thee, what is thy name, and whither dost thou
         resort?

Idleness.   Forsooth! for fault of a better (*my name*) is Due
         Disport.

Wit.   Didst not thee call thyself Honest Recreation, which
         deceived me once?

Idleness.   Why, I am a physician! If it were I—a knave shake
         my bones!

396 (?) If only I were St George.

I am a great traveller: I 'light on the dunghill like a
    puttock!   *kite*
405   Nay, take me with a lie and cut the brain out of my buttock.

Wit.   If thy name be Due Disport, I would be acquainted with
    thee; for in sport I delight.

Idleness.   Not under a couple of capons, and they must be
    white.
    But if you will be acquainted with me, as you say,
    Then must you send this companion away;
410   For you and I must walk alone.

Wit.   Why, then, sirrah! away, get you gone!

                            Exit Honest Recreation

Idleness.   So now, come on with me to a friend's house of
    mine,
    That there we may to some sport incline.

Wit.   Come on, then!

        Here Idleness, having brought him to the den of Irksom-
        ness, shall leap away, and Irksomeness enter like a
        monster, and shall beat down Wit with his club, saying,

415   *Irksomeness.*   What wight is that which comes so near his pain?

                   [Here they fight. Wit falls down

Wit.   Alas, alas, now am I stunned!

Irksomeness.   Nay, nay, no force! thou mightest a-further stood;
    If thou hadst 'scape(*d*) safe by my den,
    Thy luck were too too good.   *[Exit*

        Irksomeness leaveth him dead on the stage

        Enter Wisdom and sayeth,

420   (*Wisdom*).   Of late, abroad, I heard report that Wit makes
    many vows,
    The lady Wisdom, if he may, to wife for to espouse;
    But it I fear both Idleness and Irksomeness will sunder.
    Soft! this same is Wit, that lieth bleeding yonder.

                    [Here she helpeth him up

What, Wit! be of good cheer and now I will sustain thee.

425   *Wit.*   O, Lady Wisdom! so I would, but Irksomeness hath slain
    me!

Wisdom.   Well, yet arise, and do as I shall tell,
    And then, I warrant thee! thou shalt do well.

407 My price will be . . . etc.
415–19 This incident is so short that in production it fails to create its due
    effect unless supplemented by an amusing and well-rehearsed fight.

Wit. I thank you much; and though that I am very much aggrieved,
 Yet, since your coming, sure methinks I am right well relieved;
430 You show your courtesy herein, wherein I partly guess
 That you do know the cause right well of this my deep distress.
 My father bade me labour still your favour to obtain;
 But yet before I could you see, full great hath been my pain.
 First, Idleness, he brought me woe; then Wantonness stepped in;
435 And, last of all, foul Irksomeness his part he doth begin.

Wisdom. I think right well: for many a one hath come to sore decay
 When as it happed that Irksomeness hath met them in the way.
 For I, poor Wisdom, here am placed among these craggy cliffs,
 And he that seeks to win my love must venture many shifts;
440 But yet I bear thee great good will, and here I promise thee,
 If thou canst Irksomeness destroy, thy lady I will be;
 And to the end that may be done, which I might well afford,
 Hold here Perseverance, I say, a good and lucky sword;
 And call for Irksomeness, and let him feel thy force:
445 Be stout! for, if he overcome, he will have no remorse!

Wit. Why madam dear, behold the wight which fears not, for thy love,
 To fight with men and monsters both, as straight I shall it prove.

Wisdom. Well, do so then; the whiles I will depart.

Wit. I thank you, lady Wisdom, much! Farewell, with all my heart!

     Exit Wisdom. Wit calleth forth Irksomeness

450 Well, once more have at Irksomeness! come forth, thou monster fell!
 I hope yet now the second time thy pride and force to quell.

     Enter Irksomeness, saying,

(Irksomeness). What! Who is that that calls me forth? What! Art thou yet alive?
 If that I catch thee once again, thou shalt no more revive!

Wit. Leave off thy brags, and do thy worst;
455 Thy words may not prevail at first.

    *Here they fight awhile, and Irksomeness must run in
     a-doors, and Wit shall follow, taking his visor
     (Monster's head-mask) off his head, and shall bring it
      in upon his sword, saying,*

455 sd *visor:* Monster's head-mask. In performance, it is desirable to have a
duplicate head-mask ready with a bloody neck.

[182]

The Lord be thanked for his grace, this monster is subdued;
And I, which erst was worn with woe, am now with joy
    renewed!
Well, now before that I unto Dame Wisdom's house repair,
I will unto my father go, these news for to declare.

Exit

(PART TWO)
THE FOURTH SCENE

*Enter Idleness, halting with a stilt (crutch), and shall carry a cloth
upon a staff, like a rat-catcher, and say,*

460 (*Idleness*).   Have you any rats or mice, polecats or weasels?
    Or is there any old sows sick of the measles?
    I can destroy fulmers and catch moles;   *polecats*
    I have ratsbane, maidens! to spoil all the vermin that
      run in your holes.
    A rat-catcher, quoth you, this is a strange occupation:
465 But everywhere for Idleness they make proclamation;
    They say he shall be hanged for cozening of Wit:
    But there is a town called Hopshort; they have me not yet!
    I can go hard by their noses and never be known,
    Like a rat-catcher, till search be done.

*Here he espieth Search coming in, and goeth up and
down, saying, 'Have you any rats or mice?' as in
the first five lines*

470 *Search.*   Here is a moiling: they would have a   *painful work*
    man do more than he is able;
    One were better to be hanged than to be a constable!
    I have searched for a knave called Idleness,
    But I cannot find him for all my business:
    The knave they say has cozened Wit and
    shored him on the shelf.   *propped up*
475 *Idleness.*   Yea, if you take not heed, he will go nigh to cozen
    yourself.

Search.   What! dost thee know him, good fellow? I pray thee
    now tell.

Idleness.   Do I know? why, I tell thee I have ratsbane to sell.

Search.   Ratsbane! tut a point! Dost thou know Idleness? tell
    me!

Idleness.   Why, I tell thee I know him as well as he knows me;
480 I ween he be a tall man, and I trow he struts.
    And he be not a knave, I would he had a pound of ratsbane in
    his guts.

Search.   Yes, but where is he? canst thou tell?

Idleness.   No, faith! not well.

Search.   Yea, but methinks thou art lame.

485 *Idleness.*   Yea, you may see such luck have they
          which use game.   *play games*
  I have been at St Quintin's where I was twice kill'd;
  I have been at Musselborough at the Scottish field;
  I have been in the land of green ginger and many a-where,
  Where I have been shot through both the buttocks by an
      harquebusier:
490 But now I am old, and have nought myself to defend,
And am fain to be a rat-catcher to mine end!

> *Here shall Search take out a piece of paper and look on it*

Search.   What shall I give thee to cry a proclamation?

Idleness.   For half a score pots of beer I will cry it after the best
fashion.

> *Here shall Search reach a chair, and Idleness shall go*
> *up and make the proclamation*

Search.   Come! get up here; you must say as I say.

495 *Idleness.*   Ho! and you say I am a knave, then must I needs say
Nay.

Search.   First, cry 'Oyez' a good while.

Idleness.   Very well.

> *[He cries too long*

Search.   Enough! enough! what, hast thou never done?

Idleness.   What, didst not thee bid me cry long? I have not
scarce begun.

500 *Search.*   Go to! Cry shorter, with a vengeance!

Idleness.   'Oyez! oyez! oyez! oyez!'   *[Very often*

Search.   What? I think thou art mad!

Idleness.   Why? would you not have me do as you bade?

Search.   Why? canst thou keep no mean?

505 *Idleness.*   'Oyez!'

> *[Here he shall cry well*

Search.   That is very well said.

Idleness.   That is very well said!

Search.   What, I ween thou be'st drunk to-day!

[184]

	Idleness.	Why? did you not bid me say as you did say?
510	*Search.*	Come! Say on: 'The King's Most Royal Majesty.'
	Idleness.	John King gave a royal to lie with Marjorie. *gold coin*
	Search.	Why, what said I?
	Idleness.	Why, so!
	Search.	I say, 'The King's Most Royal Majesty. . . .'
515	*Idleness.*	The King's Most Royal Majesty!
	Search.	'Doth charge you, all his true people. . . .'
	Idleness.	What? It is not so!
	Search.	What?
	Idleness.	Why, you say there was a barge flew over a steeple!
520	*Search.*	I say, 'Doth charge all his true people.'
	Idleness.	Oh, Doth charge all his true people: that is another matter.
	Search.	'That they watch elsewhere, and see(k) in the town. . . .'
	Idleness.	That every patch that a man wears on his knee shall cost a crown.
525	*Search.*	Why, what means that? I spake no such word: 'That they watch elsewhere, And see(k) in each town.'
	Idleness.	That they watch, etc.
	Search.	'If that Idleness by any means they can find.'
	Idleness.	No, marry, you say not true.
	Search.	What is that?
530	*Idleness.*	It is not for Idleness that men sow beans in the wind.
	Search.	'If that Idleness by any means they can find.'

[Pulls him down

	Idleness.	If that Idleness, etc.
	Search.	Come down, with a pestilence! A murrain ride thee!
	Idleness.	Here is good thanks, my masters. Come, give me my fee!
535	*Search.*	Come! give me sixpence, and I will give thee eightpence.

Now shall Search run away with his money, and he shall cast away his stilt, and run after him.

535 sd In performance Idleness should hand over his sixpence to Search who then exits immediately without paying his half of the bargain: Idleness drops his disguise and gives chase.

THE FIFTH SCENE

Enter Fancy

(*Fancy*).   Like as the rolling stone, we see, doth never gather
moss,
And gold, with other metals mixed, must needs be full of
dross;
So likewise I, which commonly Dame Fancy have to name,
Amongst the wise am hated much, and suffer mickle blame,
540   Because that, waving here and there, I never steadfast stand,
Whereby the depth of learning's lore I cannot understand;
But Wit, perhaps, will me embrace, as I will use the matter;
For why? I mean to counterfeit, and smoothly for to flatter,
And say I am a messenger from Lady Wisdom sent,
545   To see if that will be a mean(s) to bring him to my bent—
But see where he doth come.

Enter Wit

Wit.   Like as the silly mariner, amidst the waving sea,
Doth climb the top of mighty mast full oft both night and day;
But yet at last, when happily he come(s) from ship to shore,
550   He seeks to sail again as fresh as erst he did before;
So likewise I, which have escaped the brunts which I have
done,
Am even as fresh to venture now as when I first begun;
A new adventure this I seek, not having run my race—
But who is this whom I behold for to appear
in place?   *on the stage*

555 *Fancy*.   God save you, gentle Mr Wit, and send you good
success!

Wit.   Fair Dame! I thank you heartily, and wish in you no
less.
What, may one be bold to ask your name without offence?

Fancy.   Yea, sir! with good will, that you may, and eke my
whole pretence:
My name is Fancy, and the cause of this my coming now
560   From lady Wisdom is to show a message unto you.

Wit.   Then are ye welcome unto me for Lady Wisdom's sake.

Fancy.   Here is the letter which she bade me unto you to take.

Here he receiveth the letter, and readeth it to himself

Wit.   My lady's will herein is this: that you should go with me
Unto a place, with her to meet, as here she doth decree.

565 *Fancy.*   Even so, good sir! even when you will I do the same
allow;
Go you before in at the door, and I will follow you.

> *Here, Wit going in, one shall pull him by the arm,*
> *whereupon he shall cry on this manner*

Wit.   Alas, I am betrayed! this sight makes me aghast!

Fancy.   Nay, nay, no force, sir! I charge you (*hold*) him fast:
Now, Wit, if that thou list to match thyself with me,
570   Thou shalt be free as e'er thou wast, and now released be.

Wit.   Alas! I am not so; Dame Wisdom hath my heart.

Fancy.   Then shalt thou lie there still, Iwis, until thou feel'st the
smart.

THE SIXTH SCENE

Enter Idleness (now dressed as a beggar)

Idleness.   This is a world! To see how fortune changeth!
This shall be his luck which like me runneth and rangeth;
575   For the honour of Artrebradle,
This age would make me swear madly!
Give me one penny, or a halfpenny,
For a poor man that hath had great loss by sea,
And is in great misery!
580   God save my good master, and my good dame,
And all the householder!
I pray you bestow your alms of a poor man
Nigh starved with cold.
Now I am a bold beggar—I tell you, the stoutest of all my kin,
585   For if nobody will come out, I will be so bold to go in!
By'r lady! here is nobody within but the cat, by the fireside:
I must needs go in; whatsoever come of it, I
cannot abide.   *stay here*

> *He goeth in, and bringeth out the porridge pot about*
> *his neck*

---

566 sd This is the climax of the scene and, in production, it will fall flat if
Wit's sexual fantasies do not materialize to tempt him in. Once inside he
is seized by a tough gaoler and clapped into irons. Wisdom and Snatch
or Catch can double in these roles. Imaginatively treated this scene can
be very theatrical and exciting.
573 cf. *Coriolanus*, IV. 4. 12, 'O world, thy slippery turns!', and Poor Tom in
King Lear.
575 Arthur Bradley, a pun, equivalent to Harry Stottle.

Ah! sirrah! my masters! how sayest thou, Hodge?
What, art thou hungry? Wilt thou eat my podge?
590   Now I provide for a dear year—this will be good in Lent;
Well fare a good mess of pottage when the herrings be spent.
A beggar, quoth you? this gear begins to fadge.
If ever I be a gentleman the pottage pot shall be
    my badge!   *coat-of-arms*
Now I am in that taking, I dare not show my head:
595   And all by cozening of Wit I am fain to beg my bread!
Well, my masters, fare you well! I may perhaps have a check,
If the good wife come forth and take the pottage-pot about my
    neck.

THE SEVENTH SCENE

Enter Doll and Lob

Doll.   Oh, the passion of God! so I shall be swinged; so, my
    bones shall be banged!
The porridge pot is stolen: what, Lob, I say, come away. and
    be hanged!
600   What, Lob, I say, come away with a foul evil!

Lob.   What a lobbing makest thou, with a   *uproar, racket*
    twenty devil!

Doll.   Thou hast kept a goodly coil, thou whoreson, hobbling
    John!
Thou keepest a tumbling of me in the barn, till the porridge-
    pot is gone.

Lob.   Nay, thou tumblest down thyself—and was
    almost bare;   *naked*
605   Nay, I will tell my dame how thou would'st needs feel my
    ware.

Doll.   Thou liest, whoreson! thou wilt be cudgelled, so thou
    wilt!

Lob.   Nay, good Doll, say thee: 'the porridge were all spilt.'

Here entereth Mother Bee with a stick in her hand

Mother Bee.   What! Where be these whore-cops?
I promise you, you keep a goodly coil;
610   I serve the hogs, I seek hen's nest,
I moil and toil!
Thanks be to God, gentlewoman, betwixt Jack and Joan,
When I come into breakfast all the pottage is gone!
I pray ye, mistress, where is the pottage-pot? is that hid away?

592 This disguise begins to please me.

615 *Doll.* Whilst Lob was kissing me in the barn, a knave stole it
away.

Mother Bee. Yea, God's bones! one can scarce go to pissing
But my man and my maid do straight fall to kissing.

                 [Here she beateth them up and down the stage

Are ye billing? what, my man Lob is become
  a jolly ruffler!   *lecherous bully*
You are billing, you! I must be fain to be a
  snuffler.   *candle extinguisher*

620 *Lob.* O, dame, dame, if you will beat me no more,
I will tell you a tale:
When I was at the town, one called you whore.

Mother Bee. Ah, whoreson! thou callest me whore by craft;
Thou art a Kentish man, I trow.

625 *Lob.* Why, Doll will not mend my breech; how would you have
me go?

Doll. He lies, Dame! He lies! he tears it neither with ploughing
nor carting
For it is not so soon mended, but he tears it out with farting.

*Enter Inquisition, bringing in Idleness, with the pottage-pot
about his neck*

Mother Bee. Soft! who have we here?
I am as glad as one would give me a crown.
630 What have I spied? by'r lady!
My porridge-pot is come to town.

Inquisition. What, is this your pottage-pot?
Do you know it, if you see it?

Mother Bee. Whether it be mine or no he had it from my fireside,
635 He cannot deny it.

                          Exit Mother Bee

Lob. O, dame, dame, so I will jerk him, if I had my whip.
Sirrah! Doll, we will accuse him of fellowship.

Idleness. Let me alone, and I will tell you who stole your eggs;
And, likewise, who stole your cock with the yellow legs.

640 *Inquisition.* Well, we will have him to a justice: dispatch! come
away!

Lob. Yea, and let him be whipped up and down the town next
market day.

                          [Go out all

THE EIGHTH SCENE

Enter Good Nurture

Good Nurture.   To them whose shoulders do support the charge
of tender youth,

One grief falls on another's neck, and youth will
have his ruth;   *sorrow, misery*

Since first I 'gan to nurture Wit full many cares hath passed,

645   But when he had slain Irksomeness, I thought me safe at
last;

But now I see the very end of that my late distress,

Is a beginning unto grief which will be nothing less:

For when I thought that Wit of late to Wisdom's house had
gone,

He came not there, but God knows where this reckless Wit is
run.

650   Nor know I where to seek him now, whereby I learn with pain

There is no grief, so far gone past, but may return again.

Here Wit crieth out in prison, and sayeth this

Wit.   The silly bird, once caught in net, if she escape alive,

Will come no more so nigh the snare, her freedom to deprive;

But rather she will leave her haunt, the which she used before;

655   But I, alas! when steed is stolen, do shut the stable door.

For being often caught before, yet could I not refrain;

More foolish than the witless bird I came to hand again.

Alas! the chains oppress me sore wherewith I now
am lad,   *held*

But yet the pain doth pinch me more wherein my heart is clad!

660   O, mighty Jove! now grant that some good man may pass this
place,

By whose good help I might be brought out of this woeful
case!

Good Nurture.   What noise is this? what piteous plaints are
sounding in my ear?

My heart doth give me it is Wit the which I now do hear.

I will draw near and see. (*He cometh near the prison.*) What
wight art thou

665   Which dost lament and thus dost pine in pain?

Wit.   My name is Wit; my grief is great—how should I then
refrain?

Good Nurture.   What, Wit! How camest thou here? O God,
what chance is this?

Wit.   Dame Fancy brought me in this case; I know I did amiss.

Good Nurture.   What! Fancy? Where is she? O, that I once might catch her!

670 *Wit.*   Would God you could, or else someone that able were to match her;
But she no sooner heard your voice, there standing at the door,
Than she with all her folks hath fled, and will be seen no more:
But I, poor soul, lie here in chains.

Here entereth and releaseth him Good Nurture

Good Nurture.   Once more I have released thee of thy pains.

675 *Wit.*   Your most unworthy schollard gives to you immortal thanks.

Good Nurture.   I pray you now take better heed you play no more such pranks;
Pluck up your spirits! Your marriage day is come even at hand.
To-morrow Wisdom shall you wed, I let you understand.

Wit.   Right so: as you think good, I shall contented be.

680 *Good Nurture.*   Then let us go for to prepare! Come on, I say, with me!

Exeunt

(SCENE NINE)

Enter Idleness like a priest

Idleness.   Ah, sirrah! my masters! There is much ado when fortune is louring;
O the passion of God! I have escaped a scouring.
Here hath been heave and shove! This gear is not fit;
In faith, I have l(*ain*) in the lurch for cozening of Wit:

685 Now shall he be married in all the haste;
When Wit and Wisdom is joined together, then I am rejected.
Well yet I can shift elsewhere, so long as I am not detected.
Detected I cannot well be; I am of that condition
That I can turn into all colours like the chameleon:

690 Although some do refuse me, and some leaden-heeled lubber will not refrain me;
And when men hath done with me women will retain me!
Idleness, the(*y*) say, is the mother of vice;
Through Idleness fell the Trojans, and the Greeks won the prize.

Idleness breedeth evil thoughts whereof come ill deeds:
695 Idleness is a cockadill, and great mischief breeds.
I give myself a good report—my masters! you may think the best;
He that loveth me shall have small joy of his rest.

683 In performance this line makes sense if his stolen vestments are much too large or too small, and if he is still putting them on while speaking his opening lines.

King Amasis made a law and bound his subjects to it fast,
To give an account whereupon they lived the year last past;
700 And if any lived idly, without any regard,
The punishment was grievous they did him award!
But now I can escape from all such peril,
And play the purveyor here in earth for the devil.
Well, my masters! I must be gone this marriage to see;
705 They that list not to work, let them follow me.

Exit

THE TENTH SCENE

Enter Severity and Wit

Severity. Well now, son Wit! the proof is plain—the clouds were ne'er so black
But the brightness of the sun, at last, might put them back.
The wind did never blow so much, wherewith the bark was tore,
But that the weather was so calm to bring the ship to shore.
710 The danger now is past. Address thyself with speed
To meet with Wisdom, thy dear wife, as we before decreed.
Wit. It shall be done as duty binds and as I bounden stand;
But see, good father; now behold Dame Wisdom is at hand.

*Enter Good Nurture and Wisdom, and Wisdom and Wit
singeth this song*

Wisdom.   My joy hath overgrown my grief,
715   My cure is past,
                  For Fortune hath been my relief
                  Now at last!
                  Tantara tara tantara,
                  My husband is at hand!
720   His comely grace appears in place,
                  As I do understand.

Wit.   My lady, thrice welcome to me,
                  Mine only joy!
                  Thy gentleness, God give it thee
725   Without annoy.
                  Tantara tara tantara,
                  Welcome, my worthy wife!
                  Thou art my part, thine is my heart,
                  My blessed limb of life!

698 *King Amasis:* of Egypt, xxvith Dynasty, a tyrant.
705 This line is verbally ironical and visually anti-clerical.

730 *Wisdom.*   As duty doth bind according to kind
                    I thank ye much;
                    For thee thy wife will spend her life,
                    She will not grutch.   grouse, nag
                    Tantara tara tantara,
735   The sum of all my bliss;
                    The welcomest wight, my chief delight,
                    That shall be and that is.

     Wit.   Let me thy comely corps embrace,
                    Dear Wisdom, now.

740 *Wisdom.*   Good Wit, I always loved the place
                    To be with you;
                    Tantara tara tantara,
                    Thou hast my heart in hold.

     Wit.   Nor do I fain, but tell thee plain,
745   I am thy own. Behold!

                                        [*Here endeth the song*

Good Nurture.   Well, now I am right glad to see you both well
     met.

Severity.   And so am I, with all my heart, that they so sure are
     set.

Both.   We thank ye both right humbly.

Wit.   And wish to marry speedily.

750 *Wisdom.*   For why? Although the turtle long were parted from
     her mate!

Wit.   Now God be thanked, they are met, in good and happy
     state;
     The Lord be thanked for his grace which gave thee unto me:
     Then welcome! nothing in heaven or earth more welcomer
     can be.

Wisdom.   And you to me, dear Wit.

755 *Severity.*   Come, now! The time requires that we depart away
     To celebrate the nuptials with joy, this wedding-day!

Wit.   Go you before, my father dear, and you, good master!
     straight,
     And then both I, and Wisdom too, upon you will await.

                                        [*Go forth all*

732 Emended from 'Thy wife for thee . . .”
751 It makes better sense for Wisdom to keep this line and for Wit's reply to
     start with line 752.

Enter Epilogue

Epilogue.   Thus have you seen, good audience! and heard the
course of youth,
760   And whoso list to try the same shall find it for a truth.
And if this simple show hath happened for to halt,
Your pardon and your patience we crave in our default:
For though the style be rough, and phrases found unfit,
Yet may you say, upon the head the very nail is hit!
765   Wherefore, the moral mark! for Finis let it pass,
And Wit may well and worthy then use it for a glass,
Whereby for to eschew his foes that always do await him,
And never hang upon the hook, wherewith they seek to bait
him.
Thus if you follow fast, (*you*) will be quit from thrall,
770   (*And*) eke in joy an(*d*) heavenly bliss—the which God grant us
all!

Amen, quoth FRA: MERBURY

FINIS

758 sd In production a final amusing and ironical touch can be achieved
here if Idleness (as Priest) returns to escort them off.

APPENDIX

The Interlude of the Student and the Girl, *c.* 1300

John Lydgate: Mummings for King Henry VI at Hertford and for the Sheriffs of London at Bishopswood, 1425-7

These three short pieces are included here partly as a reminder that the word Interlude was in use in England to describe a dramatic entertainment of a secular nature a full two hundred years before Henry Medwall wrote *Fulgens and Lucres*, and in part to illustrate what Medwall himself envisaged when he chose to make Publius Cornelius present Lucres and her father, Fulgens, with a Mumming (ii. 375-405). Francis Merbury also incorporates the idea of Mumming into *The Marriage Between Wit and Wisdom*, but at a much less sophisticated level and as the basis for slapstick; for when Idleness is tied up in a sheet and then told to tell anyone he meets that he is going mumming, the image he presents to the audience is closer to the Mummers' Play than to the Disguising of Court Revels.

The author of *The Student and the Girl* is not known. Only two brief scenes of the play survive in a manuscript now in the British Museum (Additional MS 23986). This manuscript is of the late thirteenth century (or very early fourteenth) and written in an East Midlands dialect that would allow either Beverley or Lincoln to claim it as its own. The two scenes bear a superficial resemblance to a Middle English lyric poem bearing the same title but of an earlier date (British Museum MS Harley 2253), and also to the well-known thirteenth-century fabliau, *Dame Siriʒ*. Earlier editors have suggested that *Dame Siriʒ* provides the source of the *Interlude of the Student and the Girl*, and that both may have been derived from another, still earlier interlude, now lost, that provided a common source. It is difficult, however, to credit this since the lyric poem is written in a dialect more appropriate to Herefordshire than Lincolnshire or the South Riding of Yorkshire, and since the clerk-hero of the story is an outlaw, 'far from home and also from civilization, under the forest' rather than a student 'languishing in the university', and is depicted as a bold housebreaker rather than as a timid youth who has to employ a procuress to help him win his girl.

All, therefore, that can be said with any confidence about the possible relationship of these several pieces on a similar theme is that the students of Europe's first universities from Bologna to Krakow and Oxford wrote as frequently and self-pityingly about the pangs of first love as writers of pop songs today: in doing so these young 'goliards' or '*vagantes*' provided a stock of material in part lyrical, in part comic, in part derived from personal experience and in part culled from the songs or poems of others that they had chanced to hear or read. There is thus no necessity to suppose that the English *Interlude of the Student and the Girl* was not as original as its variants from other versions of the story suggest.

What is important about it—at least to anyone seriously interested in the history of our theatre—is that this text antedates any other in the vernacular (the so-called Shrewsbury Fragments alone excepted) by at least a hundred years: [1] and this of itself serves to make nonsense of the idea, current for so long among critics and historians, that religious drama had to be 'secularized' before art of any merit in dramatic form could develop. In this context the existence of the Lydgate texts only serves to reinforce belief in the existence of an independent secular tradition, more especially if these texts are studied alongside earlier French *entremets* and the 'tregetoures' of Chaucer's *Franklyn's Tale*.

Nevertheless, Lydgate's dramatic texts were all written more than a century later than *The Interlude of the Student and the Girl* and, while equally secular in spirit, are of a distinctly different dramatic genre. Those printed here form two from a group of seven entertainments devised for the young King Henry VI, and for the Lord Mayor and Sheriffs of London and the Livery Companies of which they were members. They are neither plays nor masques. Lydgate describes one of them as,

> A letter made in wise of ballad . . . of a mumming, which the Goldsmiths of the City of London mummed in right fresh and costly (MS. *welych*) manner disguising to their Mayor, Eastfield, upon Candlemass day at night after supper; brought and presented unto the Mayor by an herald named (MS. *cleped*) Fortune.

Another is described as

> A letter made in wise of ballad . . . brought by a poursuivant in wise of mummers disguised to fore the Mayor of London, Eastfield, upon the twelfth night of Christmas, ordained royally by the worthy Mercers, citizens of London.

[1] On these lines and cues for actors see Norman Davis, *Non-Cycle Plays and Fragments with a Note on the Shrewsbury Music by F. L. C. Harrison*, ed. for E.E.T.S., 1970, pp. xiv–xxii, 1–7 and 124–33.

A third is described as

> The device of a disguising to-fore the great estates of this
> land, then being at London . . . of Dame Fortune, etc.

In each case a group of citizens have disguised themselves in
theatrical costumes to represent a group of characters deemed by
the poet to be appropriate to the occasion: their identity and the
reason for their appearance are then explained to the audience in an
introductory poem by a presenter.

In *The Mumming at Hertford* (the first of those printed in this
volume) the subject matter is the perennial conflict between husband and wife for command in the home. A Presenter supplicates to
the king on behalf of six peasant husbands who seek redress for
'the trouble and the cruelty' they have suffered at the hands of
their wives. In reply one of the six wives, acting as spokesman for
them all, counters these accusations and pleads for judgment on
their side. A third speaker, the king's advocate (possibly Lydgate
himself), then pronounces judgment by deferring sentence—

> Till there be made examination
> Of other parties and inquisition.

—and enjoins a truce. Both groups are told to return in a year's
time for the verdict—an excuse for another Mumming. All the
characters described in the text appear before the audience as
'mummers'—silent actors in costume—and mime the situations
described by the three speaking actors. Revived in this manner in
the Drama Department of Bristol University in 1961, it proved—
as a brief divertissement—to be far more entertaining than anyone
concerned had suspected.

The Mummings at Bishopswood and Eltham are written in a
very different spirit: the former is included here to show that, like
secular domestic comedy, classical mythology also found its way
into the English dramatic repertoire at least a hundred years before
the accession of Elizabeth I. It was intended as a highly stylized
May Game at which the Sheriffs of London and their friends were
to be greeted by the Goddesses Flora and Ver and by a personification of May: that at Eltham was prepared for the king and queen at
Christmas, and brings Bacchus, Juno and Ceres to earth. In both
cases the actors bear gifts from the sponsors of the *Mumming* to the
principal spectators, the allegorical nature of which is explained on
their behalf by the Presenter.

All these pieces are written in Lydgate's most Chaucerian
manner; yet even when it is granted, in the words of H. N.
MacCracken, that 'Lydgate's pen was at the service of any devout
Catholic and patriotic Lancastrian', it takes some imaginative
effort to think of the author of these texts as a monk of the Benedic-
tine Order at Bury St Edmunds.

I think it unlikely that anyone will wish to revive any of these three pieces in anything but an environment of academic research and experiment—hence the placement of them in this Appendix rather than in the body of the text: nevertheless, since their very existence has been so seriously neglected hitherto, there is as strong a case for making them more accessible to students of English literature as there is for including them in any subsequent critical discussion of the development of English drama. Students not familiar with the Middle English þ should simply substitute 'th'.

Interludium de clerico et puella has been printed several times in Middle English Readers, but in its true context of theatrical literature it has suffered gross neglect and may only be found in print tucked away in Appendix 'U' in Sir Edmund Chambers's *The Mediaeval Stage* (O.U.P., 1903), ii, pp. 324–6, inaccurately transcribed at that.

The Lydgate texts shelter no less demurely from the standpoint of the general reader (together with the four other Mummings) in Volume 2 of the Early English Text Society's *The Minor Poems of John Lydgate*, ed. H. N. MacCracken, 1911, pp. 668–701; reprinted 1934. The 'Mumming at Bishopswood' had been separately printed before then in Nicholas, *Chronicle of London*, 1837, from Bodleian MS Ashmole 59; the 'Mumming at Eltham' in Brotanek, *Die Englischen Maskenspiele*, 1902, from British Museum Additional MS 29729 and Trinity College Cambridge, MS R.3.20; and the 'Mumming at Hertford' in *Anglia*, vol. xxi, pp. 364 f., from the same manuscript sources as the Eltham Mumming.

The provenance of *Interludium de clerico et puella* is discussed by Ten Brink in his *History of English Literature*, trans. W. C. Robinson, 3 vols., 1893, i. 255 and ii. 295, and by Bruce Dickens and R. M. Wilson in *Early Middle English Texts*, 1951, p. 132. All the Lydgate texts are discussed at some length by C. M. Welsford in *The Court Masque*, 1927, and by me in *Early English Stages*, 3 vols., 1958, i. 191–206.

THE INTERLUDE OF THE STUDENT
AND THE GIRL, *c.* 1300

Hic incipit Interludium de Clerico et Puella

Clericus. Damishel, reste wel!

Puella. Sir, welcum, by Saynt Michel!

Clericus. Wer es ty sire, wer es ty dame?

Puella. By Gode, es noþer her at hame.

5 *Clericus.* Wel wor suilc a man to life,
    Þat suilc a may mithe have to wyfe!

Puella. Do way, by Crist and Leonard,
    No wil Y lufe na clerc fayllard;
    Na kep I herbherg clerc in huse no y flore,
10   Bot his hers ly wit-uten dore.
    Go forth þi way, god sire,
    For her hastu losyt al þi hire.

Clericus. Nu, nu, by Crist and by Sant Jhon,
    In al þis land ne wist I none,
15   Mayden, þat hi luf mor þan þe;
    Hif me micht ever þe bether be!
    For þe hy sory nicht and day;
    Y may say, 'Hay, wayleuay!'
    Y luf þe mar þan mi lif,
20   Þu hates me mar þan gayt dos chnief.
    Þat es noutt for mysgilt,
    Certhes, for þi luf ham hi spilt.
    A, suythe mayden, reu of me,
    Þat es ty luf, hand ay sal be!
25   For þe luf of þe mod(er) of efne,   MS. *Mod*
    Þu mend þi mode, and her my steuene.

Puella. By Crist of heuene and Sant Jone!
    Clerc of scole ne kep I none,
    For many god wymman haf þai don scam.
30   By Crist, þu michtis haf be at hame!

Clericus. Syn it n(o) other gat may be,
    Jesu Crist, bytech Y þe,
    And send neulic bot tharinne,
    Þar Y be lesit of al my pine.

35 *Puella.* Go nu, truan, go nu, go,
    For mikel canstu of sory and wo!

(*Scene 2.*)

Clericus. God te blis, Mome Helwis.

Mome Helwis. Son, welcum, by san Dinis!

Clericus. Hic am comin to þe, Mome;
40   Þu hel me noth, þu say me sone.

THE INTERLUDE OF THE STUDENT AND THE GIRL

Here begins the Interlude of the Student and the Girl
(*Molly's House*)

Student.   Fair Damsel! Rest you well!

Girl.   Sir! Welcome, by Saint Michael!

Student.   Where is your father? Where is your mother?

Girl.   In God's name, neither is here at home!

5   *Student.*   Happy were such a man to be alive
       Who such a girl might have as a wife!

Girl.   Be off with you! By Christ and by St Leonard,
       I won't have any deceitful student;
       Nor do I care to harbour him in house or hall
10   Unless his backside lies out of doors!
       Get off on your way, good sir;
       For here you've exhausted your welcome.

Student.   No, no! By Christ and by St John,
       In all this land I never knew anyone else,
15   Maiden, that I love more than you,
       As I hope hereafter to be blessed.
       For you I sorrow night and day:
       I may say 'Heigh, well-away'!
       I love you more than my life;
20   And still you hate me more than goat does knife!
       It cannot be for my misdeeds.
       Surely I am ruined for love of you.
       Ay, sweet maiden, pity me
       Who am your lover and always will be!
25   For the love of the mother of heaven
       Change your mind, and hear my voice.

Girl.   By Christ in Heaven and St John!
       I don't care for any student,
       For many a good woman have they brought to shame!
30   By Christ, you should have stayed at home!

Student.   Since it can be no other way
       I commit you to Jesus Christ,
       And may he soon send a remedy for this,
       So that I may be delivered from all my torment.

35   *Girl.*   Go now, you vagrant! Go now, go!
       For you're a maker of much grief and woe!

(*Mother Eloise's House*)

Student.   God be with you, Mother Eloise.

Mother Eloise.   Welcome, son, by St. Denis!

Student.   I have sought you out, mother;
40   Conceal nothing from me; tell me at once.

[201

Hic am a clerc þat hauntes scole;
Y lydy my lif wyt mikel dole;
Me wor lever to be dedh,
þan led the lif þat hyc ledh,
45 For ay mayden with and schen,—
Fayrer ho lond haw Y non syen.
Yo hat mayden Malkyn, Y wene;
Nu þu wost quam Y mene;
Yo wonys at the tounes ende,
50 þat suyt lif, so fayr and hende;
Bot if yo wil hir mod amende,
Neuly Crist my ded me send!
Men send me hyder, vytuten fayle,
To haf þi help and ty cunsayle.
55 þar for am I cummen here,
þat þu salt be my herandbere,
To mac me and þat mayden sayct,
And hi sal gef þe of myn ayct,
So þat hever, al thi lyf,
60 Saltu be þe better wyf;
So help me Crist! and hy may spede,
Riche saltu haf þi mede!

Mome Helwis. A, son, vat saystu? *Benedicite!*
Lift hup þi hand, and blis þe!
65 For it es boþt syn and scam
þat þu on me hafs layt thys blam;
For Yc am an ald quyne and a lam;
Y led my lyf with Godis gram;
Wit my roc Y me fede;
70 Can I do non othir dede
Bot my *Pater Noster* and my *Crede*
(To say Crist for missedede),
And myn *Avy Mary*
(For my scynnes hic am sory),
75 And my *De Profundis*
(For al that yn sin lys);
For can I me non oþir þink,
þat wot Crist, of hevene kync.
Iesu Crist, of hevene hey,
80 Gef that þay may heng hey,
And gef þat hy may se
þat þay be heng on a tre,
That þis ley as leyit onne me,
For aly wyman am I on.

. . . .

I am a student who attends the university,
Where I spend my life in heavy grief:
I had rather that I were dead
Than lead the life I do lead,
45 And all because of a maiden fair and shimmering—
None fairer have I seen in this country.
She is called maiden Molly, I think—
Now you know whom I mean.
She lives in the outskirts of the town,
50 The pleasant creature, so pretty and gracious.
Unless she will soften her heart towards me,
May Christ send me my death soon!
I have been strongly advised to come here
To enlist your help and your counsel.
55 The reason for my coming here is
That you shall be my go-between
In reconciling that maiden with me.
I will give you such rewards
That for all the rest of your life
60 You will be a wealthier woman;
So help me Christ!—if I succeed,
Profusely shall you reap your reward!

Mother Eloise.   Eh, son? What do you say? Bless us!
Lift up your hand and bless yourself,
65 For it is both sin and shame
That you should have laid this blame on me;
For I am an old crone and a cripple.
I lead my life under the wrath of God.
With my distaff I earn my food;
70 I can do nothing over and above reciting
Both my *Pater Noster* and my *Credo*
(To tell Christ of my neglected duties)
And my *Ave Maria*
(For my sins I am sorry)
75 And my *De Profundis*
(For all that dwell in sin):
For I can do no other thing for myself,
As Christ, the King of Heaven, knows;
May Jesu Christ of the heavens high
80 Grant that they may be strung up high,
And grant that I may see
That they are hung upon a tree,
They that have laid this lie on me;
For a God-fearing woman, that am I.

. . . .   *(End of fragment)*

80 *they :* The people who advised the student to employ her as a procuress.

[203]

MUMMING AT HERTFORD

*Nowe foloweþe here þe maner of a bille by wey of supplicacion putte
to þe kyng holding his noble feest of Cristmasse in þe Castel of
Hertford as in a disguysing of þe rude vpplandisshe people com-
pleynyng on hir wyves, with þe boystous aunswere of hir wyves,
devysed by Lydegate at þe request of þe Countre Roullour Brys
slayne at Loviers.*

Moost noble Prynce, with support of Your Grace
Þer beon entred in-to youre royal place,
And late e-comen in-to youre castell,
Youre poure lieges, wheche lyke no-thing weel;   *well*
5 Nowe in þe vigyle of þis nuwe yeere
Certeyne sweynes ful froward of ther   *swains, young men*
    chere
Of entent comen, fallen on ther kne,
For to compleyne vn-to Yuoure Magestee
Vpon þe mescheef of gret aduersytee,
10 Vpon þe trouble and þe cruweltee
Which þat þey haue endured in þeyre lyves
By þe felnesse of þeyre fierce wyves;   *harshness, wickedness*
Which is a tourment verray importable,
A bonde of sorowe, a knott vnremuwable,
15 For whoo is bounde or locked in maryage,
Yif he beo olde, he falleþe in dotage.
And yong(e) folkes, of þeyre lymes sklendre,
Grene and lusty, and of brawne but tendre,
Phylosophres callen in suche aage
20 A chylde to wyve, a woodnesse or a raage.   *madness; passion*
For þey afferme þer is noon eorþely stryff
May beo compared to wedding of a wyff,
And who þat euer stondeþe in þe cas,
He with his rebecke may sing ful offt ellas!   *fiddle, violin*
25 Lyke as þeos hynes, here stonding oon by oon,
He may with hem vpon þe daunce goon,
Leorne þa traas, booþe at even and morowe,   *steps*
Of *Karycantowe* in tourment and in sorowe;
Weyle þe whyle, ellas! þat he was borne.
30 For *Obbe* þe Reeve, þat gooþe heere al to-forne,
He pleyneþe sore his mariage is not meete,
For his wyff, *Beautryce Bitter sweete*,
Cast vpon him a hougly cheer ful rowghe,
Whane he komeþe home ful wery frome þe ploughe,
35 With hungry stomake deed and paale of cheere,
In hope to fynde redy his dynier;
Þanne sitteþe *Beautryce* bolling at þe nale,   *boozing at the pub*

As she þat gyveþe of him no maner tale;
For she al day, with hir iowsy nolle,   *crooked nose*
40 Hathe for þe collyk pouped in þe bolle,   *breathed in the bowl*
And for heed aache with pepir and gynger
Dronk dolled ale to make hir throte cleer;
And komeþe hir hoome, whane hit draweþe to eve,
And þanne *Robyn*, þe cely poure Reeve,
45 Fynde noone amendes of harome ne damage,
But leene growell, and soupeþe colde potage;
And of his wyf haþe noone oþer cheer
But cokkrowortes vn-to his souper.   *? chicken's feet*
Þis is his servyce sitting at þe borde,
50 And cely *Robyn*, yif he speke a worde,
Beautryce of him dooþe so lytel rekke,   *respect, care*
Þat with hir distaff she hitteþe him in þe nekke,
For a medecyne to chawf with his bloode;   *warm his blood with*
With suche a meteyerde she haþe shape him an hoode.
55 And *Colyn Cobeller*, folowing his felawe,
Haþe hade his part of þe same lawe;
For by þe feyth þat þe preost him gaf,
His wyff haþe taught him to pleyne at þe staff;
Hir quarter-strooke were so large and rounde
60 Þat on his rigge þe towche was alwey founde.   *back*
Cecely Soure-Chere, his owen precyous spouse,
Kowde him reheete whane he came to house;   *rebuke, scold*
Yif he ought spake whanne he felt(e) peyne,
Ageyne oon worde, always he hade tweyne;
65 Sheo qwytt him euer, þer was no thing to seeche,
Six for oon of worde and strookes eeche.
Þer was no meen bytweene hem for to goone;
What euer he wan, clowting olde shoone
Þe wykday, pleynly þis is no tale,
70 Sheo wolde on Sondayes drynk it at þe nale.   *alehouse, pub*
His part was noon, he sayde not oonys nay;   *once*
Hit is no game but an hernest play,
For lack of wit a man his wyf to greeve,
Þeos housbondemen, who-so wolde hem leeve,   *believe*
75 Koude yif þey dourst telle in audyence
What foloweþe þer of wyves to doone offence;
Is noon so olde ne ryveld on hir face,   *wrinkled*
Wit tong or staff but þat she dare manase.
Mabyle, God hir sauve and blesse,
80 Koude yif hir list bere here of witnesse:
Wordes, strookes vnhappe, and harde grace
With sharp(e) nayles kracching in þe face.

72 See General Introduction, p. **vi** above.

I mene þus, whane þe distaff is brooke,
With þeyre fistes wyves wol be wrooke.   *avenged*
85 Blessed þoo men þat cane in suche offence
Meekly souffre, take al in pacyence,
Tendure suche wyfly purgatorye.
Heven for þeyre meede, to regne þer in glorye,
God graunt al housbandes þat beon in þis place,
90 To wynne so heven for His hooly grace.
Nexst in ordre, þis bochier stoute and bolde
Þat killed haþe bulles and boores olde,
Þis *Berthilmewe*, for al his broode knyff,
Yis durst he neuer with his sturdy wyff,
95 In no mater holde chaumpartye;   *contention*
And if he did, sheo wolde anoon defye
His pompe, his pryde, with a sterne thought,
And sodeynly setten him at nought.
Þoughe his bely were rounded lyche an ooke
100 She wolde not fayle to gyf þe first(*e*) strooke;
For proud Pernelle, lyche a chaumpyoun,
Wolde leve hir puddinges in a gret cawdroun,
Suffre hem boylle, and taake of him noon heede,
But with hir skumour reeche hom on þe heued.
105 Shee wolde paye him, and make no delaye,
Bid him goo pleye him a twenty deuel wey.
She was no cowarde founde at suche a neode,
Hir fist ful offt made his cheekis bleed;
What querell euer þat he agenst hir sette,
110 She cast hir not to dyen in his dette.
She made no taylle, bu qwytte him by and by;   *tally*
His quarter sowde, she payde him feythfylly,
And his waages, with al hir best entent,
She made þer-of noon assignement.
115 Eeke *Thome Tynker* with alle hees pannes olde,
And alle þe wyres of Banebury þat he solde—
His styth, his hamour, his bagge portatyf—   *anvil*
Bare vp his arme whane he faught with his wyff.
He foonde for haste no better bokeller
120 Vpon his cheeke þe distaff came so neer.
Hir name was cleped *Tybot Tapister*.
To brawle and broyle she nad no maner fer,
To thakke his pilche, stoundemel nowe and þanne,
Thikker þane Thome koude clowten any panne.
125 Nexst *Colle Tyler*, full hevy of his cheer,
Compleyneþe on *Phelyce* his wyff, þe wafurer.

104 But with her ladle clout him on the head.
111 She did not argue, but paid him out immediately.
123 To thump his fur coat every now and again.

Al his bred with sugre nys not baake,
Yit on his cheekis some-tyme he haþe a caake
So hoote and nuwe, or he can taken heede,
130 Þat his heres glowe verray reede,   *ears*
For a medecyne whane þe forst is colde,   *frost*
Making his teethe to ratle, þat beon oolde.
Þis is þe compleynt, þat þeos dotardes oolde
Make on þeyre wyves, þat beon so stoute and bolde.
135 Þeos holy martirs, preued ful pacyent,
Lowly beseching in al hir best entent,
Vn-to Youre Noble Ryal Magestee
To graunte hem fraunchyse and also liberte,
Sith þey beoþe fetird and bounden in maryage,
140 A sauf-conduyt to sauf him frome damage.
Eeke vnder support of youre hyeghe renoun,
Graunt hem also a proteccyoun;
Conquest of wyves is ronne thoroughe þis lande,
Cleyming of right to haue þe hyegher hande.
145 But if you list, of youre regallye,
Þe Olde Testament for to modefye,
And þat yee list asselen þeyre request,   *seal, confirm*
Þat þeos poure husbandes might lyf in rest,
And þat þeyre wyves in þeyre felle might   *evil, cruel*
150 Wol medle amonge mercy with þeyre right.
For it came neuer of nature ne raysoun,
A lyonesse toppresse þe lyoun,
Ner a wolfesse, for al hir thyraunye,
Ouer þe wolf to haven þe maystrye.
155 Þer beon nowe wolfesses moo þane twoo or three,
Þe bookys recorde wheeche þat yonder bee.
Seoþe to þis mater of mercy and of grace,
And or þees dotardes parte out of þis place,
Vpon þeyre compleynt to shape remedye,
160 Or þey beo likly to stande in iupardye,
It is no game with wyves for to pleye,
But for foolis, þat gif no force to deye!

Takeþe heed of þaunswer of þe wyves

Touching þe substance of þis hyeghe discorde,
We six wyves beon ful of oon acorde,
165 Yif worde and chyding may vs not avaylle,
We wol darrein it in chaumpeloos by bataylle. *settle; open field*
Iupart oure right, laate or ellys raathe.   *early*
And for oure partye þe worthy Wyff of Bathe   *soon*
Cane shewe statutes moo þan six or seven,
170 Howe wyves make hir housbandes wynne heven,
Maugre þe feonde and al his vyolence;   *despite*

For þeyre vertu of parfyte pacyence
Parteneþe not to wyves nowe-adayes,
Sauf on þeyre housbandes for to make assayes.
175 Þer pacyence was buryed long agoo;
Gresyldes story recordeþe pleinly soo.
It longeþe to vs to clappen as a mylle,   *prattle, chatter*
No counseyle keepe, but þe trouth oute telle;
We beo not borne by hevenly influence
180 Of oure nature to keepe vs in sylence.
For þis is no doute, euery prudent wyff
Haþe redy aunswere in al suche maner stryff.
Þoughe þeos dotardes with þeyre dokked berdes,   *cut short*
Which strowteþe out as þey were made of   *stick*
   herdes,   *coarse flax*
185 Haue ageyn hus a gret quarell nowe sette,
I trowe þe bakoun was neuer of hem fette,   *carried, fetched*
Awaye at Dounmowe in þe Pryorye.
Þey weene of vs to haue ay þe maystrye;
Ellas! þeos fooles, let hem aunswere here-to;
190 Whoo cane hem wasshe, who can hem wring alsoo?
Wryng hem, yee, wryng, so als God vs speed,
Til þat some tyme we make hir nases bleed,   *?our own noses*
And sowe hir clooþes whane þey beoþe to-rent,
And clowte hir bakkes til somme of vs beo shent;   *patch*
195 Loo, yit þeos fooles, God gyf hem sory chaunce,
Wolde sette hir wyves vnder gouuernaunce,
Make vs to hem for to lowte lowe;   *bow*
We knowe to weel þe bent of Iackys bowe.
Al þat we clayme, we clayme it but of right.
200 Yif þey say nay, let preve it out by ffight.
We wil vs grounde not vpon wommanhede.
Fy on hem, cowardes! When hit komeþe to nede,
We clayme maystrye by prescripcyoun,
Be long tytle of successyoun,
205 Frome wyff to wyff, which we wol not leese.
Men may weel gruchche, but þey shal not cheese.   *grumble; choose*
Custume is vs for nature and vsaunce
To set oure housbandes lyf in gret noysaunce.
Humbelly byseching nowe at oon worde
210 Vnto oure Liege and Moost Souerein Lord,
Vs to defende of his regallye,
And of his grace susteenen oure partye,
Requering þe statuyt of olde antiquytee
Þat in youre tyme it may confermed bee.

*þe complaynte of þe lewed housbandes with þe cruwell aunswers of
þeyre wyves herde, þe kyng yiveþe þer-vpon sentence and iugement*

215 Þis noble Prynce, moost royal of estate,
Having an eyeghe to þis mortal debate,
First aduerting of ful hyeghe prudence,
Wil vnavysed gyve here no sentence,
With-oute counseylle of haste to procede,
220 By sodeyne doome; for he takeþe heede
To eyþer partye as iuge indifferent,
Seing þe paryll of hasty iugement;
Pourposiþe him in þis contynude stryffe
To gif no sentence þer-of diffynytyff,
225 Til þer beo made examynacyoun
Of oþer partye, and inquysicyoun.
He considereþe and makeþe *Raysoun* his guyde,
As egal iuge enclynyng to noo syde;
Not-with standing he haþe compassyoun
230 Of þe poure housbandes trybulacyoun,
So offt arrested with þeyre wyves rokkes,   *spindles*
Which of þeyre distaves haue so many knokkes;
Peysing also, in his regallye,   *Weighing*
Þe lawe þat wymmen allegge for þeyre partye,
235 Custume, nature, and eeke prescripcyoun,
Statuyt vsed by confirmacyoun,
Processe and daate of tyme oute of mynde,
Recorde of cronycles, witnesse of hir kuynde:
Wher-fore þe Kyng wol al þis nexst(e) yeere
240 Þat wyves fraunchyse stonde hoole and entier,
And þat no man with-stonde it, ne with-drawe,
Til man may fynde some processe oute by lawe,   *argument*
Þat þey shoulde by nature in þeyre lyves,
Haue souerayntee on þeyre prudent wyves,
245 A thing vnkouþe, which was neuer founde.
Let men be-ware þer-fore or þey beo bounde.
Þe bonde is harde, who-so þat lookeþe weel;
Some man were leuer fetterd beon in steel,   *rather, better*
Raunsoun might help his peyne to aswaage.
250 But whoo is wedded lyueþe euer in seruage.
And I knowe neuer nowher fer ner neer
Man þat was gladde to bynde him prysonier,
Þoughe þat his prysoun, his castell, or his holde
Wer depeynted with asure or with golde.

EXPLICIT

NOTE At the following lines these stage-directions occur in the MS: 25
showing six rustics; 55 *showing a cobbler*; 91 *showing a butcher*; all in
Latin. Then in English: 115 *showing the tinker*; 156 *distaves*. The last is
probably a cue for the entry of the wives.

*Nowe here nexst folowyng ys made a balade by Lydegate, sente by
a poursyvant to þe Shirreves of London, acompanyed with þeire
breþerne vpon Mayes daye at Busshopes wod, at an honurable
dyner, eche of hem bringginge his dysshe.*

(1)

Mighty Flourra, goddes of fresshe floures,
    Whiche cloþed hast þe soyle in lousty grene,
Made buddes springe with hir swote showres
    By influence of þe sonne so sheene;
5   To do pleasaunce of entent ful clene
Vn-to þestates wheoche þat nowe sitte here,
Haþe Veere dovne sent hir owen doughter dere,   *Spring*

(2)

Making þe vertue þat dured in þe roote,   *survived*
    Called of clerkes þe vertue vegytable,   *sap*
10 For to trascende, moste holsome and most swoote,
    In-to þe crope, þis saysoun so greable.
    þe bawmy lykour is so comendable
þat it reioyþe with þe fresshe moysture
Man, beeste, and foole, and every creature   *bird*

(3)

15 Whiche haþe repressed, swaged, and bore dovne
    þe grevouse constreinte of þe frostes hoore;
And caused foolis, ffor ioye of þis saysoune,
    To cheese þeire makes þane by natures loore,   *choose; mates*
    With al gladnesse þeire courage to restore,
20 Sitting on bowes fresshly nowe to synge
Veere for to salue at hir home comynge;   *spring, salute*

(4)

Ful pleinly meninge in þeire *ermonye*
    Wynter is goone, whiche did hem gret payne,
And with þeire swoote sugre melodye,
25   Thanking Nature þeire goddesse souereyne
    þat þey nowe have no mater to compleyne,
Hem for to proygne every morwenyng
With lousty gladnesse at *Phebus* vprysinge.

(5)

And to declare þe hye magnifysence
30   Howe Vere inbringeþe al felicytee,
Affter wynters mighty vyolence
    Avoydinge stormys of al adversytee;

[210]

For sheo haþe brought al prosperitee
To alle þestates of þis regyoun
35 At hir comynge to-fore youre hye renoun:

(6)

To þe mighty prynces þe palme of þeire victorie;
And til knighthode nowe sheo doþe presente
Noblesse in armes, lawde, honnour, & glorie;
Pees to þe people in al hir best entente,
40 With grace and mercy fully to consente
Þat provydence of hye discressioun
Avoyde descorde and al devysyoun.

(7)

Wynter shal passe of hevynesse and trouble,
F(l)owres shal springe of perfite charite,
45 In hertes þere shal be no meninge double,
  Buddes shal (blosme) of trouþe and vnytee,
  Pleinly for to exyle duplicytee,
Lordes to regne in þeire noble puissance,
Þe people obeye with feythful obeyssaunce.

(8)

50 Of alle estates þere shal beo oone ymage,
  And princes first shal ocupye þe hede,
And prudent iuges, to correcte outrages,
  Shal trespassours const(r)eynen vnder drede,
  Þat innocentes in þeire lowlyhede
55 As truwe comvnes may also beo þeire socour,
Truwly contune in þeire faithful labour.

(9)

And by þe grace of Oure Lorde Ihesu
  Þat Holly Chirche may have parseueraunce,
Beo faythfull founde in al (vertu),
60 Mayre, provost, shirreff, eche in his substaunce;
  And aldremen, whiche haue þe governaunce
Over þe people by vertue may avayle,
Þat noone oppression beo done to þe pourayle. *poor and lowly*

(10)

Þus as þe people, of prudent pollycye,
65 Pryncis of þe right shal governe,
Þe Chirche preye, þe iuges iustefye,
  And knighthode manly and prudently discerne,
  Til light of trouþe so clerely þe lanterne:
Þat rightwysnesse thorughe þis regyoune
70 Represse þe derknesse of al extorcyoune.

[211]

(11)

Þeos be þe typinges, wheoche þat Weer haþe brought,   *Ver*
   Troubles exylinge of wynters rude derknesse;
Wherfore reioye yowe in hert, wille, and thought,
   Somer shal folowe to yowe off al gladnesse;
75   And siþen sheo is mynistre of lustynesse,
Let hir beo welcome to yowe at hir comyng,
Sith sheo to yowe haþe brought so glad typinge.

(12)

Þe noble princesse of moste magnifisence,
   Qweene of al ioye, of gladde suffisaunce,
80 May is nowe comen to Youre Hye Excellence,
   Presenting yowe prosperous plesaunce,
   Of al welfare moste foulsome haboundance,
As sheo þat haþe vnder hir demayne
Of floures fresshe moste holsome and soueraine.

Lenvoye to alle þestates present

(13)

85 Þis Princesse haþe, by favour of nature,
   Repared ageine þat wynter haþe so fade,
And foolis loustely recvvre   *birds*
   Þeire lusty notes and þeire enemye glade,   *Þenvoye*
   And vnder braunches vnder plesant shade
90 Reioyssing þaire with many swote odoures,
And Zepherus with many fresshe (*shoures*).

(14)

Topyted fayre, with motleys whyte and rede,   *Tufted, crowned*
   Alle hilles, pleynes, and lusty bankes grene,
And made hir bawme to fleete in every mede,   *abound*
95   And fury Tytane shewe oute heos tresses sheene,
   And vppon busshes and hawthornes kene,
Þe nightingale with plesant ermonye
Colde wynter stormes nowe sheo doþe defye.

(15)

On *Parnoso* þe lusty muses nyene,
100   Citherra with hir sone nowe dwellis,
Þis sayson singe and þeire notes tuwyne
   Of poetrye besyde þe cristal wellis;
   Calyope þe dytes of hem tellis,   *songs*
And *Orpheus* with heos stringes sharpe
105 Syngeþe a roundell with his temperd herpe.

[212]

(16)

Wher-fore to alle estates here present,
  Þis plesant tyme moste of lustynesse,
May is nowe comen to fore yow of entent
  To bringe yowe alle to ioye and fresshnesse,
110   Prosparitee, welfare, and al gladnesse,
And al þat may Youre Hyenesse qweeme and pleese,   *gratify*
In any parte or doone youre hertes eese.